D0968530

British Politics in Perspective

Contents

BRITISH POLITICS IN PERSPECTIVE

BRITISH POLITICS
IN PERSPECTIVE

*Edited by R. L. Borthwick
and J. E. Spence*

WITHDRAWN

ST. MARTIN'S PRESS, NEW YORK
1984

First published in 1984 by Leicester University Press
First published in the United States of America in 1984
by St. Martin's Press, Inc., 175 Fifth Avenue, New York, NY 10010

Designed by Douglas Martin
Set in Linotron Imprint by Alan Sutton Publishing Ltd., Gloucester
Printed and bound in Great Britain at
The Pitman Press, Bath

Library of Congress Cataloging in Publication Data

Main entry under title:

British Politics in Perspective.

Includes index.
1. Great Britain–politics and government–1979
addresses, essays, lectures. 1. Borthwick, R.L.
11. Spence, J.E. (John Edward)
JN231.B725 1984   320.941   83-40608
ISBN 0-312-10508-8

CONTENTS

NOTE: Places of publication are given only for works published outside the United Kingdom. Commonly used abbreviations such as *J.* for *Journal*, *Rev.* for *Review*, have been used in references.

PREFACE

ANYONE proposing to add to the already considerable volume of literature on British politics ought to have good reason for their temerity. Ours would be that British government is in a period of change and the chapters that follow offer some reflections on those changes. Conventional wisdom has it that change in British politics comes slowly; it is perhaps as true that change, when it does come, comes surreptitiously. In the 1980s there are signs that the system is moving in directions that are either new or have been unfamiliar in recent times.

Themes that have been brushed aside in the past, such as the control of public expenditure, have returned to the centre of the political stage. Equally, confidence about the consensual nature and convergent direction of our political parties has been greatly shaken by developments during the 1970s. Even where change comes more slowly, for example in Parliament, there are signs that the 1980s will prove to be very different from recent decades. All these and other internal changes take place against a background of great uncertainty about our relationship with the European Community and a renewed interest in Britain's role in the wider world.

What we are offering here is not a textbook providing a comprehensive coverage of the subject; rather it is an attempt to provide discussion on a selection of topics that seem to us important within that wider field. Inevitably our choice of topics will not meet with universal acclaim. Every reader could no doubt draw up a different list.

We would like to thank Peter Boulton, the Secretary of Leicester University Press, for suggesting the theme of this volume to us. We are also grateful to both him and his staff for the patience and consideration they have shown both editors.

R.L.B.
J.E.S.
June 1983

NOTES ON CONTRIBUTORS

GEOFFREY ALDERMAN is Lecturer in Politics and Government at Royal Holloway College, University of London. His previous publications include *The Railway Interest* (1973), *British Elections: Myth and Reality* (1978), and *The Jewish Community in British Politics* (1983). In 1979 he acted as election analyst for Independent Television News. He has recently completed a book on British pressure groups, and he is currently researching into the relationship between Jews and New Commonwealth immigrants in Britain.

JAMES BARBER is Master of Hatfield College, Durham. Previously he was Professor of Political Science at the Open University. His publications include *South Africa's Foreign Policy* (1973), *Who Makes British Foreign Policy?* (1977), and *The Uneasy Relationship: Britain and South Africa* (1983).

RODNEY BARKER is Senior Lecturer in Government at the London School of Economics and Political Science. He is the author of *Education and Politics: a study of the Labour Party* (1972) and of *Political Ideas in Modern Britain* (1978).

R.L.BORTHWICK is Senior Lecturer in Politics at the University of Leicester; he has also taught in the United States. He is a member of the Study of Parliament Group and has been a Chief Examiner for the J.M.B. 'A' level British Government and Politics. He has written articles in *Parliamentary Affairs* and *Teaching Politics* and has contributed to *The Commons Today* (1981), *The House of Commons in the Twentieth Century* (1979) and *Multi-Party Britain* (1979).

H.M.DRUCKER is Senior Lecturer in Politics at the University of Edinburgh. He is author of *Doctrine and Ethos in the Labour Party* (1979) and *Breakaway: the Scottish Labour Party* (1978) and editor of *Multi-Party Britain* (1979) and *Developments in British Politics* (1983).

WYN GRANT is Senior Lecturer in Politics at the University of Warwick where he has taught since 1971. He is the co-author of *The Confederation of British Industry* (1977) and author of *Independent Local Politiccs in England and Wales* (1977) and *The Political Economy of Industrial Policy* (1982). He has written numerous articles on pressure groups in such journals as *Political Studies*, *Government and Opposition* and the *Journal of Common Market Studies*.

PETER M. JACKSON is Director of the Public Sector Economics Research Centre and Head of the Economics Department, University of Leicester. He has been an Economic Adviser to the Treasury and is currently consultant to the Department of the Environment. His publications include (with C.V. Brown) *Public Sector Economics* (1978), and *The Political Economy of Bureaucracy* (1982).

MICHAEL SHACKLETON was formerly lecturer in Government at the Open University, and is at present administrator in the Secretariat of the European Parliament in Luxembourg. His publications include 'Oil and the British foreign policy process' in the *Journal of International Studies* (1978) and 'The Common Fisheries Policy' in Wallace C., Wallace, W. and Webb, C. (eds.), *Policy-making in the European Communities* (1982).

J.E.SPENCE is Professor of Politics and Pro-Vice-Chancellor at the University of Leicester. His publications include *Republic Under Pressure: the Study of South African Foreign Policy* (1965), *Lesotho: the Politics of Dependence* (1968), *Investment in South Africa: the Political and Military Framework* (1975), and a variety of contributions on Southern African themes.

1 THE RISE AND ECLIPSE OF THE SOCIAL DEMOCRATIC STATE

Rodney Barker

TO BEGIN an account of British politics with a discussion of the state may seem like opening an English cookery book with a recipe for horse meat. In Britain, the state is regarded in much the same way as force-feeding geese, eating snails or cooking with garlic: something odd and probably unnatural that is characteristic of foreigners. As Mr Podsnap put it in regard to another matter, 'Other nations do, sir, I regret to have to say it, as they do.' States are things that foreigners have, particularly foreigners in Eastern Europe and, earlier in the century, German foreigners. For F.A.Hayek, writing in 1944, the advance of state power in the United Kingdom was the result of the triumph of German collectivist ideas over English liberal ones. In the 1930s even those who were enthusiastic about the possibilities of state economic planning looked elsewhere, to the Soviet Union, for their example of its practice and benefits. The state as a distinct, directing institution was not something to be found here. The British manner of doing things was, it was supposed, quite different, and public affairs were managed in a far looser and more elusive manner. A reader would in consequence search with little success for accounts of the state in most of the writing on government and politics in the United Kingdom. The state has held a place rather like that of the dog in Conan Doyle's story 'Silver Blaze'. Sherlock Holmes had drawn Dr Watson's attention to the significance of the behaviour of the dog during the night. Watson protested that the dog had done absolutely nothing – to be told that that was precisely the point. What was remarkable was the absence of activity. Similarly when descriptions have been given of the political arrangements of the United Kingdom, they have not normally used or appeared to use the concept of the state, and it is this very silence which is remarkable. This is odd, for the state, both as a theoretical and a practical entity, is central to political science. It is certainly present in the descriptive accounts of continental European, and particularly French and German, writers.[1] The government of the United Kingdom, on the other hand, has been presented as a diverse process, emerging from the interaction of a number of institutions, rather than as the activity of a cluster of institutions acting in some kind of accord or with some common direction or style. The descriptions have, in other words, been concerned with the relations between the various institutions of government rather than with the relations between those institutions on the one hand, and the governed on the other. The internal relations rather than either the external action or the overall coherence of government have been what were seen and discussed.

The setting of these accounts has been both broader and narrower than would make the use of the word 'state' appropriate. It is broader because the entire political life and culture of the nation is sketched out piece by piece. Parties, Parliament, ministers, media, are all part of the complex pattern, and if divisions are made, other than between the generality of the whole and the particularity of the parts, they are made between central and local, formal and informal, government and individuals. In such accounts the state is dissolved, its constituent parts having no more connection with one another than with other components of the picture. Alternatively, it is presented as a box empty of character or purpose, into which the pressures and demands of society flow, and out of the balancing and interplay of which, policies emerge. It is narrower because if the object of discussion is the institutions of government (and I beg a question with that 'is'), we are inside the whale, looking at its digestion and its circulation, but ignoring its motion through the ocean and its consumption of plankton or prophets. Since the development of the modern managing and social service state in the United Kingdom, and until the development of the academic discipline of social administration, there has been remarkably little examination of the actions and consequences of the state. And it is to the analysis of the actions of the institutions of government upon those whom they govern, and on the overall character of that action, rather than to the understanding of the inter-relation of the various parts of government, that the conception of the state is most appropriate.

One way of describing the significance of the dog's silence (and without extending the metaphor to suggest that political science lies deep in intellectual night) would be to say that descriptions of politics and government in the United Kingdom have been a-theoretical. In writing about this country, political scientists have perhaps become severed from their conceptualizing colleagues. But this will not do. Those who have written on politics and government may not have articulated or discussed their concepts, but they have had them nonetheless. It is a matter of asking not why this area of political science has been a-theoretical, but rather what the particular perceptions of the subject have been that have caused so little attention to be paid to what for others working in different areas has been a major preoccupation: the state. The problem is not the absence of theory, but the presence of a theory which did not 'see' the state.

A part of the explanation is the particular historical experience of the state in the United Kingdom. The people of this country, with the exception of some of those in Northern Ireland, have never experienced the alien and occupying presence of a Bismarckian state in any or all of its simplicity. At the end of the nineteenth century public power may have been intrusive but it was also slight and local in most of its impact on any particular person. Moreover, it developed or appeared to do so in response to democratic demands for its assistance and services. There was a substantial body of collectivist argument to sustain the impression that factory legislation, public education or municipal gas were all the expression of a popular demand, and that little independent attention need be paid to the agency through which that demand was met. The gradualness of the extension of public power, and the appearance of an extension in response to public need, meant that there was no conception of a state which was distinct from its subjects, and which had styles and purposes of its own. Not all the institutions and functions of government had this appearance of immediate agency about them. But those that did not were both so distant and so habitual as to rest on bases of legitimacy which were neither directly perceived nor directly enquired into. The new functions, on the other hand, could be seen as, in effect, functions of the governed rather than of the governors. If there was no point, historically, at which the state could be seen to have begun its old functions or taken up its new ones, nor was there any clear point at which in terms of power or authority the state's territory began and the citizens' ended. This was particularly so because the extension of power, and the very agencies whereby it was extended, were *ad hoc*, as in the case of the school boards and the Poor Law guardians.

In the present century this historical experience has expressed itself in a view of government which is both democratic and pluralist. Whilst on the one hand the overmighty state was seen as the antithesis of liberal democracy, on the other, political science has developed as a profession largely sympathetic to the modern state. Those who have sought to describe the institutions of government have done so because they regarded such knowledge as important mapwork for the subject, who is presented as a citizen. The distinction is an important one, for the subject is regulated and controlled by a state seen as sufficiently coherent to define him or her as one comprehensive governed person, whereas the citizen is a person with a variety of purposes for whom the institutions of government are no more than the various instruments whereby those purposes may be attained. The English tradition has thus been empirical, reformist and collectivist, a combination which has placed political scientists both conceptually and practically within the limits set by the present order, rather than with both feet, or even one foot, outside them. It is not necessarily the case that those who are sympathetic towards the state do not 'see' it. Idealist political thought has always drawn attention to the state as the expression of the 'real' will of the citizens. But it has not given an account of the state as a historically active set of institutions, but rather as a justifying principle for actions and actors which have gone largely unexamined. On the other hand, those who have been unsympathetic to the state, and they have been few, have not by and large undertaken detailed examination of the operations of the object of their hostility, but have engaged in discussions of what they believe to be its unfortunate consequences. Anarchists and libertarians have been more concerned to delineate the erosion of freedom than to analyse the state, just as modern churchmen diagnose sin, but ignore the devil.

Whilst what is normally thought of as political science in the

United Kingdom has thus been characterized by democratic optimism, one branch of the discipline has displayed the other aspect of the outlook which engenders a neglect of the state – pluralism. To talk of constitutional theory as a branch of political science might seem to constitutional theorists both historically inaccurate and intellectually uncongenial. Constitutional theory can be presented as having precedence in terms both of chronology and progeniture. Moreover, in one sense there has always been an awareness of the state, or of the possibility of the state, in the arguments of constitutional theorists. Institutional pluralism has, to this extent, been advocated as an alternative and an antidote to the potential tyranny of an integrated state. An optimist naturally believes that the concentration of powers which such theories sought to banish, and with which the conception of the state seems closely associated, is no longer present in this country. As Geoffrey Marshall put it, 'for republicans the struggle to subject the executive to law begins with a conceptual struggle to separate and clarify what the term "state" confuses'.[2] Laski's early attempts to dissolve or at least loosen the hegemony of the modern state took the shape of a criticism of the idea of undivided sovereignty. But the conditions for such an attempt were already there in British constitutional theory where, as Marshall points out, 'it seems a moot question whether there is any such notion' as the state. He is able to quote Maitland in support of the belief that the state is 'a person whose personality our law does not formally or explicitly recognise'.[3] The nearest that constitutional theory comes to recognizing or conceptualizing the state is with the doctrine of the crown. It is by using this doctrine, in another kind of book, that Richard Rose seems almost to be talking of the state.[4] But there are difficulties with the notion of the crown, even in the wide definition used by Wade and Bradley who suggest that it represents 'the sum total of governmental power and is synonymous with the Executive'.[5] Constitutional theory is concerned to determine coherent principles, and as such the notion of the crown has a limited use since it cannot be employed over a wide range of constitutional behaviour without losing precisely that coherence, and referring to powers which are separate, conflicting or independent of one another.

But it is a mistake to seek for an account of the state in constitutional theory, because this branch of political science is not engaged in the kind of task which would produce such a descriptive notion. It is doing something else. The discussions of lawyers and of constitutional theorists are about the coherence of articulated and legitimate accounts of government. The accounts are articulated in that they are expressed in common or statute law, or in recognized and acknowledged convention. They are legitimate in that they are accounts of proper functions, of rights and of obligations. It is sometimes supposed that they are accounts of what happens, but they are in fact accounts of what ought to happen, of conduct which can be considered legitimate. It is impossible to treat constitutional writing of this kind as solely or even principally descriptive, in the sense of describing observable practices and events. Of course a part of the prescriptive force of the constitution may be supposed to derive from its grounding, origin and maintenance in continued practice. But much that would be included in a description of government in the United Kingdom would in no way be either articulated or legitimate, despite the fact that no such description could ignore the actual and influential presence of constitutional norms. Constitutional theory is an account of the legitimate structure of the state, rather than of its function. It is about rights, and describes moral capacity, whereas a description of the state would be concerned with historical capacity.

But if a conception of the state is like the barkings of Conan Doyle's dog, then the animal has not been entirely silent. There are occasional snuffles and pants, even the odd bark, if you listen carefully. There can be found in both political writing and in more diverse forms of expression some notion of the state as an independent institution which affects the lives of its subjects, and which moves with purposes peculiar to itself, and different from theirs. And inasmuch as the more fortunate members of a household have the more secluded and comfortable bedrooms, whilst the servants sleep in attics and cellars less insulated against disturbance, so it is those at the bottom of the social pile who have been aware of the canine yelps, whilst those at the top have been able to declare with calm astonishment, 'Dog? What dog?' In 1909 Stephen Reynolds reported amongst his working-class friends a view of the state which was both simple and strong, even though lacking in theoretical precision. Out there, or rather up there, were officials, inspectors, policemen, who regulated and intruded upon the poor, imposing upon them standards of another class. Social reform, for such people, meant 'police'.[6] It is a notion of 'them' similar to that reported, nearly half a century later, by Richard Hoggart in *The Uses of Literacy*:

'Them' includes the policemen and those civil servants or local-authority employees whom the working-classes meet – teachers, the school attendance man, 'the Corporation', the local bench. Once the Means Test Official, the man from 'the Guardians', and the Employment Exchange officer were notable figures here. To the very poor, especially, they compose a shadowy but numerous and powerful group affecting their lives at almost every point: the world is divided into 'Them' and 'Us'.[7]

Alan Sillitoe's Arthur Seaton expresses much the same opinion:

Factories and labour exchanges and insurance offices keep us alive and kicking – so they say – but they're booby-traps and will suck you under like sinking sands if you aren't careful. Factories sweat you to death, labour exchanges talk you to death, insurance and income tax offices milk money from your wage packets and rob you to death. And if you're still left with a tiny bit of life in your guts after all this boggering about, the Army calls you up and you get shot to death. And if you're clever enough to stay out of the Army you get bombed to death. Ay, by God, it's a hard life if you don't weaken, if you don't stop that bastard government from grinding your face in the muck, though there ain't much you can do about it unless you start making dynamite to blow their four-eyed clocks to bits.[8]

This is much like the image of authority presented in popular children's comics. In the *Dandy* and the *Beano* is a world of anarchically free working-class children opposed by a loose alliance of cane-, slipper- and truncheon-wielding teachers, parents, and policemen. Dennis the Menace and Babyface Nelson have more to say about legitimate coercion than does most constitutional theory. Over the last five years, similar images have begun to appear in popular music. It is some way from the genial anti-bureaucracy of the 1950s 'Hole in the Road' to the Tom Robinson Band's 1979 'Whitehall, up against the wall'.

Whilst most of these perceptions of someone or something oppressive, up there, seem commonest amongst the working class, since they are the most governed class, they are not restricted to them. The concept 'flea' may only be necessary to those who itch, but most people feel the need to scratch at some time in their lives. When tax inspectors employ their power to enter and search, when speed limits are imposed on motorways, when children are allocated to the less exclusive secondary schools by local authorities, then those higher up the social scale begin to perceive a group of people who oppress them with the legitimacy of public authority. The more powerful or more privileged begin to scratch.

Some conception of the state is employed, too, in everyday political language. 'State control' is a usual journalistic term to describe the activities of the public corporations, and there are occasions when the word state is used in the pronouncements of ministers. Speaking of his decision to deport Philip Agee and Mark Hosenball, the Home Secretary Merlyn Rees talked in 1977 of the need to ensure the security of the 'state'. By this he seems to have meant both something like 'the realm', the territorial nation politically governed and guarded, and the institutions of government. It is not a common usage in this country, yet when the word is so used, there is no sense of strangeness. There is also the implication that the institutions of governing and guarding are at least as much in need of protection as are the territory and people they are presumed to be guarding. Whilst Rees was not using the term 'state' with any academic precision, the implication of what he was saying was clear.

Sometimes, on the other hand, it has been the very ambiguities of official language which have been illuminating. In 1973 the Home Office, in a classified circular to local authorities, spoke of the primary purpose of 'Home Defence' as being 'to secure the United Kingdom against any internal threat'.[9] In one sense, this is simple nonsense. The United Kingdom as a nation territorially defined can be defended against alien incursion, or against nationalist secession of parts of the territory. But it cannot threaten itself. What may of course be threatened, is the current political and governmental order, and those who direct and administer it. What is happening here, then, is the familiar device of dignifying a particular institution – the incumbent state – with the aura of the whole citizen body and their territory. The Home Office becomes England, and the Ministry of Defence our national heritage.

Awareness of the state, or of something very like it, in twentieth-century Britain, has had two dimensions: location and time. In general the working class are, and feel themselves to be, governed to a degree not experienced by, for instance, the professional middle classes. The citizens of Derry are, and feel themselves to be, governed to a degree not experienced by the citizens of Derby. There is more legitimate coercion by the police in Brixton than in Bournemouth. Awareness of the state varies, too, over time. It has been slight, during most of the present century, but has increased steadily over the last quarter of a century.

Though the state was far smaller, and less active, in the nineteenth century, people were more sharply aware of it than they have been in much of the twentieth. There was less government, but what there was was clearly separate from, and a constraint on, subjects. At the same time, the experience of the state had a social dimension. The local bench may have been a coercive control for poachers, but for the gentry it was a means of defending their property and the tranquillity of their communities between lunch and dinner. So the developing conception of the state depended upon not just simple chronological change, but an alteration in the groups and classes which experienced the state, and in the intensity with which they experienced it.

The history of this change is directly related to that of the social democratic state. The term social democracy has been used in recent years by the Social Democratic Party to indicate a mixture, in no very precise proportions, of liberalism, democratic elitism, social reform, a mixed economy, and piecemeal social engineering. But to seek the meaning of the term here is like trying to study the architecture of castles amongst the battlements of Disneyland. The term 'social democracy' has been most commonly used in Europe in the way in which it was used in the nineteenth century. It denotes an extension of democracy from the world of politics, to that of social and economic relations. The powers which the people enjoyed in a political democracy, were to be enhanced by social and economic powers exercised on their behalf by a state which they legitimated and whose policies they chose. In this way democracy would be extended, and the capacities of the citizens themselves would be enhanced by the ending of inequalities of social and economic power and advantage. Political democracy would be complemented by social democracy. And at the same time, the enhancement of popular power which social democracy created, would make political democracy a realizable end. The social democratic state developed in response to industrialism, socialism and political democracy. It has grown in response to the needs of an industrial society and of a democratic one, where a substantial section of the population, and its health and skills, are a major economic resource, and a resource, moreover, whose approval and support is necessary for the continuance of party government.

But the electorate which the social democratic state sought to manage was neither a variegated crowd of individual citizens, nor a constantly shifting pattern of groups organized by status, principles, geography or religion. The electorate was increasingly from the beginning of the twentieth century, organized along lines of occupational class. The principal division was between the manual working class and the middle class. This division, which occurred in the official relations of state and citizens in class voting, appeared in the unofficial relations of state and society also. As Keith Middlemas has argued, the present century has seen the steady incorporation of the organized working class in the system of government of the United Kingdom.[10] The system of governing and making policy sometimes described as corporatism has its origins before the First World War, and the attention which it has received from the 1970s onwards represented not its emergence, but its maturity. Not only was class the principal organizing category of politics, but it was also a central category of government. National efficiency and economic progress involved the state investing in the capacities of its subjects, and the categories in which they were ordered for this purpose were those of economic status.

But though the state which developed in the United Kingdom in the twentieth century can be termed social democratic, it is important not to confuse this with any direct extension of popular power. Like all liberal democratic nations, the United Kingdom has of necessity employed a system of indirect or representative democracy, which has taken the form similar to Schumpeter's democratic elitism, but which had been characterized at the end of the last century by Fabian Socialists such as Shaw and the Webbs as a relationship between elite, expert producers of government, and its democratic, relatively unskilled, consumers. Moreover, the social democratic state was not a creation of a democratic electorate, but a reaction of an already existing state and ruling class to that electorate and to its economic – and military – function. Indeed, as Mosei Ostrogorski had argued in 1902, the very political parties which presented themselves as representatives of electoral demands upon the state were, rather, supporters' clubs created by one section within the ruling system, to organize popular support for their continued predominance.[11] The provision of technical education in the 1890s was a response to German and American economic competition. The provision of school medical inspection and school meals before the First World War was an investment in the military kindergarten of a nation faced with German military competition.

The changing experience of the state – who has been aware of it, how, and when, can be historically related to the rise and decline of the social democratic state. Between 1880 and the outbreak of the First World War there was a heightened awareness of the state amongst those individualists and conservatives for whom a new concern, initially by regulation rather than by provision, for the material well-being of the population threatened the economic liberties and the distribution of wealth and power to which they had become habituated, and from which they drew substantial advantage. Individualism was predominantly a doctrine of the propertied, of the person whom Michael Oakeshott, writing on being conservative three-quarters of a century later, described as 'aware of something to lose which he has learned to care for'.[12] It was a fact which sometimes caused embarrassment to its more disinterested proponents. As Wordsworth Donisthorpe put it in 1889,

> the lovers of liberty are not without questionable allies, men who are open to the charge of protesting against State interference with the industry in which they are themselves interested, lest such interference should favour their weaker fellow workers . . . . Let the poverty-stricken be defended against the rapacity of the merciless pawnbroker; but it is preposterous to tolerate the claim of the helpless widow and children whom a railway accident has left destitute, for be it known that I am a railway king. One can hardly blame those demagogues who stigmatise individualism as selfishness.[13]

But there was hostility too amongst the property-less, which arose when a state which as yet seemed to provide little, nonetheless intruded into their privacy. The socially regulating and inspecting state appeared to Stephen Reynolds' working-class friends as simply 'police'.[14]

By the end of the First World War the new responsibilities of the state were established. The resistance of the propertied had become romantic and impractical at a general level, though in more particular ways it survived in the adherence to classical liberal economics. The resistance of the property-less faded as the state's appearance as 'police' became enclosed more and more in a sugar coating of social services. The end of the First World War saw the end of working-class libertarianism, just as it marked the last breaths of socialist pluralism. Between 1918 and the outbreak of the Second World War, although the activities of the state did not develop in a single direction or at a single rate, reaction to them was slight. By the end of the Second World War, on the other hand, substantial changes in the activities of the state had been accompanied by similar changes in awareness of it. The classical liberal economics which had seen state expenditure as a drain, albeit a sometimes necessary one, on the vitality of the cultivation of production and profit, had been challenged if not replaced by a Keynesianism which saw the market as in part the creation of the state's management of demand. This, together with the actual extension of economic management and social provision by the war-time government, and the possibility, soon realized, of an electorally approved extension of social democracy, revived the fears of those whose conception of liberty was of the unregulated distribution of wealth. From the mid-1940s therefore, the prospect of a state with enlarged responsibilities, no longer justified by war-time expediency nor guaranteed in its moderation by Churchill's premiership, but launched on further potential expansion with the double legitimacy of war-time precedent and peace-time electoral choice for social democratic advance, led to a reiteration of libertarianism, though without the forthrightness or lack of qualification with which it had been expressed by Spencer and his followers. But like Spencer's, the response was essentially conservative, calling for a ban on radical change, and a politics of 'consensus'. The opponents of social democracy, fearing its successes, called for an 'end to ideology' or, not quite in the same breath, for the pursuit of a free market economy.

A different awareness of the state arose in the later 1950s, and in the 1960s, amongst those socialists who were dismayed or frustrated not by the successes but by the failures of social democracy.

The new Left did not pay as much attention to the state as had its libertarian and conservative predecessors, nor as much as had the guild socialists in the first quarter of the century. Its first concern with social democracy was that it had not created the material well-being which it had promised, or that it had corrupted the people with a mere materialism which had left them culturally deprived so that even their bread was sliced, and their circuses were all on television. But it also had something to say about political power. Neatly reversing the convergence theories which had been associated with the 'end of ideology' approach, the new Left described a gathering of power in the hands of a few ruling groups which characterized the state systems of both East and West. As socialists they wished to extend public control and services for the promotion of equality. As anarchists and liberals they wanted to disperse public power, and to make it more openly and accountably exercised.

Finally, those who saw the social democratic state as in part a fraud perpetrated on the working class, developed a neo-Marxist account of the state's activities. In this view, economic management and social services were designed to maintain the conditions necessary for capital accumulation, and to preserve the legitimacy of the social order. It is this last development which has produced the most substantial body of writing on the state in the present century.

The libertarian reaction against the social democratic state in the 1940s and 1950s occurred at a time of its likely expansion. The socialist and new Left criticism occurred when that expansion was supposed, under the 1945–51 Attlee government, to have taken place, but had not produced the expected changes in the lives of ordinary people. The neo-Marxist criticism occurred when, after the decline and discrediting of the rhetoric of consensus, both Labour and Conservative governments, but particularly the long managerial administration of Harold Wilson, had settled down to govern a mixed economy.

But the real crisis of the social democratic state was still to come. Its democratic rationale had rested on an extension of power to the citizens as a collectivity. Since democracy operated through majorities rather than through unanimity, and since the working class was both the majority class and the deprived class in an electorate which had come to vote along class lines, social democracy was deeply enmeshed with the political power of the working class, and with social reform aimed at improving that class's material conditions. In addition, the social democratic state as a cultivator of the economic and military resource of labour was, as in its democratic mode, specifically linked with the working class. Social democratic politics were class politics, and the social democratic state was a state governing a class society. From around 1968 onwards, however, demands began to be placed upon the state which, whilst drawing on the promises of social democracy for equality and opportunity, did not come from groups organized in the categories it recognized. These new categories were race, religion, national identification and sex.

The social democratic state was not able easily to respond to these claims. First, because they came from members of racially, religiously, nationally or sexually identified groups they were made on behalf of those with whom the state had not been accustomed to deal, for whom it had no mechanisms of reform, and of whom it had taken little or no notice in its political incorporation of citizens, an incorporation which had been organized on a class basis. Second, the demands made were subversive either of the existing arrangements of the state, or of the patterns of social advantage and the advantages of social groups, with which the state was enmeshed. Third, the demands were made at a time when the state's provision was levelling off, and was about to be reduced. The new material austerity was presaged by Ralf Dahrendorf in his 1974 Reith Lectures, when he called for an acceptance and an exploitation of the need for a shift from 'expansion to improvement'.[15]

The demands made in Northern Ireland in 1968 provide a clear illustration. The Northern Ireland Civil Rights Association demanded that the formal equality in voting, the allocation of housing, employment and the general provision of social services, which social democracy offered, be implemented for the Roman Catholic minority. But whereas the extension to the working class of education, better housing, improved working conditions and better medical services could be seen as strengthening the social order, any move towards the equal treatment of Roman Catholics in Northern Ireland was seen by large numbers of Protestant Unionists as strengthening the position of a group which could never be incorporated and which, the more its conditions were improved, the greater the threat is presented to the régime. The demands of women and of blacks had similar implications and consequences within the United Kingdom as a whole. Equal treatment in employment and promotion for blacks meant the acceptance by whites of personal and cultural styles which were different from theirs, yet which could not be regarded, as could those of an assimilable working class, as temporary consequences of inadequate or incomplete socialization. Similarly the consequences of an end to the distribution of power and rewards according to sex had radical consequences for the position of men in both the household and paid employment, which could not be viewed as simply one further extension of social democracy. Had the working class ever presented itself in any sustained way as the possessor of an alternative culture, then the difference between class demands and the new demands would not have existed. But nor would a social democratic state have been possible.

Not only, however, was the state unable readily to meet these new demands, but the demands were made by those who were to challenge, or simply ignore, the legitimacy which class claimants on the social democratic state had nearly always accepted. In these circumstances the state responded with a degree of coercion which it had not employed in class politics, and which, by presenting a quite different face to its subjects, was the occasion for a new and far more hostile experience by them of the state. In particular, the politics of religion and nationalism in Northern Ireland, from 1968 onwards, and the politics of race on the mainland from around 1979, made it possible to see the state as essentially a coercive rather than a providing institution. In 1971 the government, in an attempt to defeat the Provisional I.R.A. and bring to an end the violence in the province, introduced internment without trial for those suspected of terrorist activities, or of supporting terrorist activities. Those who, on the evidence of the beliefs or suspicions of police officers were considered to be in some way associated with terrorism, were held and detained without being charged with any offence or brought before a court. The effect of this was greatly to increase the numbers of people with direct or indirect experience of the state as a coercive and intrusive institution arbitrarily intruding on their privacy and security. The hostility towards the police and the army within the Roman Catholic community was increased, as was support for those who attempted to gain their nationalist and republican goals by violence. Internment without trial achieved precisely the opposite of what its authors intended. The numbers ready to help the Provisional I.R.A. against what was increasingly regarded as an oppressive and alien state, were increased, and deaths by political violence rose to their highest level before or since.[16]

On the mainland of the United Kingdom, the changing conduct of the police in dealing with political demonstrations, particularly those with a racial aspect, led to major erosions of legitimacy. The police have altered their tactics by the establishment of Special Patrol Groups and other similar units which are removed from the normal style of policing. When dealing with crowds, the Special Patrol Groups have acted as flying columns whose function is the rapid application of physical force, a policing of intervention rather than of regulation. As such their response both to situations in which they have been instructed to act, and to any resistance to their intervention, has been different from that of the normally organized and deployed police. Their style has been to pounce, and in the disturbances which took place at Southall in April 1979, whilst the normal police used cordons, the Special Patrol Group of the Metropolitan Police used the quick dash, the snatch squad and the charge. The method of policing used by the S.P.G. presents the citizen with an attacking force, rather than with a regulating power. The response of citizens has to this extent already been determined by the manner in which the police themselves behave. This response reached its highest point in the summer of 1981. In nearly every major British city, but most violently in London and Liverpool, crowds of young men, both black and white, confronted police who used riot shields, motor vehicles and gas. The relationship between the police and the crowds was utterly different from that which has normally existed in the United Kingdom. The crowds treated the police not as the legitimate enforcers of law, but as invading enemies. The police treated the crowds as the occupiers of hostile territory which was to be subdued.

Since 1968, the coercive agencies of the state, the police and the army, have been increasingly present before the attention of citizens. At the same time their actions have become both more violent and more invasive. Nor have the consequences of the most violent relations between state and subjects, those in Northern Ireland, been limited to that part of the United Kingdom. By a series of Prevention of Terrorism Acts, the normal procedures whereby the police investigate suspected crimes, and hold suspects, have been altered so as to reduce the restraints upon the police and to erode the rights of the subject. For ministers in the Home Office, the connection is clear. Following the riots in the St Paul's area of Bristol in 1980 the Home Secretary William Whitelaw told Parliament that there would be no 'no-go areas' in British cities – a phrase borrowed from the urban politics of Belfast and Londonderry. The riots which took place in the cities of mainland Britain in the summer of 1981 led to a party of chief constables visiting Belfast to see how what was clearly considered to be a similar situation was dealt with there.

Insofar as the increasingly incursive conduct of the police and the army has led to a greater awareness amongst subjects of the state itself as an incursive institution, this view has been substantiated by a separate but related development. As Spencer had argued in the nineteenth century, there was a close relation between external and internal compulsion, and between the military expansion of the state, and reduction of the liberties of its domestic subjects. Since the end of the Second World War, three further changes have strengthened this relationship. First, the withering of the empire and the appearance of military nationalism in Ireland has meant that the armed forces have become less of a weapon against the nation's external enemies, and more an instrument for combating the state's internal ones. Second, and particularly during the 1950s, the cold war gave a foreign relations dimension to political and ideological differences, so that to be on the Left, and particularly to be associated with Communism, became cause for suspicions about one's loyalty to one's country. The defence of the nation came to be a justification for the policing of political beliefs. Third, although there had always been attempts to maintain some secrecy about the strength and disposition of the armed forces, the development of a strategy increasingly reliant on nuclear missiles vastly increased this policy. Nuclear weapons have been characterized by both secretive spending – from the atom bomb through to the Chevaline project – and secretive deployment. In the promotion of this secrecy, the citizen has become an alien in his or her own country, treated as a potential enemy from whom information is to be hidden, and whose surveillance and supervision is justified in terms of the state's military strategy. So the development of a form of warfare which is both elite and secret, in a way that labour-intensive warfare never can be, has been accompanied by a growing use of espionage by the state against its own subjects.

The consequences of this have been a new consciousness of the state as a distinct and governing institution, resistance to it, and denials of its legitimacy. It has sometimes been argued that the modern state has maintained its legitimacy by providing for the material needs of its citizens. In the United Kingdom, on the other hand, it has maintained its legitimacy by not disturbing the habitual deference of its subjects to its own power. The provision of social services did not purchase legitimacy. Rather, by emphasizing the caring, providing work of the state, it drew attention away from its other functions, particularly the raw and ultimate function of coercion. When the state itself draws attention to this last function, however, its subjects are compelled to recognize and respond to government as something external to their lives, which yet intrudes upon them. The novelty of such coercion makes it appear more harsh, too, than might be the case were it a familiar part of life in the United Kingdom.

Thus whilst academic writing has concentrated on the class role of the social democratic state, awareness – and resistance – at a political level falls outside the boundaries of traditional class politics. It has come from groups for which the social democratic state has had least relevance, and it opposes forms of state action which, being straight-forwardly coercive, draw attention to an aspect of the state which had been eclipsed by the paternalism of twentieth-century government.

The point at which awareness of the state develops so that the whole household hears the barking of the dog may prove to be the point at which the dog has been replaced by something fiercer and less benign. Perhaps inside every St Bernard is a bloodhound trying to get out. The household itself, when the dog slept, or seemed to many people to do so, was an ordered community whose inequalities were lodged within a single social structure. But the new barks and growls come at a time when the household is breaking up into a far looser collection of competing social and political interests, so that the traditional cohesion cannot perhaps be maintained. If that is so, then the hound may assume a very different purpose.

NOTES

1. See e.g. K.Dyson, *The State Tradition in Western Europe* (1980).
2. G.Marshall, *Constitutional Theory* (1971), 34.
3. *Ibid.*, 12.
4. R.Rose, *Politics in England Today* (1974); *Politics in England: an interpretation for the 1980s* (1980).
5. E.C.S.Wade and A.W.Bradley, *Constitutional Law* (7th edn., 1966), 166.
6. S.Reynolds, 'What the poor want', *Quarterly Rev.*, CCXII (Jan. 1910), 422.
7. R.Hoggart, *The Uses of Literacy* (1958 edn.), 53.
8. A.Sillitoe, *Saturday Night and Sunday Morning* (1960 edn.), 176.
9. D.Campbell, 'Who cares if the Bomb Drops?', *New Statesman* (19 Sept. 1980).
10. K.Middlemas, *Politics in Industrial Society: the experience of Britain since 1911* (1979).
11. M.Ostrogorski, *Democracy and the Organisation of Political Parties* I, (1902).
12. M.Oakeshott, *Rationalism in Politics and Other Essays* (1962), 169.
13. W.Donisthorpe, *Individualism, a system of politics* (1889), 76.
14. S.Reynolds, *ibid.*, 422.
15. R.Dahrendorf, *The New Liberty: survival and justice in a changing world* (1975).
16. R.Rose, *Northern Ireland: a time of choice* (1976), 24–5.

2 THE ELECTORAL SYSTEM

Geoffrey Alderman

THERE is probably no facet of British government more in need of reform than the electoral system by which the nation chooses its representatives at Westminster. But the likelihood of such reform taking place in the immediate future – say within the next decade – is problematic. The Liberal party has long advocated electoral reform, and in March 1981 the new Social Democratic party announced its support for proportional representation.[1] However, these two parties combined can only muster some 42 M.P.s. Unless some form of Liberal-Social Democratic alliance can achieve a balance of power the future of electoral reform will remain in the hands of M.P.s from the Conservative and Labour parties. Past experience teaches that their overriding consideration will not be the justice of electoral reform, or its desirability from the national point of view, but its effect on their own political fortunes.

Yet politicians must also face realities. It is beyond dispute that the present electoral system has grave imperfections, the consequences of which extend far beyond the electoral process itself. For the system provides the backcloth against which political argument, economic debate and social and industrial dialogue must all take place. If it is true that since 1945 British society has been dogged by needless industrial strife, sterile political argument and absence of realistic economic and financial policies, it is equally true that the electoral system has contributed to all these shortcomings.

No major reform of the British electoral system has taken place since the Representation of the People Act of 1948; that measure established the principle of one vote only per elector, abolished the special representation of the universities in the House of Commons and conferred a limited right of postal voting upon the civilian electorate. The extension of the franchise to persons aged over 18 but under 21, carried out by the Labour government in 1969, added about 800,000 voters to an electorate of 39 millions; this made a difference of about two per cent to the size of the voting population and, though an important reform, it cannot be termed fundamental. Women, who were allowed to vote at the age of 30 or over under the Representation of the People Act of 1918, were given equality of the franchise with men in 1928.

The method of compiling the electoral register last underwent a major overhaul in 1918, save that the 1918 Act provided for the compilation of two registers a year, in the spring and autumn, whereas since 1948, on grounds of cost, only one register has been compiled annually.[2] Because there is now only one re-compilation of the register each year, it can take as much as 16 months of residence in a constituency before an elector qualifies for the vote. The effect of reducing the number of registers per year from two to one is in fact to disfranchise between three and four per cent of eligible voters.[3] In this respect, the system in operation in the 1980s is demonstrably worse than that in force at the end of the First World War.

Broadly speaking, therefore, the present electoral system dates from the first half of the twentieth century, and much of it is based upon the Act of 1918, with just such modifications of detail as have been thought necessary, on political grounds, to accommodate changing views of adult political maturity or to curry favour with sections of the population from whom it was hoped political benefits might be derived. The 1918 Act had indeed been revolutionary in one respect: it had increased the electorate from 7.5 millions to nearly 20 millions. Beyond that, however, it had built upon pre-1914 notions of representation and election procedure, some of which still govern the workings of the present-day electoral system.

Among these, the most basic is the very act of dissolving a Parliament and calling a general election. Although the Parliament Act of 1911 reduced the maximum period between general elections from seven years to five, it left the timing of an election entirely in the hands of the government of the day, and in particular of the Prime Minister.[4] So there is no such thing as a fixed-term Parliament, though at local government level the principle of a fixed term has long been accepted. The result is that the timing of a general election is a political act, and there have been occasions when economic decisions which possessed little merit in themselves have been taken with a view to preparing the way for an election victory. In May 1955, for instance, Sir Anthony Eden called a general election (though one need not have been held for another 17 months) in the hope of capitalizing on a reduction in the standard rate of income tax the previous month. At other times, general elections have been held, or postponed, for the sake of party advantage. In the summer of 1978 James Callaghan put off a general election which it was generally expected – even by some of his Cabinet colleagues – would take place in the autumn, partly because he hoped that lower tax rates and higher child benefits (due to come into effect in mid-November) would help Labour to victory at the polls early in 1979.[5]

The basis upon which a political party appeals to the electorate is its election manifesto, and a party which wins a majority of seats in the House of Commons claims a 'mandate' to carry into law those of its policies which were included in its manifesto. Nothing illustrates more clearly the wholly artificial nature of the election contest than the doctrine of the mandate, a peculiarly twentieth-century device used to endow with a moral sanction beyond question the right of the governing party to pass into law whatever its election manifesto might have contained. At first glance such a proposition might be thought entirely reasonable. But in two major respects the proposition is entirely fraudulent.

First, manifestos are often deliberately drawn in woolly and vague phraseology, capable of many interpretations; manifestos also contain many policy commitments, and it can hardly be supposed that every voter voting for a particular party therefore agrees with every one of the manifesto commitments that party makes. These commitments have been growing alarmingly in number. The 1979 Conservative manifesto included 74 specific commitments, while Labour's manifesto contained no less than 133.[6] Yet on three important election issues in 1979 (the prohibition of secondary picketing; a free vote in the Commons on the restoration of capital punishment; and the sale of council houses to sitting tenants) a majority of Labour voters actually supported Conservative policies.[7]

Many manifesto promises are ignored, and others are cynically broken. The Labour governments of 1964–70 acted contrary to manifesto pledges on three issues: the Common Market; housing; and the maintenance of a free health service.[8] The 1970 Conservative manifesto, *A Better Tomorrow*, declared, 'We will stop further nationalization'; yet Rolls-Royce was nationalized by Edward Heath's government a mere eight months later. The manifesto also stated: 'We utterly reject the philosophy of compulsory wage control'; in November 1972 such a philosophy was implemented. Within a year of coming to office in May 1979 Margaret Thatcher's government had announced its determination to break three of its manifesto commitments. It abandoned its promise to introduce a register of those Commonwealth wives and children entitled to entry for settlement in the United Kingdom under the 1971 Immigration Act.[9] It broke a manifesto pledge to introduce a quota system covering all immigrants from outside the Common Market. And it reneged on a manifesto promise to have all Welsh language television programmes put out on the new fourth television channel in Wales. Little wonder, therefore, that, some months before the 1979 election, the Advertising Standards Authority let it be known that it would not deal with complaints about claims made in political advertisements.[10]

There may of course be very sound pragmatic reasons why it is better that some manifesto promises are not kept. In the cases of the register of immigrants and the problem of Welsh language television programmes, the government's reasoning was that grave technical problems lay in the way of the promises being fulfilled. The promises themselves, it was admitted, had been rash and mistakes had been made.[11] If so, why did politicians of great experience make the promises in the first place? Why give hostages to fortune?

So far as Welsh language television was concerned, the government badly miscalculated public opinion in the principality. The President of Plaid Cymru, Gwynfor Evans, threatened to starve himself to death unless the government's decision was reversed. There was a very real possibility of civil disobedience and public violence. So in September 1980 William Whitelaw, the Conservative Home Secretary, announced that the manifesto pledge was, after all, to be kept. This honouring of a written commitment was hailed as a 'climb-down' and a 'capitulation'; one Conservative M.P. called it 'a concession to blackmail'.[12] Certainly the cause of parliamentary democracy was badly served. But the blame lay squarely with the politicians, not with the electors.

At one level the manifesto is a 'house' publication, a document drawn up for internal party consumption, perhaps to ensure party unity as election time approaches, certainly to provide candidates with a ready answer to awkward questions from constituents and the press. At another level the manifesto is drawn up to attract votes. There is in fact no evidence that manifestos do attract votes.[13] This is hardly surprising in view of the fact that, apart from politicians and academics, very few people read them. But party workers *believe* that manifestos sway voters. And there is plenty of evidence (discussed below) that the failure of politicians to keep faith with their voters has contributed towards the sharp decline in public respect for the political process in recent years.

The second major reason why the doctrine of the mandate is false is that it is based upon a view of democracy which has no basis in reality. The party which 'wins' the election forms the government. But what does 'winning' actually mean? In the British context it means being able to command a simple majority of the M.P.s (at present 635) in the House of Commons. These M.P.s, in turn, 'win' their seats by obtaining, not a majority of the votes cast in their individual constituency contests, but merely the *largest number* of votes cast, irrespective of the votes obtained by other candidates. This is the essence of the first-past-the-post, or plurality, system which has in recent years come under increasingly critical scrutiny. By this system it is possible – indeed common – for candidates to win seats with less than 50 per cent of the votes cast. In October 1974, 59.8 per cent of the seats were won by a minority vote, and in May 1979 the proportion was 32.4 per cent.[14] At Inverness in May 1979 the victorious Liberal candidate, Russell Johnston, polled only 33.7 per cent of the vote; at Belfast North John McQuade won the seat for the Democratic Unionists with only 27.6 per cent of the votes.

The overall effect of this system is that, since the National Government's victories of 1931 and 1935, no British government has polled more than half the votes cast, yet all but one have obtained more than half the seats in the Commons. The post-war picture is given in Table 1. It will be seen that the plurality system not only distorts the wishes of the electorate, by delivering power into the hands of parties which do not have the backing of a majority of those who bother to vote. It can, on occasion, prevent the party with the largest share of the vote from forming a government, by giving more seats to another party. In 1951 Labour obtained a larger share of the votes cast than the Conservatives, but ended up with fewer seats; in February 1974 the Conservative share of the poll was higher but the number of seats lower than Labour's.

The minor parties undoubtedly suffer most under this system. The Liberal party, in particular, has been systematically and repeatedly robbed of its true entitlement to seats at Westminster. In February 1974 the Liberals obtained 19.3 per cent of the votes but only 2.2 per cent of the seats. In May 1979 they polled 13.8 per cent

Table 1: Votes and seats for the governing party, 1945–79

Election	Government	Votes cast (%)	Seats obtained (%)
1945	Labour	47.8	61.4
1950	Labour	46.1	50.4
1951	Conservative	48.0	51.4
1955	Conservative	49.7	54.6
1959	Conservative	49.4	58.0
1964	Labour	44.1	50.3
1966	Labour	47.9	57.6
1970	Conservative	46.4	52.4
1974 Feb.	Labour	37.1	47.4
1974 Oct.	Labour	39.2	50.2
1979	Conservative	43.9	53.4

of the votes but were rewarded with a mere 1.7 per cent of the seats; the Scottish National party obtained only two seats (0.3 per cent of the Commons) for 1.6 per cent of the votes. At the European Assembly elections of June 1979 the gross inequalities of the plurality system were even more pronounced. Table 2 gives the results of the Euro-elections in Great Britain (Northern Ireland did not have the plurality system, but polled by proportional representation). As a result of the plurality system, the British Liberal party has no representation at all in the European Parliament, nor has Plaid Cymru; the only British minor party to be represented is the Scottish National party, with one seat.

Table 2: European Assembly elections, June 1979 (excluding Northern Ireland)

Party	Votes (%)	No. of seats	% of seats
Conservative	50.6	60	76.9
Labour	33.0	17	21.8
Liberal	13.1	0	0.0
Scottish & Welsh Nats.	2.6	1	1.3
Others	0.7	0	0.0
	100.0	78	100.0

The plurality system, therefore, not only distorts the true state of political opinion among the voters. It give the impression, and transforms that impression into political power, that two major parties alone dominate the nation's politics, that the nation is split into two political groupings, and that all political debate must be conducted in an adversarial framework as a contest between two stark alternatives. The very shape of the House of Commons, with two rows of seats facing each other, itself reflects this view: Her Majesty's Government on one side and Her Majesty's Opposition on the other; two 'sides' advocating different and opposing policies, between which the electors must make their choice at the polls. The broad middle ground is squeezed out. Compromise politics are consequently in short supply. Unpleasant measures are taken early on in the lifetime of a government, in the hope that popularity can be recouped nearer the time of the next general election; because, at that election, 'the winner takes all'.[15] Politics has, in this way, become an auction in which the only two bidders are the Conservative and Labour parties.

In fact there has never been a two-party system in modern British politics. But, just as nature abhors a vacuum, so the electoral system abhors third parties, and tries its best to eliminate them by slashing their representative strength at Westminster.[16] Table 3 charts the combined electoral support of the Conservative and Labour parties at each general election since 1970, and compares this support with the percentage of parliamentary seats both parties obtained. Nothing could indicate more clearly how unfairly the present electoral system bestows power at Westminster, and how unjustly, in 1974, a quarter of the voters – that is, over seven million persons – were treated.

Table 3: Support for and Parliamentary representation of the Conservative and Labour parties (combined), 1970–9

Election	Combined share of the votes (%)	Combined share of the seats (%)
1970	89.5	98.1
1974 Feb.	75.1	94.2
1974 Oct.	75.0	93.9
1979	80.8	95.6

Would a different system of counting votes produce a fairer result? Proportional representation (P.R.) is less of a mystery now than it was to most voters a couple of decades ago, and some of the fears about it have been dispelled. It used to be said, in condemnation of P.R. (1) that P.R. would never produce a majority for any one party at Westminster; (2) that consequently it would lead to coalition government; (3) that coalition governments are inherently unstable; and (4) that therefore P.R., though mathematically more attractive than the plurality system, would lead to instability and uncertainty in government, which were evils far worse than lack of proportionality in election results. The present system, according to this argument, provides strong government even if it does not provide representative government.

The general truth of the first of these four propositions cannot be denied. The two systems of P.R. favoured most by British electoral reformers are the Single Transferable Vote (S.T.V.) and the Additional Member System (A.M.S.). Under S.T.V. voters would express preferences for candidates in large, multi-member constituencies. A.M.S. would retain single-member constituencies, as at present, but would add to them a number of larger, regional constituencies for which additional M.P.s would be elected proportionately to the votes cast for their parties in each region.[17] In 1966 S.T.V. would have given Labour a working majority of between 10 and 20 seats, rather than the 96-seat majority the party actually obtained. In 1955 and 1959 A.M.S. would have produced small but workable Conservative majorities, instead of the majorities of 58 and 100 seats respectively which the party obtained at these elections. At all other general elections since 1945, under either system of P.R., coalition or minority governments would have been the rule rather than the exception. In 1979, for instance, P.R. would have given a pivotal position in Parliament to the Liberals, so that the resulting government might have been a Liberal-Conservative or a Liberal-Labour coalition.[18]

The second proposition is therefore probably also true. But it would be wrong to suppose that coalition or minority governments cannot be produced under the present system. Since the First World War there have been four minority governments (1924; 1929-31; March–October 1974; and April 1977—May1979[19]) and there were coalition governments between 1918 and 1922, from 1931 to 1940, and during the Second World War. The National governments of 1931-40 and Churchill's wartime coalition were particularly strong administrations.

The third and fourth propositions are therefore open to question. Politicians brought up under the plurality system are certainly capable of entering into coalitions when political necessity and overriding national considerations force them to S.T.V., which is

the system of P.R. officially promoted by the Electoral Reform
Society and the Liberal party, was rejected by only seven votes in the
House of Commons in 1917. Between 1918 and 1945 it was used for
the university seats, and Edward Heath's Conservative government
prescribed it as the system by which the short-lived Northern
Ireland Assembly was to be elected. It was also used for the election
of Northern Ireland's three Euro-M.P.s. There can therefore be no
question that S.T.V. might be too complicated for electors to
understand. A.M.S., a variant of the West German electoral system,
is the method of P.R. preferred by the Hansard Society's Commission on Electoral Reform, which reported in October 1976.[20] It has
the merit that, though the counting of votes is admittedly complex,
it would involve no new departure so far as the mechanics of voting
are concerned; voting would take place exactly as at present.

But it is not only the relative party strengths that would alter
under a system of P.R. Voting habits would probably undergo a
revolution. Under the present system votes given for minor parties
are usually wasted votes. The realization that this is so deters many
voters from giving minor parties their support. Some voters feel
themselves forced to vote 'tactically'; that is, they do not vote in
support of the party they want to see in power, but cast their votes so
as to ensure (they hope) the defeat of the party they most dislike.
Tactical voting may mean that a Liberal supporter, living in a
constituency which the Liberals have no hope of winning, will
decide to vote Conservative in order to keep Labour out; or that a
Labour supporter will vote Conservative in order to help prevent a
nationalist victory. In October 1974 tactical voting by about 35,000
voters in England and Wales cost Labour 25 seats.[21] In May 1979
there was evidence of tactical voting by Liberal supporters in
England and by Labour and Liberal supporters in Scotland.[22]

Under P.R., voting behaviour would be very different. Far fewer
votes would be wasted, because minority parties would be guaranteed a much fairer representation in Parliament. Minor parties
would, in turn, probably feel justified in putting up more candidates. Some important consequences would follow. The present
electoral system fails to recognize that in the majority of parliamentary seats, the 'safe' seats, the selection by a relatively few party
activists of the candidate of the prevailing party is tantamount to
election. In May 1979 only 72 seats changed hands; thus the
outcome of the election was decided by only four million or so voters
out of a total of 41 million persons on the electoral register. Not only

are local party selection procedures open to abuse. Even when the procedures are technically sound, those who are selected are very often not representative of general opinion in the party, and sometimes even less representative of party support in the consti- tuency. Though there have been a few cases of local parties (all Conservative) instituting 'primary' elections, allowing local party members to choose the candidates, the results – in terms of active participation – have not been encouraging.[23] Under a system of P.R. (particularly S.T.V.) where a local party was deeply divided, it would be possible for the party to put up candidates representing different points of view, thus allowing the electors to choose between them.

We might also note that under S.T.V. many more constituencies would become 'marginal', because at least one of the seats – and perhaps two – in a multi-member constituency would be winnable by a minor party. M.P.s would therefore have a much greater incentive than at present to pay attention to the views of their constituents. And, partly as a consequence, it is more likely that under P.R. the style of electioneering would also change. It would be rash for a party to make sweeping categorical promises of what it would do if brought to power because, in all probability, it would have to share power with other parties. Manifestos would be more realistic and down-to-earth. The dialogue between electors and elected would therefore be franker and certainly more honest.

The inequitable system of representation in the House of Com- mons is the single most important deficiency to be found in the present electoral arrangements in the United Kingdom. A system of P.R. would do much by way of remedy. But it would not be a complete answer. There is, indeed, a danger that other deficiencies might be ignored or glossed over should the campaign for P.R. gain real momentum. And if, for reasons of party advantage, politicians are adamant that P.R. must be resisted, there are other reforms which they might be persuaded to undertake. These reforms fall into three broad areas of election law and administration: the delineation of constituency boundaries; the registration of voters; and the regulation of election finance.

The way in which constituency boundaries are drawn up can affect the result of an election as profoundly as the manner in which votes are cast and counted. In the nineteenth century franchise reform was usually accompanied by a redistribution of seats. The 1918 Act, in general terms, redrew constituency boundaries so that most parliamentary seats had the same number of electors, but it was not until the Redistribution Act of 1944 that permanent machinery to review boundary arrangements was set up. The 1944 Act (amended in 1946 and 1948) established four Boundary Commissions, one each for England, Wales, Scotland and Northern Ireland, continually to review and alter boundaries. Each Commission was to establish an electoral quota by dividing the total electorate by the number of seats available. Northern Ireland was to have not less than 12 seats, Scotland not less than 71, Wales not less than 35, and the total number of seats in the United Kingdom was not to be substantially greater than 625. Once the electoral quotas had been established, the task of the Commissions was to recommend boundaries to produce constituencies with electorates as near the quotas as practicable.

The work of the Boundary Commission has been bedevilled with technical and political difficulties, and the ideal of roughly equal-sized constituencies has never in practice been attained. The technical difficulties stem from the terms of reference of the Commissions and the various constraints which the law imposes upon their work. Originally the Commissions were enjoined to keep electorates within 25 per cent of the quota in order to respect local government boundaries; but in 1958 a Redistribution of Seats Act released them from this obligation. The Act also increased the period between general reviews to a minimum of 10 and a maximum of 15 years. Moreover, under the original Act of 1944, the calculation of the quota is based upon the number of qualified electors, not upon the total population, and the Commissioners have no power to take into account projected population movements when redistributing seats.

The result is – predictably – that very substantial differences in constituency size can develop between boundary revisions. In 1979 Gateshead West (electorate 29,037) and Glasgow Central (19,826) each returned one M.P., but so did Newton (102,885), and Bromsgrove and Redditch (104,375).[24] On average the Labour party polled 42,871 votes for every candidate elected, whereas the successful Conservative candidates polled only 40,406 votes each. The principle of 'one man, one vote' has been acccepted, but that of 'one vote, one value' certainly has not.

This omission is at its most glaring when one considers the apportionment of seats between England, Scotland, Wales and Northern Ireland. Scotland and Wales are over-represented at Westminster. Scotland has had 71 seats (excluding unversity seats) since 1918. Welsh representation has remained at 36 seats since 1948. Northern Ireland, on the other hand, is under-represented; its Westminster representation, 12 M.P.s, was fixed in 1922. Table 4 illustrates the present disparities in the parliamentary representation of the four constituent countries of the United Kingdom.

Table 4: Unequal parliamentary representation in the U.K.

	Electorate (May 1979)	Seats	Seats if constituencies were equal
England	34,189,115	516	528
Scotland	3,813,835	71	59
Wales	2,063,108	36	32
Northern Ireland	1,027,204	12	16
	41,093,262	635	635

The under-representation of Northern Ireland did originally have sound reasoning behind it. Under the Government of Ireland Act of 1920 Northern Ireland enjoyed internal self-rule through the Stormont Parliament. Stormont was dismantled in 1972. Its successor, the Northern Ireland Assembly, lasted less than a year. In 1974 Northern Ireland, in common with the rest of the United Kingdom, came to be ruled directly from Westminster. In these circumstances British politicians recognized that the under-representation of the province was no longer tenable. Legislation increasing the number of Northern Ireland seats to 17 (with provision to vary the number between 16 and 18)[25] was passed in March 1979 but was not to come into effect until the general election *after* that due in 1979.

The over-representation of Scotland and Wales is also deliberate. The number of seats allotted to these countries, as determined in 1918, was about right, given the difficulties of amalgamating mountain and island constituencies. But over the past 30 years the over-representation has been tolerated because it is in the interests of the two major parties that it should be. It is felt that nationalist sentiment must be accommodated lest a reduction in Scottish and Welsh representation is exploited by Plaid Cymru and the Scottish National party. Labour relies heavily on its Celtic representation; in October 1974 it won 41 of the Scottish seats and 23 of the Welsh. The Celtic fringe is also important for the Conservative party. In May 1979 the Conservatives won 22 Scottish seats and 11 in Wales –

the largest number of seats won by the Conservatives in Wales this century. Had there been equal-sized constituencies at the 1979 election, Conservative representation in Scotland and Wales would have fallen by five seats, and Labour representation by 10 seats. Though the Conservatives would probably have balanced these losses by winning an extra seven seats or so in England, Labour would only have gained an extra five English seats. Moreover, these calculations assume that the same percentage of seats in England, Scotland and Wales would have been won by each party. Were a reduction of Scottish and Welsh representation to be followed by an upsurge of nationalist support, the few extra English seats gained would undoubtedly be swamped by heavy Scottish and Welsh losses. So the cutting down to size of Scottish and Welsh representation is a political risk neither party is willing to take.

Politics governs the entire mechanics of delineating parliamentary constituency boundaries. The Boundary Commissioners merely make recommendations. It is for Parliament, and the government, to give them legal sanction. The boundary revisions of 1948 aroused great controversy, for the English proposals involved – quite rightly – the transfer of seats from depopulated city centres to growing suburban areas; it has been estimated that the proposals cost Labour between 20 and 30 seats at the 1950 election.[26] The boundary proposals of 1969 were actually rejected by the Labour Home Secretary, James Callaghan, and vetoed by the Labour majority in the Commons.[27]

In the United States of America a series of Supreme Court decisions has curbed the power of politicians to influence electoral boundaries and has laid down the maxim that all voters must enjoy equal political strength.[28] The subordination of the United Kingdom Boundary Commissioners to the dictates of the politicians at Westminster needs to be similarly dealt with. The Speaker of the House of Commons is *ex-officio* chairman of each Commission, and a judge is deputy chairman; other members are chosen for their expertise in demography and their independence of party politics, and the Commissions have the assistance of the Director of the Ordnance Survey and the Registrar-General of Births, Deaths and Marriages. There is no reason why the recommendations of such Commissions should not have the force of law, subject of course to the overriding authority of Parliament to reverse boundary decisions with which it did not agree. In practice, the government of the day would have to make out a very strong case indeed for setting aside the Boundary Commissions' rulings. Moreover, given the rapidity with which population changes can occur, the maximum period of 15 years between boundary revisions is clearly too long, especially when one remembers that revisions, even when approved by Parliament, do not take effect until the next general election; thus the general election of 1970 was fought on boundaries approved in 1954 and researched at an even earlier date. Boundary revisions should take place about as frequently as general elections have to, i.e. every five years; once fixed, new boundaries should take effect at once. Most important of all, the Boundary Commissions must be empowered to take account of *projected* population movements when redistributing seats.

Boundary revisions are closely observed by local party workers, keen to preserve their 'territory' intact and often unwilling to accept constituency revisions which would necessitate the merger of adjacent party organizations. For the voter a boundary change can be dramatic. An elector living in a safe seat might suddenly find himself in a marginal constituency; his political influence and the degree of attention which parties, candidates and the media will give to him will be much greater.

At the outset, local party workers will want to make sure that he is entitled to vote. It is not sufficient simply to live in a constituency and be over 18 years of age at the time of an election. The right to vote has to be claimed and registered. Reference has already been made to the deficiencies created by the fact that nowadays only one register of electors is compiled each year. It is generally reckoned that the register (which is already out of date when it comes into force on 16 February, having been compiled the previous autumn) deteriorates in accuracy at the rate of about one half per cent each month, so that on its last day of validity (15 February of the following year) it is only 85 per cent accurate.[29] Given that there is only one register per year, some of this inaccuracy is nonetheless preventable.

Registration depends, in the first instance, on the completion and return of the registration forms distributed to heads of households. It is an offence not to fill in and return such a form, but prosecutions are extremely rare. The accuracy of the register therefore depends on the honesty and intellectual ability of heads of households. Sometimes heads of households fail to return the forms because they do not wish to be called for jury service (names for which are drawn from the electoral registers). Landlords who allow their dwellings to become overcrowded with tenants do not want to advertise the fact on the registration forms. Many Commonwealth immigrants do not understand the registration procedures, or are ignorant of their rights, or may suspect the motives of those who seek information, or fear the consequences of giving it. A survey conducted at the time of the October 1974 election in seven English constituencies with a high density of Afro-Caribbeans and Asians in their populations showed that whereas only six per cent of eligible white voters were not registered, 24 per cent of eligible coloured voters were not on the register.[30] By the time of the election of May 1979 the position had improved only slightly. A survey of 24 constituencies at that election revealed that 22 per cent of non-white respondents were not registered, compared with seven per cent of white respondents.[31]

A Home Office Working Party on the Electoral Register, which reported in February 1978, recognized that there was room for improvement in the reliability of the register, and made a series of recommendations – such as the use of other sources of information, including Post Office records – to bring about greater accuracy. Many of the recommendations were accepted by the government, but the necessary legislation has still to be passed into law. The Working Party's report was, however, characterized by excessive deference to the alleged needs of political parties. Continuous updating of the electoral register was rejected partly on the grounds that party canvassers needed definitive 'frozen' lists of voters as soon as an election was called; and the argument of national party agents was accepted, that 'an essential part of the registration procedure is a claims and objection stage', which a continuously-updated register would make more difficult.[32] The Working Party concluded: 'Although the concept of continuous updating of the electoral register is technically attractive . . . The usefulness of the register as a working document for those concerned with elections might be seriously impaired.'[33]

This attitude can hardly be called satisfactory. It is made worse by the apparent determination of those in authority to acquiesce in other, avoidable, discrepancies. Thus, although aliens living in the United Kingdom are supposed to be disenfranchised, many can in fact vote. The largest group of enfranchised aliens are citizens of the Irish Republic. By a historical anomaly which no British government has had the courage to put right, every citizen of Eire resident in the United Kingdom, and otherwise qualified to vote, may do so. Other aliens find their way onto the electoral register because, once the registration forms are returned to the Registration Officer, few checks are carried out by his staff into the question of eligibility. During the district council elections of May 1976 it was discovered at one college campus that, in a student population of 1,300 the names of 30 aliens had been entered on the electoral register. The college authorities had simply returned to the Registration Officer a list of all students in residence, without deleting the names of foreign students; the registration officials had accepted the list without question.

In other ways too the compilation of the electoral register is slapdash. There is no provision for the automatic deletion of deceased voters. Consequently, since there is no necessity to bring to the polling station any evidence of identity (not even the official 'Polling Card' sent to every voter), it is possible to vote more than once using the names of deceased voters. 'Polling the dead men' is a favourite election pastime in Northern Ireland. By contrast, eligible voters who move from one constituency to another must wait until the next annual re-compilation of the register before they can vote in their new constituency. It ought to be possible for a person moving house to have his name removed from one register and added to another at once.[34]

However, of all the anomalous restrictions upon the right to vote the most unjust are certainly those surrounding the postal vote. Seamen and members of the armed forces do of course have the right to vote by proxy or by post, as do persons incapacitated by blindness or illness. But for other people who know they will be away from their constituency on polling day, the law makes a curious distinction. The 1948 Act, which greatly extended the postal voting provisions, permits a vote by post to anyone whose occupation would make it impossible for him to be at home to vote in person. But those who will be away from home for other reasons, such as a holiday, are not allowed to vote by post.

When the taking of an annual holiday was the exception rather than the rule, and confined to the well-to-do, this distinction was perhaps tenable. Nowadays it is not. The Labour party has always been keener to maintain the distinction than the Conservatives, who actually proposed in 1964 to extend the postal vote to holiday-makers. But in 1967 the Speaker's Conference on Electoral Law ruled against the idea. Postal ballots are not counted separately; however, the general belief is that they divide 2:1 in favour of Conservatives.[35] On this assumption, the efficient organization of the postal vote by local Conservative activists in May 1979 may have been responsible for as many as 11 victories over Labour and three over the Scottish Nationalists.[36] Be that as it may, it is a great pity that the postal vote has become a political battleground, and that the Labour party has adopted in this matter an attitude which is excessively partisan. If a fully qualified voter, who happens to be on holiday at the time of an election, has enough civic responsibility to want to vote, the facility of the postal ballot really ought not to be denied him.

We have seen that in relation to boundary revision and to voter registration, as well as to plurality voting, reform has very often been blocked on political grounds. When one examines the law relating to finance at elections, there can be no doubt that political considerations have led to the framing of very unjust rules. The spending of money by candidates during the period of a general election or by-election (that is, between the issuing of the writ and the day of the poll) is strictly controlled. A distinction is drawn between borough and county constituencies, and the permitted expenditure per candidate is composed of a fixed sum plus an amount related to the number of electors in the constituency. These amounts are periodically reviewed to allow for inflation, though in fact the limits are rarely reached in practice; in May 1979 the average expenditure was £1,394 per candidate, though the permitted averages are substantially higher.[37]

But these limits bear no relation whatsoever to the amount of money which may quite legally be spent by the political parties nationally. National publicity campaigns promoted from party headquarters are not subject to any financial restrictions. Thus in May 1979 the total election expenses of all candidates amounted to £3,557,000, but several million pounds more were spent by the Conservative, Labour and Liberal parties in national press publicity, broadcasting, additional headquarters' expenses, private opinion polls, and so on.[38] Moreover, the legal restrictions on expenditure do not apply outside the three- or four-week period of the election. Local parties are careful to refer to their candidates as 'prospective' until the writ for the election has been issued. In this way none of the expenses incurred by a 'prospective' candidate in nursing his constituency can be legally chargeable to his election expenses.

The anomalies of election finance strike deeper than this. Although a candidate's constituency election expenses are controlled by law, there is no restriction on the amount of money which may be spent by private bodies which are not themselves political parties, provided they are not seen to favour one political party as against another, and provided the money is not spent in support of particular candidates. Thus in 1970 Aims of Industry, an avowedly anti-socialist organization, spent £134,000 during the general election on propaganda which clearly favoured the Conservative cause, but which escaped the election expenditure laws.

Private organizations also make large grants to political parties for general election purposes. In 1979, in addition to the usual hefty donations from trade unions, the Labour party received £80,000 from the League Against Cruel Sports 'in appreciation of the section of the manifesto with regard to cruel sports'; the Rowntree Trust gave large grants to the Liberal party.[39] Similarly, in the summer of 1978, when it was widely expected that a general election would be called in the autumn, the 'Campaign Against Building Industry Nationalisation' (CABIN), a consortium of building and civil engineering employers, spent a great deal of money distributing circulars attacking the Labour party's plans to take large sections of the building industry into public ownership and control. No legal action was taken to stop this propaganda.[40]

There is, then, a great deal of pious humbug in the legal restrictions on election finance. Candidates must meticulously record every penny spent on petrol, postage stamps and envelopes, and occasionally have been known to do public penance in the courts when a few pounds of expenses not recorded in the proper manner have come to light. But the vast amounts spent on the national campaign are totally uncontrolled, and so is the expenditure of national pressure groups. Locally, however, pressure groups are not so free to campaign as they think fit. It is illegal to incur unauthorized expense to *procure* the election of a candidate. The legality of unauthorized expense to *prevent* the election of a candidate is less clear.

Much depends on the way election literature is worded. In October 1974 three members of anti-fascist organizations in the Manchester and Bolton areas distributed leaflets advising 'Don't Vote National Front, Don't Vote Fascist'. The House of Lords, reversing a decision of the Divisional Court, judged them to be guilty of a breach of electoral law.[41] But leaflets distributed by the Association of Jewish Ex-Servicemen at the same general election, giving information about National Front leaders and exhorting 'Don't give these men a chance to get their hands on our Government' were never made the subject of legal proceedings.

The Law Lords themselves have not clarified the issue beyond question. Lord Diplock, delivering the judgment referred to above, made some pointed observations about 'disparaging another candidate', and it seems that the defendants in that case overstepped an invisible line, drawn by the Law Lords, in trying to prevent the election of particular candidates. Lord Fraser, though he agreed with the judgment, nonetheless added that there might be circumstances in which he would be prepared to enter verdicts of not guilty against defendants charged with similar offences.

After the Ilford North by-election of March 1978 Phyllis Bowman, of the Society for the Protection of the Unborn Child, was successfully prosecuted for breaching electoral law by distributing leaflets – headed 'Protect The Unborn: Vote for Life' – which printed the views of the Conservative, Labour and Liberal candidates on the subject of abortion law reform.[42] Yet no action was taken in respect of a leaflet distributed, at that same by-election, by the Anti-Nazi League, which advised: 'Don't Vote Nazi Say No to the National Front'. This legal confusion is clearly unsatisfactory. At the very least it ought to be possible for local pressure groups, or individuals, to distribute factual information about candidates they would prefer not to see elected, and to add to this factual information some expression of their own opinion, without legal penalty. It cannot be right, in a country which sets great store by freedom of expression, to restrict during a parliamentary election the exercise of that freedom by individuals and private organizations, while maintaining it virtually unfettered for politicians and political parties.

The privileges enjoyed by political parties and politicians at an election are clearly considerable, and some are worth a great deal of money. Every candidate has the right to one free delivery by the Post Office to every elector in his constituency; election addresses can be distributed free in this way. Party broadcasts on radio and television, agreed by the parties and the broadcasters in a Committee on Party Political Broadcasting, are entirely free so far as broadcasting time is concerned. The parties only pay for such films, professional advice and production teams as they might wish to use in addition to the studio facilities provided by the broadcasting networks. Advertising time, which would cost the private citizen hundreds of thousands of pounds, is given to major and minor parties without cost and, it might be added, without legal obligation.[43]

In these circumstances, the calls which have been heard ever more frequently over the past couple of decades, for state financing of political parties, seem entirely out of place. In 1975 the Labour government set up a committee, under the chairmanship of Lord Houghton of Sowerby, to examine the possibility of state subventions to political parties. A majority of the committee recommended annual grants to the central party organizations on the basis of five pence per vote cast for each party at the previous general election, and the payment of half of each candidate's permitted expenses in parliamentary and local government elections; the payments towards election expenses would be made to all candidates polling at least one-eighth of the votes cast, and would be payable to independent candidates as well as to those belonging to political parties.[44]

The financial implications of these proposals would by themselves seem to preclude their implementation. On the basis of the May 1979 election figures, the cost to the nation in central grants would be well over £1.5 millions; the payment towards election expenses would have cost about £1.7 millions for the general election alone. But beyond the cost to the taxpayer there are other considerations weighing heavily against the implementation of the Houghton Committee's recommendations. For the notion of state subsidies cannot easily be reconciled with the voluntary nature of politics in the United Kingdom. It cannot be right that Labour taxpayers should be made to finance the Conservative party, and vice-versa; or that taxes raised from coloured voters should be used to bolster the activities of parties and candidates advocating the repatriation of immigrants. Only Labour has welcomed the Houghton proposals, for reasons which have little to do with political principles but derive largely from the unhealthy state of Labour party finances.

The foregoing overview of the British electoral system has not been comprehensive, but it has been deliberately selective.[45] My purpose has been to focus upon the major features of the present arrangements, as a preliminary to relating the system as a whole to wider considerations of British government and society as the twentieth century nears its end. The system may be summarized as follows: the manner in which votes are cast and counted is manifestly unfair, and produces fraudulent results; in particular, it enables a party with less than half the votes cast (and with the support of much less than half the electorate) to rule the country for up to five years. The winning party will have based its popular appeal on a manifesto, and will claim a mandate to carry into law its manifesto commitments. But it is frequently the case that the manifesto contains ill-informed, unresearched or vague and misleading commitments which may bear little relation to the realities of government and which are often cheerfully discarded, abridged or forgotten as soon as power is achieved. Those voters (usually the majority) who did not vote for the party in power have no hope of influencing government decisions, except in the case of a minority government (as between 1974 and 1979) or when government losses at by-elections are especially heavy.

The plurality system, moreover, is directly responsible for a situation in which Westminster politics is dominated by only two major parties. These parties not only have a vested interest in maintaining the present system of voting. They see to it that the justice of boundary changes is compromised to their own political advantage. The rules governing election expenditure favour political parties and discriminate against local independent pressure groups. And we may also note that proposals currently being considered, to raise the election deposit which must be paid by all candidates (and which is returned only to those gaining at least one-eighth of the valid votes cast) from £150 to about £1,000, is likely further to favour the large parties against the small ones and the independents.[46] Typically, the large parties, with considerable financial resources behind them, are trying to tighten their grip on the present electoral system by excluding the poorer candidates and parties. We have also seen that the voter-registration arrangements are lax and lead inevitably (and, in part, deliberately) to the disenfranchising of several millions of voters.

What wider effects does this sorry state of affairs have upon the way in which the country is governed? So far as Westminster politics is concerned, it is clear that the present electoral system nourishes the dominance of the House of Commons by two parties, whose dearest wish is to be seen as opposing and irreconcilable alternatives, offering mutually exclusive policies between which the electors must choose. The politics of divisiveness and confrontation, which have so often been seen in industrial relations and economic strategy in the nation at large, begin at Westminster. The system does not rule out compromise, but it makes compromise exceedingly difficult, because (especially as general elections or crucial by-elections approach) it is not in the interests of either major party to be seen to be in any sort of agreement with the other.

The system would not be quite so pernicious if there were indeed only two parties worth bothering about at elections. But in fact the

United Kingdom has a multi-party system. It is only the mechanics
of the electoral arrangements which make it appear as if British
politics were a two-horse race. The proportion of the electorate
supporting the Conservative and Labour parties has fallen dramatically since the 1950s, as Table 5 shows.

Table 5: Share of the electorate supporting the Labour and Conservative parties 1950–79 (%)

1950	74.9
1951	79.2
1955	73.8
1959	73.4
1964	67.4
1966	68.2
1970	64.4
1974 Feb.	59.2
1974 Oct.	54.7
1979	61.4

In these circumstances, the risk that the electorate may become
alienated from the parliamentary system must grow. And there are
some disturbing signs that such development is already taking place.
The ballot paper is, after all, a means by which politicians and their
voting publics conduct a dialogue. Voting reinforces conviction in
the reality of political participation, and this helps underpin the
citizen's belief in the legitimacy of the governmental system and
allegiance to it. Non-voting is a repudiation not merely of the
party-political establishment but of the constitutional framework
within which politicians operate. The number of non-voters has
grown in size. In the five general elections between 1950 and 1964
non-voters averaged 20.2 per cent of the electorate; in the five
general elections since 1966 they have averaged 25.6 per cent.

These figures reflect creeping public disillusion with representative democracy in this country. To them may be added the results of
a number of surveys which have shown that, among ordinary
voters, there is a widespread feeling of political impotence and a low
opinion of politicians and of parliament.[47] A Gallup survey for
B.B.C.Television a week before the 1979 general election revealed
that 21 per cent of respondents felt their opinion of politicians had
gone down as a result of the campaign. A Gallup survey the
following October showed that though confidence in the honesty of

doctors and police officers remained high, so far as M.P.s were concerned it was low.[48] Though it is clear that a whole range of factors have produce responses such as these, the distorting effects of the electoral system form a basic element which has produced such responses. A national sample of electors in June 1980 placed 'the political system' second only to 'class division and snobbery' in a list of national characteristics and institutions they regarded as 'bad'.[49] A majority of voters do not feel that elections force governments to pay attention to what people think. Hence the increasing resort to pressure groups, protests and 'direct action'.

These tendencies cannot but be deeply disturbing to all who care about the survival of parliamentary democracy in this country. What likelihood is there of the electoral system being changed to make it more representative? At first glance, the possibility that the Conservative and Labour parties might agree to reforms which would weaken their own parliamentary positions, and perhaps prevent either of them from being able, ever again, to form a single-party government, seems remote. But there are a number of factors which might cause them to change their minds.

The first is Northern Ireland. The disappearance of the apparent political consensus in Northern Ireland in the late 1960s convinced Westminster politicians that the plurality system was no longer appropriate there, and so it was swept away, not only for internal local authority elections but also for elections to the European Assembly. More recently, the claim of Northern Ireland to extra Westminster M.P.s has also been recognized. Political realities in the province have therefore caused Westminster politicians to view electoral reform with less hostility than was formerly the case; and the smooth functioning of the S.T.V. system in Northern Ireland must surely have dispelled the fears of those who once argued that P.R. was too complicated for voters in the United Kingdom.

The second factor is what might be called the European dimension. The United Kingdom is a member state of the European Economic Community, or Common Market. The 78 British members of the European Parliament are elected by the plurality system, but the elected members for every other member state, and for Northern Ireland, are elected by various systems of P.R.[50] From the Euro-elections of 1984 it was the intention that one common system of voting should prevail in all member states. At the time of writing Conservative and Labour leaders are adamant that Britain shall not have a system of P.R. even for the European Parliament.[51] This attitude is likely further to alienate British politicians from their voters, especially if the European Parliament gains in status and authority and comes to be seen as an important forum within which issues of direct concern to the British economy are thrashed out.

Third, there is the possibility of a major realignment of British political parties, stemming from the divisions within the Labour party following Labour's 1979 election defeat. These divisions have led to a group of Labour moderates forming the Social Democratic party, which at its inception in March 1981 had 14 M.P.s (13 ex-Labour and one former Conservative). Electoral reform is high on the agenda of this new party. It is just possible that, in combination with the Liberals, it might force such reform through a 'hung' Parliament, but only, it must be added, if its performance at a general election reflects the national grass-roots support it appeared to have at its foundation.[52]

Finally, there are the possible consequences of maintaining the present system virtually intact – that is, of doing nothing. Political alienation may well grow to dangerous proportions. Since industrialization in this country there has only been one occasion upon which revolution could be sniffed in the air. That was in the winter of 1830–1, following the refusal of the House of Lords to permit the second reading of the Whig Reform Bill. The idea of a revolutionary situation developing in the Britain of the 1980s because of the absence of electoral reform seems at first glance too absurd to contemplate. But in fact there has already been an instance of mass refusal to obey an Act of Parliament, in 1971, when the response of the Trades Union Congress to the Industrial Relations Act (for which the Conservative government claimed a 'mandate') was to tell trade unionists to ignore it and frustrate its implementation, which they did. We might also point to the threats of violence and civil disobedience in Wales (see above, p. 22) which caused the present Conservative government to honour its election promise concerning Welsh language television.

To the very real possibility of political alienation if the present electoral system is not reformed other consequences, hardly less sinister, must be considered. At the May 1979 general election it was clear that the pro-Conservative swing had not been as great in the north of England as in the south. To that extent the English electorate split on geographical lines. But the effect of the plurality system was grossly to exaggerate this cleavage. Table 6 compares seats and votes in the South-East and North-West regions of

England in 1979. In the South-East the Conservatives obtained about half the votes but three-quarters of the seats; in the North-West Labour obtained more seats than the Conservatives even though the party did less well in terms of popular support. The electoral system thus produced, in Parliament, the appearance of a geo-political divide which was not nearly so great in reality. This is not only unfair. It is dangerous.

Table 6: Seats and votes in the South-East and North-West regions, May, 1979*

Region	Seats(%)				Votes(%)			
	Con.	Lab.	Lib.	Other	Con.	Lab.	Lib.	Other
South-East	75.6	23.8	0.6	—	51.5	31.7	15.3	1.5
North-West	39.7	57.7	2.6	—	43.7	42.6	13.0	0.7

We have already seen how the plurality system discriminates against minor parties. But even in its treatment of each minor party the present system is not even-handed. If support for a minor party is territorially or culturally concentrated, the system may allow it a reasonable parliamentary representation. But if its support is more evenly spread, and more broadly based, as with the Liberals, the parliamentary representation will be token only, as indicated in Table 7, which compares the popular support and parliamentary representation obtained by the Scottish National party in Scotland, Plaid Cymru in Wales and the Liberal party in England at the October 1974 election. Both nationalist parties did relatively better in terms of seats won than the Liberals in England; Plaid Cymru obtained a much larger percentage of Welsh seats than the Liberals did of English seats, even though its relative popular support was much less.

There are therefore strong grounds for arguing that the present electoral system favours narrowly-based nationalist minor parties against broadly-based minor parties.[53] Should a future general election held under the present system produce another 'hung'

* Adapted from D.Butler and D. Kavanagh, *The British General Election of 1979* (1980), 356. The regions are the Standard Regions as defined by the General Register Office before the 1974 re-organization of local government. The swing to the Conservatives in 1979 was 6.8 per cent in the South-East but only 3.2 per cent in the North-West.

Table 7: Representation of Liberals, Welsh and Scottish Nationalists, October 1974

	Popular Support	Parliamentary representation
Liberals	20.2% of English votes	1.6% of English seats
Plaid Cymru	10.8% of Welsh votes	8.3% of Welsh seats
S.N.P.	30.4% of Scottish votes	15.5% of Scottish seats

Parliament (as in 1974) there is indeed every likelihood that the
balance will be held by introspective territorially-founded nationalist
groups from Scotland and Wales (and from Northern Ireland, whose
representation will in any case be increased). The experience of the
1974–9 Parliaments is that these groups will use such political
muscle as comes their way to feather their own nests, rather than to
work for the good of the United Kingdom as a whole. No one, least
of all Conservative and Labour M.P.s, can be happy with such a
prospect. And if the major parties come to be convinced that the
present electoral system is a political liability, might they not
conclude that it has, after all, outlived its usefulness?

It would be quite wrong to argue that electoral reform could solve
the nation's problems. It would not of itself reduce inflation, create a
satisfactory balance of trade, bring down interest rates, do away with
industrial stoppages, increase productivity or reduce unemployment. But it would create a climate of opinion, in the country and in
Parliament, in which all these problems, and many more, could be
tackled sensibly, with moderation and without confrontation. It is
astonishing to think that the basis of the electoral system in force
today has remained unchanged since 1918, and that that system had
previously been condemned by both Houses of Parliament.[54] The
very foundation of parliamentary democracy in the United Kingdom
still awaits modernization.

Postscript

This essay was completed prior to the general election of 9 June
1983. But the results of that election have reinforced the essay's
major conclusions. The election was fought on new and drastically
revised boundaries, giving seven extra seats to England, two to
Wales, one to Scotland and five to Northern Ireland. However, the
650-seat House of Commons elected in 1983 was a cruel distortion of

the wishes of the electorate. At 72.7 per cent, turnout was lower than at any time since 1970. The Conservative share of the vote (42.4 per cent) gave the Conservatives over 60 per cent of the seats, and the Labour party won 32 per cent of the seats with only 27.6 per cent of the votes. The S.D.P.-Liberal Alliance polled over a quarter of the votes, and was rewarded with the handsome total of 23 M.P.s! Thus, on a turnout lower than in 1979, and with fewer voters supporting it than in 1979, the Conservative party 'achieved' (by courtesy of the electoral system) an overall majority of 144 seats. This majority the media at once graced with the title 'landslide', while Conservative politicians lost no time in declaring that the voters had given them a 'mandate' for their policies.

In the opinion of the author, therefore, the case for electoral reform is stronger than ever; he reiterates in the strongest possible terms the essay's concluding sentence.

NOTES

1. *The Times*, 27 March 1981, 2.
2. Between 1926 and 1948 there was only one register a year, also for reasons of economy.
3. I expound upon the reasons for this in G.Alderman, *British Elections: Myth and Reality* (1978), 44–5.
4. The 1911 Act gave and gives to the House of Lords the absolute and unfettered power to veto (and not merely delay) any bill passed by the Commons to postpone an election beyond five years. This power has never been used, but those who advocate a unicameral legislature often fail to provide for an alternative method of ensuring that no parliament can prolong itself indefinitely.
5. D.Butler and D.Kavanagh, *The British General Election of 1979* (1980) [cited hereafter as Butler and Kavanagh, *1979*], 45–6.
6. S.E.Finer, *The Changing British Party System, 1945–1979* (Washington, D.C. 1980) [cited hereafter as Finer, *Party System*], 122.
7. *Ibid.*, 124.
8. R.Rose, *The Problem of Party Government* (1974), 411.
9. *The Times*, 7 Dec. 1979, 2.
10. *The Times*, 8 Aug. 1978, 13: letter from the chairman of the Authority.
11. The government admitted that its manifesto promise concerning Welsh language television programmes was 'ill-advised': *Daily Telegraph*, 28 Aug. 1980, 10.
12. *The Times*, 18 Sept. 1980, 1.
13. Alderman, *op.cit.*, 25–6.
14. The highest number of minority-vote victories since 1945 was in Feb. 1974, when 408 (64.3 per cent) of the seats were won in this way.

15. These themes are explored in S.E.Finer (ed.), *Adversary Politics and Electoral Reform* (1975) [cited hereafter as Finer, *Adversary Politics*], especially in the introductory essay by Professor Finer.

16. A socially and territorially broad-based party needs to poll about 34 per cent of the votes before it begins to achieve reasonable parliamentary representaton; anything less would give it many near-misses but few actual victories.

17. The mechanics of these systems are explained in Alderman, *op.cit.*, 34–8.

18. J.Curtice and M.Steed, 'An Analysis of the Voting', in Butler and Kavanagh *1979*, 430–1.

19. In Oct. 1974 Labour was returned with a majority, on paper, of three seats. The loss of the Stechford by-election in April 1977 led effectively to the disappearance of this majority, because Labour also provided the Speaker, who normally does not vote.

20. *The Report of the Hansard Society Commission on Electoral Reform* (1976), 46–7. A.M.S. is also the system favoured by Roy Jenkins, one of the leading figures in the foundation of the Social Democratic party: *The Times*, 18 March 1981, 2.

21. M.Steed, 'The Results Analysed' in D.Butler and D.Kavanagh, *The British General Election of October 1974* (1975), 339–40.

22. Curtice & Steed, *loc. cit.*, 406, 417.

23. Alderman, *op.cit.*, 82–3.

24. In 1980 there were 11 English constituencies with more than 100,000 electors, and 14 with fewer than 40,000: *The Times*, 5 Jan. 1981, 3.

25. The Times, 20 April 1978, 1. The Northern Ireland Boundary Commission is empowered to fix the number of Northern Irish seats at between 16 and 18.

26. H.G.Nicholas, *The British General Election of 1950* (1951), 4.

27. The Labour party feared that the proposals would deprive them of city-centre seats; the Conservative opposition therefore supported them. Ironically, the boundary changes of 1969, applied by the Conservative government in time for the Feb. 1974 election, produced a net gain to Labour of between 16 and 22 seats: Alderman, *op.cit.*, 63.

28. M.Busteed, *Geography and Voting Behaviour* (1975), 9–21.

29. Alderman, *op.cit.*, 44–5.

30. Community Relations Commission, *Participation of Ethnic Minorities in the General Election October 1974* (1975), 13–14.

31. M.Anwar, *Votes and Policies: Ethnic Minorities and the General Election, 1979* (1980), 35.

32. *Report of the Working Party on the Electoral Register* (1978), 5–6.

33. *Ibid.*, 13.

34. There does exist a complicated procedure by which a qualified elector, whose name has been omitted in error from the electoral register, may apply to the High Court for an Order of Mandamus obliging the appropriate Registration Officer to allow him to vote. On polling day, 3 May 1979, a barrister and his wife used this procedure. It cost them

£12.50 each in court fees, took up most of the day, and is certainly not to be recommended for those unversed in the law; it also requires a great deal of patience and a letter of consent from the Registration Officer against whom it is directed: *Daily Telegraph*, 4 May 1979, 1.

35. An Independent Television News-Opinion Research Centre survey in May 1979 found that electors in marginal seats who said they had voted by post divided 5:3 in favour of the Conservatives.

36. Butler and Kavanagh, *1979*, 314.

37. £3,050 in boroughs and £2,725 in counties: *The Times*, 29 June 1979, 2.

38. M.Pinto-Duschinsky, in *The Times*, 10 March 1980, 6, has estimated the cost of the national campaign by the Conservative party at the 1979 general election at approximately £2.3 millions, and Labour party national expenditure at about £1.5 millions.

39. *Ibid.*

40. *Sunday Times*, 9 July 1978, 3.

41. *The Times*, 28 May 1976, 10.

42. *The Times*, 21 Aug. 1978, 2; *Daily Telegraph*, 9 March 1979, 3.

43. M.Pinto-Duschinsky (see n. 38 above) has estimated the value of the free broadcasting time and free postage given to the Conservative, Labour and Liberal parties in 1979 at £7.8 millions.

44. *Report of the Committee on Financial Aid to Political Parties* (Cmnd. 6601, 1976), xv.

45. The interested reader should consult the bibliographies in Alderman, *op.cit.*, and Finer, *Party System* for further reading material on all aspects of the electoral system.

46. *The Times*, 19 March 1980, 2.

47. See F.Stacey, *A New Bill of Rights for Britain* (1973), 149–57 and Lord Hailsham's 1976 Dimbleby Lecture, reported in *The Times*, 15 Oct. 1976, 4. See also Finer, *Party System*, 130–1.

48. Both surveys are reported in *British Public Opinion*, i (1980), 25.

49. *The Times*, 10 Sept. 1980, 4.

50. For an explanation of these systems see *Your Vote in Europe* (European League for Economic Co-Operation, 1979), 8–11. The method of election in Greenland (part of Denmark) is by the plurality system, but since Greenland has only one Euro-M.P., proportional representation is not appropriate. The Greek Euro-M.P.s are (for the time being) appointed by the Greek parliament.

51. In December 1977 a proposal to have a form of P.R. throughout the United Kingdom for the first Euro-elections was defeated by 97 votes in the House of Commons: *The Times*, 14 Dec. 1977, 1.

52. See the article by I.Crewe in *The Times*, 23 March 1981, 12.

53. As if to press home the point, in the 1979 Euro-elections the Scottish National party had one Euro-M.P. elected, but the Liberals none at all.

54. M.Steed, 'The Evolution of the British Electoral System', in Finer, *Adversary Politics*, 46.

3 PARLIAMENT

R.L.Borthwick

IT HAS become a commonplace observation that the twentieth century has been hard on legislative bodies. The reasons for this are not hard to find (though they may be harder to measure); they include the increasing complexity of more technologically advanced societies, the greater interdependence of societies and the growth of demands made upon the state alongside a greater reluctance to accept the guidance offered by traditional sources of authority. Not only do these problems present difficulties in themselves but they tend to give rise to responses which are in turn challenges to the position of a legislative body as, for example, in the growth of bureaucracy and the increased importance of interest groups.

In the case of the British Parliament, or at least of its dominant element the Commons, an essentially subservient role is not new. Indeed formal recognition of such a position is almost as old as the century itself. The procedural reforms of 1902 formalized the government's dominant position in the House in return for recognition of the place of the Opposition and, to a lesser extent, backbenchers. This, it might be argued, provided a framework which suited the demands of the twentieth century. While it could hardly be claimed that changes have occurred in society because of the way in which relations between executive and legislature were ordered at the outset of the century, it may be that some of those developments were thereby facilitated. Certainly Parliament has not acted as a major obstructive force – though some would argue that even to express matters in those terms is to be unfair to Parliament. What may be as true is that governments have been insufficiently checked because the 1902 reforms encouraged a shared view on the part of the leadership of the major parties that the relationship between Parliament and executive was basically sound because the electoral system happened to provide each of the major parties, whether Liberal and Conservative or Labour and Conservative, with the prospect of office and therefore with the opportunity of controlling the executive side of the relationship. What was perhaps lost in this was any concept of Parliament as a separate entity, or more particularly of the House of Commons as having any corporate identity.

Of course in the absence of any separation of powers this may be quite understandable: the focus of ambition, for example, of the average M.P. is usually held to be ministerial office. What specifically House of Commons job could compete with this? Similarly because the British system tends to operate as a two-party system, or at least under the belief that it is, or ought to be, a two-party system, it is understandable that frontbenchers, whatever their apparent party differences, would wish to keep the machine running in much the same way. In that respect the significant division in the House of Commons is as much between front and backbenchers as it is between parties. However, given a tradition of loyalty by backbenchers to party, alongside the shared values of the frontbenchers, it is easy to see why the role of Parliament has been seen as one of assenting and support rather than one of initiation and checking.

In that respect a textbook view of Parliament as a legitimizing body, rather than a legislative one, has much to commend it as a description of reality. Parliament has worked as it has in the twentieth century because governments have had the initiative, both in substantive and procedural terms, and because Parliament, by and large, has been content to act as a critic, a body prepared to air individual or general grievances and occasionally to make a fuss. It could be argued that the qualifications required to play such a role have become more demanding, and the role itself less playable, as the century has advanced. The volume of activity to be scrutinized, the technical complexity of much of that activity, along with the speed of change and perhaps the intractability of problems, together with society's raised expectations (and acccompanying difficulty of meeting them) have combined to make Parliament seem more peripheral in our national life.

Parliament's difficulties have arisen not just from the increase in the volume and technical complexity of issues to be dealt with; in part they derive from specific features of the growth of government. One of these is the gulf – paradoxical in the absence of the separation of powers – between the executive and the legislative assembly. The close intermeshing of ministers and civil servants is paralleled by the gap between the bulk of civil servants and the bulk of M.P.s. In part this gulf may be due to specifically British features of bureaucratic recruitment and training, in part it may be simply due to a recognition (self-fulfilling though it be) that civil servants are often better informed than M.P.s, but both aspects have been reinforced by the tradition of ministerial responsibility. In its simplest form this has held that ministers are answerable for the work of their departments; they are to be praised or blamed while their servants are to be regarded as anonymous, politically neutral, disinterested guardians of the public good. Given the absence of much in the way of institutional links between civil servants and backbenchers, it is easy to see how this separation has been possible.

The tendency of bureaucracy to keep M.P.s at arm's length has been reinforced by a tradition of secrecy. The picture here is unclear however: how much is due to this and how much to M.P.s' failure either to use existing information sources or to pursue adequately existing avenues is a matter of debate. It is likely however that a natural bureaucratic caution has been strengthened by certain features of the British civil service tradition.

Here as elsewhere in this context much of the argument is of the chicken and egg variety. For example one of the clearest phenomena of recent years in British government has been the preference on the part of governments to deal directly with interest groups. Is this because M.P.s have little to offer or do they have little to offer because they are effectively excluded from the processes that matter? At one level the rise of interest group politics is inevitable: M.P.s cannot know all that the interest group know or be as useful in securing acceptance of government decisions with group members; but the system perhaps does not need to have gone so far in appearing to exclude M.P.s from any positive role in the policy-making process. A measure of tri-partism, for example, as Wyn Grant shows elsewhere in this volume, is part and parcel of twentieth-century governing; the question is rather whether Parliament can hope to shape the outcome of that process or whether it must simply accept and sanctify what is presented to it.

This has tended to produce a situation where effectively decisions are taken outside Parliament, and perhaps, though not necessarily, presented to Parliament for approval ('legitimized'). Despite this, the time occupied by Parliamentary sittings is no less and therefore what fills this time must often be second-order activity. Parliament has had increasing difficulty in making its voice heard (the mass media for the most part have until very recently taken it at one remove) and perhaps too much that occupies time there is not cost-effective in substantive terms or even in political ones, which may be the more usual way of measuring it. In part this is because Parliament so often seems to be talking to itself, or to be demonstrating its belief that talking in itself is self-evidently valuable. The tradition of debate and oratory exercises a powerful myth in British politics; but with a few exceptions it seems agreed that it is rarely to be found in the Commons nowadays. Unless it reaches an audience, which will rarely be present in the flesh in the House, debate is destined for instant obscurity.

To its credit Parliament has shown much more awareness in the past 15 years that not all is well in its relations with the executive and the outside world. Accordingly the rest of this chapter is devoted to a consideration of how Parliament has responded to this situation. So far Parliament has been used as a collective term. In practice the Commons and the Lords are so different in their powers and status that it seems simpler to consider them separately. Accordingly the bulk of what follows considers the part played by the Commons with a modest postscript devoted to the Lords.

1. Responses to the growth of government

It is difficult to say precisely how the House of Commons has responded to the growth of government activity in the present century. In the nature of things one cannot be sure what the connection is or, if the growth had been less, how the work of the Commons today might be different. There are some obvious comparisons that can be made. For example the House now sits on average for about 170 days a year compared with an average of 129 days before 1914,[1] an increase of almost one-third. The House's day is nominally of eight hours' duration from Mondays to Thursdays (2.30 p.m. – 10.30 p.m.) with a shorter sitting of five and a half hours on Fridays (9.30 a.m. – 3.00 p.m.). In practice the House often sits for longer than its 'normal' hours; the overall average length of a sitting (including Fridays) being something over nine hours. In session 1980–1 the House sat after midnight on about 70 days, including one monstrous sitting lasting 25 hours which caused the loss of the following day's sitting.

Another aspect of the response to pressure has been that more happens off the floor of the House than used to be the case. For example the normal procedure on legislation since 1945 has been for the committee stage to be taken in standing committee, whereas this was much less true before the Second World War. The power to take most bills in standing committee had been in Standing Orders since 1907 but they were not fully used until after 1945.[2]

The increase in legislation is not so much a matter of numbers as of the length of statutes. At the beginning of the century Public Acts amounted to around 200 pages a year; in 1980 they accounted for 2867 pages in the annual compilation. Moreover the number and volume of statutory instruments (subordinate legislation) has also grown. According to Rush they have doubled in number since 1900;[3] in 1980 'general' instruments numbered 2,051 and occupied some 7,390 pages.

It could be argued that the House of Commons has been able to cope with the pressure which the above figures suggest only by means of firm executive leadership. This has been exercised by a kind of tacit consent between the front benches of the two major parties. The Whips' offices in both parties are an accepted part of the machinery of the House (symbolized in the payment of Opposition Whips by the state). Of course the term 'Whip' gives these individuals a more disciplinarian sound than is appropriate. Essentially they are a necessary medium of communication within the House.[4] In both parties somewhere from 250–350 individuals have to be kept informed of forthcoming business and have to have a chance to express their views about party activity privately. Thus the Whips act as a channel of information, gossip and grievance while at the same time acting in concert to organize the work of the Commons. It is one of the paradoxes of the House that outwardly its procedures are highly adversarial while behind this a great deal proceeds by comity. For example, the arrangements for forthcoming business in the House are given to the Opposition before they are publicly announced; likewise there is much agreement about the timing of and subject of debates. The 'usual channels' are an important lubricant, and arguably one of the most important weapons an Opposition has is its threat not to operate the system with its tacit bargains and its pairing arrangements. But like all weapons it must be used sparingly because probably before long the parties will find their roles reversed. In practice much legislation is now passed under voluntary timetables, although when these prove inadequate and compulsory timetables have to be resorted to (guillotine resolutions) great is the outcry from the Opposition of the day.

British political parties have long been regarded as highly disciplined entities. Indeed some American observers have looked with envy at their degree of discipline. For much of the post-war period party voting has been the norm and government defeat regarded as exceptional, except perhaps for defeats in standing committee and those could usually be reversed. Governments with small majorities were able to operate effectively (as in 1950–1 and 1964–6) though at some cost to those who fell ill. However, this comfortable predictability seems to be becoming a thing of the past. Not that every vote has become a quasi-free vote – far from it – but M.P.s are now, it seems, more prepared to vote against their party. This pattern developed under the Heath government of 1970–4 and then under the Labour government of 1974–9: when there was either a minority government or a government with a very small majority, it became almost a regular feature of life for the government to be defeated. According to the researches of Norton, between July 1905 and March 1972 'there were 34 government defeats in the division lobbies . . .'; while 'between April 1972 and April 1979 . . . there were a total of *65 Government defeats*' (6 between 1970–4; 17 in the 1974 Parliament and 42 in the 1974–9 Parliament).[5] Apart from defeats, of course, there was also a good deal of dissenting voting that did not result in defeat: whereas in every post-war Parliament up to 1970 except one the percentage of divisions with dissenting votes was in single figures, subsequent Parliaments have shown percentages of 20(1970–4), 23(1974) and 28(1974–9). Moreover, where defeats occurred these were sometimes on major issues. For example, the Government lost major elements of its legislative programme by defeat, as with an important part of the Dock Work Regulation Bill and the Aircraft and Shipbuilding Nationalisation Bill. Even a whole bill was defeated on Second Reading (Reduction of Redundancy Rebates Bill), while the major piece of legislation of a session (the Scotland and Wales Bill) had to be withdrawn after the failure to carry a guillotine resolution. Many bills were heavily amended against the government's wishes and even parts of the government's budget were rejected. All this adds up to a substantial change in the behaviour of the Commons. Even a government with a substantial majority after 1979, though more protected against actual defeat, still found M.P.s less amenable. Thus there were problems as early as June 1979 over M.P.s' pay while dissent or the threat of it was enough to secure changes on sanctions against Iran, M.P.'s pensions and the rates of duty on DERV. Other issues produced substantial dissent – for example, the Employment Bill of 1979–80.

Explanations for this weakening of the habit of party voting are several. It obviously owes something to the presence in the 1970s of a number of cross-cutting issues – that is, issues which did not fit into the conventional party categories but tended to split both parties – notably entry into the E.E.C. and devolution. It owed something too to the party balance between 1974 and 1979 where obviously a dissenting vote was likely to be more valuable in its impact. More important perhaps has been the revelation that government defeats do not result in government resignations unless the defeat is on a vote of confidence – as that in March 1979 was. Thus M.P.s have had made clear to them that one of the traditional arguments for supporting a government – that otherwise defeat might lead to a general election and loss of office – is no more than a myth. It is hardly surprising if they draw the appropriate conclusions. Perhaps too, one should give some weight to the changes taking place in the party system. It is probably not coincidence that M.P.s of both parties began to show more signs of independence at a time when both parties were losing some of their popular appeal, when the Labour party in particular was showing signs of division that eventually produced a split in the party, and when the party system in general appeared to be sinking in popular esteem. A further factor is undoubtedly the changing nature of M.P.s themselves. Both parties have lost their uncomplaining foot-soldiers: their traditional solid body of, in the case of Labour, union sponsored ex-manual workers and in the case of the Conservatives the country squires and military officers. Both groups had limited political aspirations but a strong sense of instinctive loyalty to party; their replacements are more likely to be drawn from the professions and business world, less willing to abide by advice and instruction. Thereby the life of the party Whip has been made more difficult but the behaviour of the institution more interesting.

2. The work of the House

Traditionally the House of Commons has aired grievances, assented to legislation and sanctioned the raising and spending of money. These have all tended, except on rare occasions, to be rather formal functions. The House spends a good deal of time debating issues, asking questions and discussing legislation as well as, away from the floor of the House, spending even more time on legislation, investigation and assorted other duties through its committee system.

Debates

Apart from debates on legislation the House spends a good deal of time discussing major or less major issues of the day. The occasions for these debates vary: at the start of each session of Parliament several days are set aside to debate the government's programme as set out in the Queen's Speech; during the session time is provided by the government for major debates and by the Opposition, who have 19 days at their disposal. Originally these were Supply Days linked at least formally to the discussion of Estimates of expenditure but this 'peg' became less and less plausible and in recent years they have been devoted simply to an area of government activity that the Opposition wishes to see discussed. In addition to these major slices of debating time which are largely frontbench-controlled, there are a number of occasions when backbenchers have the chance to raise issues that concern them. The most obvious is the half-hour at the end of each day's sitting when M.P.s can air a topic that concerns them. In addition there are adjournment debates before each recess, and a further opportunity is provided after the second reading of Consolidated Fund Bills (a symbolic seeking for the redress of grievance before the granting of Supply) as well as the time set aside for Private Members' debates on a specific number of Fridays and Mondays in each session. Moreover, it is possible for any M.P. to seek to move the adjournment of the House to debate a matter of urgent importance; in practice such requests are rarely acceded to. In 1980–1, for example, only one out of 48 requests under this procedure was successful. More recently there have been suggestions that the procedure is somewhat abused. If granted, the House interrupts its prearranged business for three hours on the following day (or very exceptionally on the same day). This last type of debate has a considerable symbolic importance for backbenchers, though it is doubtful whether frontbenchers are quite so enthusiastic, even though these debates provide an opportunity to embarrass the government of the day on occasions – indeed on one occasion in 1980–1 the unsuccessful applicant was the Leader of the Opposition.

While, as we have seen, the House devotes much time to debate, it is difficult to be sure how valuable this activity is. At the most general level it is obviously important that issues can be aired, that opposition from within or without the governing party be given a chance to express itself, that ministers be open to challenge and that M.P.s have a chance to express their own and their constituents' views. None of this is to be despised but whether it need take up as much time as it does is less clear. The House has made rather a fetish of debate; oratory has been preserved as a value in itself (whether or not actually found in practice in the House) and it may be that too much value is placed on the possession of purely verbal skills both for ministers and backbenchers. Moreover, the framework of much debate is such as to encourage the making of routine party points. These are likely to have little effect in influencing any votes within the House, and to be relatively ineffective in reaching any audience outside the House, let alone influencing them. Indeed the inside audience may be very small (a matter of some concern to some observers, though by no means to all), and the more cynical would say that M.P.s make speeches mainly in the hope of attracting an invitation to be interviewed on radio or television and thereby to reach a real audience for their views.

Questions

Nowhere has the pressure exerted by the growth of business in the House of Commons been more apparent than in relation to Parliamentary Questions. Overall something like 40,000 Questions are now tabled each year compared with about 15,000 in the 1950s.[6] The growth in the number of Questions for oral answer has been restricted partly by the simple fact that fewer Questions have been answered. It is common now for less than 20 Questions to be dealt with in a Question Time, less than half of the figure for 30 years ago and less than one third of the inter-war figure.[7] The conflict between the number of Questions answered and the length of each answer is obvious, but the matter has been affected also by increasing the restrictions on the tabling of Questions. The real growth in recent years has been in Questions for written answer. These have mushroomed from around 20 a day from the beginning of the century to the 1950s to between 100 and 200 a day in recent years and on some occasions more.[8] This explosion can be explained partly by the diminishing prospect of securing oral answers to Questions (though questions for oral answers have the advantage from the questioners' point of view of having to be answered by a particular date), partly by the realization on the part of M.P.s that written answers could be used to mount publicity campaigns on particular issues and partly by the increased employment by M.P.s of research assistants who can be used to dream up Questions. One variation on the written answer has been to have some Questions (indicated by a 'W') which have a date for answer attached to them.

In conventional wisdom Question Time is regarded as one of the high spots of parliamentary government. In popular mythology a critical House of Commons is holding a cowering minister (and, through him or her, a government) to account. The reality is a good deal less impressive. Although public and parliamentary attention is still focused on Question Time the advantage in the sparring lies with the minister rather than the questioner. Of course it is important to see Question Time as a political contest rather than a source of information. As a device for the latter purpose Question Time has obvious shortcomings: ministers are under relatively little pressure to divulge information they do not want to, the M.P. has probably only a single supplementary to follow up his original Question and, while the minister and his advisers cannot be certain what supplementary questions will be asked (whereas on the original question they have a good deal of notice), in practice the civil servants are able to prepare answers to a range of likely supplementaries. Moreover, the pressure of time means that further exploration of a particular topic can only be at the expense of other M.P.s' Questions being unanswered.

Question Time has come to be regarded as a part of the party political battle: to that extent it has become less of a backbench occasion and more one where frontbenchers are expected to join in – if not perhaps to table the original Questions. All of this applies with particular force to Prime Minister's Questions, the twice-weekly occasion of a quarter of an hour when the Prime Minister is open for questioning. Here the object is quite unambiguously political: the Questions are frequently of the most open-ended sort, for example 'To ask the Prime Minister if she will list her official engagements for (that day)' or 'To ask the Prime Minister if she will pay an official visit to (the questioner's constituency)'. The result is a twice-weekly period of exchange which is either exhilarating or depressing according to one's taste and politics. An average of three or four Questions are dealt with in the 15 minutes, about half the number of 20 years ago.[9] It is interesting that the broadcasting authorities initially regarded this as one of the features of parliamentary life that should be broadcast live. In many respects it is one of the least productive parts of parliamentary activity, though those who find that a too jaundiced view would argue that it is an important safeguard in a democracy to have the head of government answerable (whatever that may mean) twice a week while Parliament is sitting. Certainly recent American Presidents have often gone many months without *choosing* to face a press conference. In practice it would be politically difficult to dispense with Prime Minister's Question Time, though arguably little public knowledge would be lost if it were abandoned.

Overall there is no answer to the perennial dilemma of Question Time: is it better to have more Questions answered or fewer Questions answered more deeply? To increase the time would be likely merely to produce a parallel growth in demand. Moreover, it is not clear that Question Time is so valuable that more time should be given to it. However, it is important to see Question Time not just as a political weapon but also as a part of the process whereby M.P.s can hope to represent their constituents. In that context it is one of a variety of devices that M.P.s have to bring pressure on ministers. The ultimate threat (though there are further stages possible such as an adjournment debate or referral to the Ombudsman) of public ventilation of an issue may help an M.P. in his use of informal consultation or letter writing to a minister. Here it is important to see Question Time perhaps in the light of the 'village society'[10] of Whitehall where public embarrassment is duly noted and this may be more important than being a source of information.

Legislation

The growth of legislation is an obvious manifestation of the increased role of the state. Not only do governments legislate in more areas, they are constantly under pressure to legislate more than they do. Few problems arise in society that are not felt somewhere to be matters that government should do something about. As we have seen, since the end of the Second World War the House has operated on the principle that unless a bill was of great importance, or extremely urgent, or very unimportant, then its committee stage should take place off the floor of the House. This has meant that as far as the House as a whole is concerned the substantial legislative stage is the second reading and increasingly there has been pressure to minimize the time spent on the post-committee stages of report and third reading. Committees thus take the bulk of the detailed consideration of bills. Ryle has pointed out that 'debating committees on bills and other matters held 576 sittings in 1979–80, compared with 66 in 1951–52'.[11] Though formally unspecialized, these committees are constituted afresh for each bill referred to them and therefore can contain those with knowledge of or interest in the subject matter of the particular piece of legislation. In the immediate post-war period standing committees usually consisted of 45–50 M.P.s; it is normal for them now to be made up of only 17 or 24 M.P.s. On the whole this has been a change for the better, since the larger size of committees meant that many there were pressed men (or women) who had little interest in the proceedings and who, at least on the government side, had an obligation to be seen but not heard.

Even so the powers of the Committees are somewhat restricted: they operate entirely as creatures of the House. The principles of the bill have been agreed at second reading and the standing committee is bound by that. Moreover the power of party discipline, though in some respects more fragmented in a smaller body, is nevertheless the norm. In effect the committees are used as a forum for amendments (very largely from the government) rather than as a source of amendments.[12] In that respect it is a political exercise and not a neutral academic exercise in legislative improvement. The possibility of taking second readings and report stages in committee exists but in practice little use is made of this. For non-contentious bills the saving in time would be minimal while for more important bills it would be seen as an infringement of the position of M.P.s as a whole. It is significant that even the existing rules are hedged round with protections to allow a small number of backbenchers to block any referrals of second readings or report stages that might result from frontbench collusion. The idea that the House might adjourn one afternoon a week to enable committees to meet, while formally part of the House's Standing Orders, has never been put into practice. This is perhaps indicative of the political value of time on the floor of the House compared with time in committee.

The effects of the growth of state activity are seen not only in the volume of legislation passed through Parliament but also in the volume of subordinate legislation made under statutory authority. Parliament has always found the task of keeping some measure of control over this rather difficult. For many years the House of Commons had a select committee whose task was restricted to matters of technical form: debate on substance (if it took place at all) took place on the floor of the House. In practice a relatively small proportion of statutory instruments were dealt with in this way (whether under the negativing or take note procedures). More recently there has been a change by way of joining forces with the House of Lords (which had a longer tradition of inquiry in this area) in the matter of technical inquiry to produce a Joint Committee while allowing debate on the merits of statutory instruments to take place in a series of specially composed standing committees. This has enabled more items to be discussed (previously debate on the floor had been limited to 1½ hours per topic and usually at very late times in the day) but the possibility is still there for debates to be held on the floor and for formal decisions there on instruments debated in standing committee. However, the feeling persists that what has been achieved has been a saving of time on the floor of the House rather than an increase in the House's control over delegated legislation.[13]

Select Committees

Given the importance which the House attaches to its plenary sessions and to what happens on the floor of the House, it is not perhaps surprising that for much of the twentieth century (though not the nineteenth) relatively little use was made of select committees. Apart from committees concerned with matters internal to the House itself (such as procedure privileges or catering), for much of the post-war period the select committees amounted to little more than the two concerned with finance (Public Accounts, and Estimates – later Expenditure), that dealing with delegated legislation, and the Select Committee on Nationalised Industries established in 1955. As we have seen, the committee dealing with delegated legislation had a mainly technical role, while the Public Accounts Committee had a well-established tradition of concern with past expenditure and its propriety which appeared to make its role relatively uncontroversial. For the other two committees there was a theory that they were concerned with administration rather than policy and thus it could be said that even for such committees as existed a low profile was in order.

The expansion of select committee activity in the second half of the 1960s (evidenced in the establishment of committees dealing with Agriculture, Education, Science and Technology, Race Relations, Overseas Aid and Scottish Affairs) though largely a response to a particular set of political circumstances, represents the first major advance for the protagonists of increased scrutiny of executive activity by means of select committees. Half-hearted though the experiment proved to be, and ill-thought-out as it now tends to be judged, nevertheless enough survived from that period into the 1970s to suggest that select committee activity was at least not the dangerous foreign threat that its opponents sometimes tried to label it in the years before 1966. The conversion of the Estimates Committee into the Expenditure Committee in 1971 allowed wider terms of reference and what seemed like a new line of approach through specialized sub-committees rather than separate committees. In fact the sub-committees were too few to be effective overall and the general verdict on the Expenditure Committee is that its success was very limited.[14]

These committees did not, with some exceptions, tackle the major issues of the day. They were regarded as peripheral, rightly pehaps in view of the fact that political reputations were unlikely to be made there. In this respect, however, their plight was not as bad as that of standing committees where service was almost regarded as a punishment. Committee reports were frequently ignored and even the long-established committees had severe limitations on their effectiveness. Much effort was extended by academics, clerks of the House and a small number of M.P.s in arguing for a more ambitious system of committees but overall one might say that certainly until the mid-1960s and probably beyond, the prevailing view was that the British system of parliamentary government would be harmed rather than helped by the development of such a system.[15]

3. Europe

Accession by the United Kingdom to membership of the European Communities has offered interesting new challenges to the British Parliament in recent years. These are considered more fully in chapter 8 of this volume. To the House of Commons in particular it has meant an additional area of work that has to be squeezed into an already crowded timetable and posed the teasing problem of how to have an effective voice on matters to be decided at the European level. The solution to the time problem has been twofold. First, a select committee is used to examine secondary legislation (in effect a new kind of delegated legislation) with a view to drawing the House's attention to matters of concern. Second, there is the possibility of debates on the floor of the House with a time limit again of $1\frac{1}{2}$ hours per topic. More generally of course, Europe has occupied much time on the floor in a less specific way (through debates and questions for example). The other problem, that of ensuring the House an effecive voice is more difficult: not only is it hard for the House to act quickly enough in many cases for its voice to be heard, but there is the more serious problem that ministers are participating at the European level in a decision-making process which not only allows little place for the national parliaments but is also one which involves compli-cated bargaining that makes it impossible for Parliament's voice, even if expressed, to be adhered to. Thus there is little scope here for even the illusion of parliamentary control. Throughout this field there is a great problem with the sheer volume of information, and with its accessibility and complexity. It could be said that Europe provides an extreme version of the problems facing the House of Commons as it seeks to find its role in the political system of the late twentieth century.

4. The new mood

Despite a certain amount of tinkering, the formal structures and procedures of the House of Commons changed relatively little during the 1960s and 1970s. New committees were set up but not all survived, experiments with morning sittings were quickly aban-doned, new arrangements were made to deal with the Finance Bill involving some saving of the House's time and minor changes, of a cosmetic nature, were made in the procedures involving Committees of the Whole House. New problems such as Europe and Northern Ireland imposed new demands; but specific procedural responses were confined to the margins of the House's life.

Less easily identified but perhaps more important were the changes taking place behind the scenes. The complacency which had characterized the 1959 Procedure Committee Report and the re-sponse to it gave way over the course of the next decade and a half to a growing mood of self-doubt. Partly this was due to the changing personnel of the House: the new M.P.s who entered the House from 1964 onwards were perhaps less in awe of the institution, less willing to be socialized into its ways. (It is interesting that over the same period a similar process was taking place in the United States Congress where old maxims about the need 'to go along to get along' have been effectively buried along with associated notions of appren-ticeship.) It was not merely that the new M.P.s were somewhat different in background but also that their expectations in terms of resources and facilities have in themselves produced great changes in office, secretarial and research facilities. At the most trivial level, it is relatively recently that M.P.s have ceased to have to pay out of their own pockets the cost of postage when writing to constituents; though the situation has changed in many respects very dramatically, M.P.s remain very modestly provided for by the standards of many Western democracies.

Over a somewhat longer period it could be argued that M.P.s have come to adopt a more 'service' relationship with their constituents. Most M.P.s now find it expedient to hold regular surgeries and there is little doubt that the volume of demands made on M.P.s by constituents and others has increased greatly. At the same time their capacity to respond to these demands has also been improved.[16] A further reflection of these increased demands has been the growth of the 'full-time' M.P. – the person for whom service in the House is itself a career.

At the same time that the nature and consequent expectations of M.P.s have been changing, there has been a realization that Parliament is not as effective in reality as it has tended to be regarded both in the minds of M.P.s and in high liberal theory. Those who had argued that the House of Commons lacked the capacity to be an effective critic of the executive, that perhaps the House was not widely listened to and so on, found themselves attracting more attention. It was no longer possible to dismiss all this as the sour criticism of those who did not really understand the House. Events in the 1970s made the decline in Parliament's status inescapably obvious. The power of groups outside Parliament seemed to assume greater importance, for example in the challenge offered to laws passed by Parliament by trade unions opposed to industrial relations legislation or by local authorities opposed to legislation on council house rents. Moreover, groups seemed willing to challenge the legitimacy of elected governments by their willingness to strike for political purposes and even to welcome the idea that strikes might bring about the downfall of a disliked government. Less dramatic perhaps, but in the long run more important was the decision to make a reduction in the rate of income tax for the whole community depend not on the voice of the House of Commons but on the agreement of the T.U.C. to a policy of 'voluntary' wage restraint. In effect the assent of Parliament could be assumed, and it could be assumed to be subordinate to the assent of outside interests. But these were only the tips of the icebergs: the more frequent reality, and many more M.P.s came to recognize it, was that the House of

Commons lacked the detailed knowledge and the political will to mount an effective challenge or check to the executive.

Realization of Parliament's reduced status was brought home too by the use of the referendum as a device to secure an acceptable decision on two of the most difficult and persistent issues of the 1970s: membership of the European Community and devolution. Although these referendums were technically advisory, they acquired a legitimacy (as was intended) which suggested that the mere verdict of Parliament was no longer sufficient.

These developments, together with the greater sense of unease about whether Parliament was not becoming more remote from the effective channels of communication with the public, and whether it was merely the forum for the negative and introverted exchanges between parties whose credibility with the electorate was declining, provided the background for an important examination of the House's affairs by a Select Committee on Procedure between 1976 and 1978. In their Report the Committee frankly acknowledged the problem: 'the balance of advantage between Parliament and Government in the day to day working of the Constitution is now weighted in favour of the Government to a degree which arouses widespread anxiety and is inimical to the proper working of our parliamentary democracy'.[17] In order to improve on this the Committee recommended a number of changes in the House's arrangements. Most notably they suggested that a new system of select committees be introduced covering virtually all the activities of government. In addition the Committee suggested changes in the legislative process to allow standing committees to take evidence rather than be confined to debate. The Procedure Committee drew back, however, from following the logic of their arguments any further and recommended against a single system of committees combining both legislative and evidence-taking roles.

As far as select committees were concerned, the substance of the Committee's proposals was accepted (after a considerable delay and an intervening General Election) by the House in June 1979. The result is that the House of Commons now has for the first time a comprehensive system of committees covering, with only minor exceptions, the whole range of government activity. To the original twelve committees (Agriculture; Defence; Education; Science and Arts; Employment; Energy; Environment; Foreign Affairs; Home Affairs; Industry and Trade; Social Services; Transport; Treasury and Civil Service) were added committees covering Welsh and

Scottish Affairs. The powers granted to the committees have not, however, been increased. The suggestion that Ministers might be compelled to attend, as the Procedure Committee had suggested, was not accepted nor was the idea that committees might have powers to ensure debate of their reports on the floor of the House.

Potentially these moves represent the most important change in the House's work since the Second World War (if not in a longer period). Not only is it the first time that all government departments have been shadowed by a select committee but the change represents an explicit acknowledgement of the importance of committee work. Of course it would be easy to be cynical. Acceptance of the idea was probably less than whole-hearted by both government and civil service; for the latter in particular it represents a good deal of extra work and perhaps in the long run a challenge to some of their assumptions about the rules of the game. Acceptance owed a good deal to the happy coincidence of a newly elected government pledged to reform and a Leader of the House who took that pledge seriously enough to secure the agreement of his colleagues to its implementation, an agreement which probably owed something, to the need, as after 1966, to find employment for backbenchers in a substantial government majority. It is also true that as a system it must be judged by its results rather than its shape and, moreover, not just within the life of a single Parliament.

However, the fact that members of the new committees were appointed for a whole Parliament, that some of the committees fairly quickly achieved some impact and that members appear to have an interest in their committee's work (though naturally this varies a good deal from committee to committee) suggests that we may be seeing an important addition to the House's armoury. It may even lead to the establishment of committee loyalty and even committee careers, though whether committees can develop loyalties which transcend party loyalties is doubtful. Certainly the earlier evidence from the Nationalised Industries Committee is not encouraging here in the shape of voting against a report on the floor of the House that some Committee members had accepted in committee.

Already the committees have shown themselves capable of having an impact. The Home Affairs Committee's investigation in the 'sus' law, the Education Committee's contribution to solving the dispute over the Promenade Concerts and its concern for the future of *The Times Supplements*, the Treasury and Civil Service Committee's contribution to the debate over monetarism and the Foreign Affairs

Committee's inquiry into the patriation of the Canadian Constitution are but a few examples of important investigations made by the committees.

A second change which is potentially of less significance has been the acceptance of the idea that standing committees (in the form of Public Bill Committees) should be able to operate for up to a maximum of three sittings per bill in select committee form. This represents a step away from the notion that legislation is best considered in debating form and is some acknowledgment of the need for the House to improve its sources of information regarding legislative proposals. Instead of allowing interested parties to communicate only via the civil service and ministers or via M.P.s informally, it is now possible for evidence to be offered openly and directly to the Committee members. The procedure was used three times in 1981 and once in 1982.

Clearly then, the House of Commons is changing not only in its membership but also in its procedures and in its facilities. At the same time, while the House remains a body whose life is party-oriented, there have been signs as we have noted, that M.P.s are more willing to vote against their parties. Of course much pressure continues to be informal: the use of Whips in this process we have already noticed. Important also are the Conservative 1922 Committee and meetings of the Parliamentary Labour party as well as the backbench subject committees in each party, as vehicles for the airing of concern. All have a dual role in the educating of M.P.s as well as keeping leaders aware of the feelings of their followers.

While the House has shown more awareness that its channels of communication with the outside world are not all they might be, broadcasting of parliamentary proceedings has proved very much a double-edged weapon. While extracts from proceedings help to make radio and television reporting more lively, and in some cases live broadcasting has helped to bring Parliament on to the stage at first hand rather than second, public reaction has tended towards deploring much that passes for traditional behaviour in the Commons. The baying, booing and cheering have seemed particularly unfortunate on radio. Some of the early hopes of live broadcasting have been disappointed, as evidenced in the decision of the broadcasting authorities to revise their view of the desirability of broadcasting Prime Minister's Question Time. This always seemed a singularly unhappy choice to be given prominence both because of the implicit emphasis which it gave to what was deemed important in the House and because it is perhaps that part of the House's work most certain to be subject to noisy interruptions.

5. The House of Lords

Perhaps no aspect of the Parliament has remained so controversial for so long as the House of Lords. Its problems arise both from composition and functions and the combination of the two has proved remarkably immune from change. The growth in governmental activity has affected the Lords but much of its work remains seasonal. The system as a whole might be said to suffer from the absence of full bi-cameralism. Despite attempts to shift the imbalance of work so that, for example, more bills are introduced in the Lords, in practice it has proved difficult for political reasons to achieve a great deal and thereby to avoid the situation where the peak of the Lords' work comes when bills reach them from the Commons in mid-summer and even early autumn. For example in 1980 the Lords worked through September to deal with the backlog of work from the Commons. Annually there are pleas and plans to avoid this next year but, apart from a minor experiment with Public Bill Committees for the committee stage of a few bills, little has been achieved by their lordships themselves in this area.

It is the case not only that the House sits for longer hours than it used to but also that more peers attend. In 1980–1 for example, the House sat on 143 days for almost 920 hours, an average sitting of $6\frac{3}{4}$ hours. Twenty-five years ago typical figures were about 110 days a year, a total of around 400–450 hours and an average sitting length of about $4\frac{1}{2}$ hours. Average daily attendance in 1980–1 was 290 (very similar figures were recorded in the previous few sessions) whereas 25 years ago average daily attendance was around 100.[18] This increase may owe something to the existence and the level of the daily attendance allowance but probably it is due also to the fact that the House has become much more of a working House with life peers prominent in its activities. It is of course very easy for those peers not interested in the work of the House either to apply for leave of absence or not to respond to the writ of summons or simply not to attend.

Little has been achieved by way of altering the composition of the House, apart from the introduction of life peerages, the acceptance of Scottish peers as full members, and the introduction of peeresses associated with the 1963 Act that enabled existing peers to renounce their titles and gave subsequent inheritors a year within which to make up their minds on that subject. The House therefore still looks very odd and few would defend its composition particularly at a time when its powers and composition have so alienated sections of the Labour party that the House is faced with the threat of abolition. The decisions of Labour party Conferences in the 1970s (and in 1980) were overwhelming in this direction and the proposal was kept out of the 1979 Labour manifesto only, we are given to understand, as a result of the veto of the then Leader of the party.

The very existence, as well as the possibility of reform, of the House have therefore become live political issues. This is not very surprising in the light of the fact that during the 1974–9 Labour government's period of office, the House took a much more active view of its responsibilities than it had done for many years. The prevailing doctrine, that proposals that were deemed to have been approved of by the electorate should not be resisted unduly by the Lords, was modified by arguing that the 1974 Labour government was in a minority much of the time, that it had, at best, the support of a mere 39 per cent of the voters and of only 27 per cent of the electorate. In terms of strict democratic theory the Lords' argument had a good deal to be said for it, though it was inevitably regarded as coming badly from those who had never been elected by anyone.

At any rate the issues on which the Lords most famously clashed with the Commons: Dockwork Regulation, Aircraft and Shipbuilding Nationalisation (over the proposed nationalization of ship-repair firms), Education, and Pay Beds in the National Health Service were ones where in some cases their actions were subsequently endorsed by the House of Commons and where, though it is difficult to be certain, they probably enjoyed considerable support among the general public. Inevitably with the return of a Conservative government matters became less dramatic, but important modifications were made to Conservative legislation, most notably over the issue of charging for school transport in rural areas.

Controversy over the composition and powers of the Lords, and even over its very existence, tends to obscure the solid virtues of the House. While one may discount some of the more grandiose claims sometimes made for it, that for example its debates are vastly superior to those of the lower house, as being at least difficult to prove and depending much on the taste of the observer, there is no doubt that the House does much useful if unspectacular work. Issues are debated in the Lords that the Commons does not have time for;

debates on legislation may reveal views unheard in the lower house but more particularly the House is valuable on the details of legislation where clauses get the benefit of second thoughts or in many cases of discussion which they did not receive at all in the Commons. For example the Scotland Bill of 1978–9 arrived in the Lords with 61 of its 83 clauses undebated in the Commons, thanks in part to the capricious effect that guillotine resolutions can have on the discussion of legislative detail. It is generally agreed that the Lords did a much better job on this Bill (and on the Wales Bill) than did the Commons.[19] Moreover, this is an area where the Lords' relative lack of political muscle matters less. It is true that their amendments can be overturned by the Commons but in practice many are not.

The House also plays a useful part in the parliamentary process by taking consideration of some legislation before it goes to the Commons. In principle this saves the latter's time, though how much is difficult to measure. More recently the House has developed its select committee work particularly in areas where the Commons is weak. The Select Committee on the European Communities for example is a more elaborate body than its Commons counterpart; not only does the Lords Committee make much more use of sub-committees but it is also much more concerned with the merits of proposed European legislation than is the Commons committee.

It remains to be seen whether the less publicized work of the House is sufficient to safeguard its existence in the future. Many are the plans for reform: since the Crossman reform proposals of 1968–9, embodied in the White Paper and the Parliament (No.2) Bill of that time, for a nominated House and a reduction in its delaying power to six months, there have been proposals from all parties for change.[20] Unless the nettle of election to a reformed House is grasped, for which devolution at one time seemed to provide the opportunity, it would seem that some variation on the Crossman theme remains the most hopeful direction in which to move. On past evidence, however, no change remains an even safer prediction.

NOTES

1.   M.Rush, 'The Members of Parliament', in *The House of Commons in the Twentieth Century*, ed. S.A.Walkland (1979), 73.
2.   S.A.Walkland, 'Legislation in the House of Commons', in Walkland, *op.cit.*, 263–4.

3. Rush, in Walkland, *op.cit.*, 73.
4. P.Norton, 'The Organization of Parliamentary Parties', in Walkland, *op.cit.*, 60.
5. P.Norton, 'The Changing Face of the British House of Commons in the 1970s', *Legislative Studies Q.*, V (1980), 339. See also the same author's *Dissension in the House of Commons 1974–1979* (1980).
6. M.Ryle, 'The Legislative Staff of the British House of Commons', *Legislative Studies Q.*, VI (1981), 497–8.
7. D.N.Chester, 'Questions in the House', in *The Commons Today*, eds. S.A.Walkland and M.Ryle (1981), 197.
8. *Ibid.*, 185 and P.Norton, *The Commons in Perspective* (1981), 111–12.
9. See G.W.Jones, 'The Prime Minister and Parliamentary Questions', *Parliamentary Affairs*, XXVI (1973), 264.
10. For a discussion of this idea see H.Heclo and A.Wildavsky, *The Private Government of Public Money* (2nd edn, 1981).
11. Ryle, *op.cit.*, 498.
12. This topic is dealt with in J.A.G. Griffith, *Parliamentary Scrutiny of Government Bills* (1974).
13. See P.Norton, *The Commons in Perspective* (1981), 96–9.
14. See A.Robinson, *Parliament and Public Spending* (1978).
15. See N.Johnson, 'Select Committees as Tools of Parliamentary Reform: some further reflections', in Walkland and Ryle (eds.), *op.cit.*, 203–36.
16. This development has been discussed in M. Rush and M. Shaw (eds.), *The House of Commons: Services and Facilities* (1974).
17. First Report from the Select Committee on Procedure, 1977–78 (H.C. 588–I) para. 1.5.
18. Figures for 1980–1 taken from House of Lords Sessional Statistics. Figures for earlier periods from J. Morgan, *The House of Lords and the Labour Government 1964–1970* (1975), appendix: table 5, and the White Paper *House of Lords Reform* (1968), Cmnd. 3799.
19. See, for example H.M.Drucker and G.Brown, *The Politics of Nationalism and Devolution* (1980), 117.
20. These are considered briefly in J.Morgan, 'The House of Lords in the 1980s', *The Parliamentarian*, LXII (1981), 18–26.

4 THE POWER OF THE PRIME MINISTER

James Barber

THE BRITISH Prime Minister has a formidable array of roles – head of government, party leader, chairman of the Cabinet, Britain's chief representative in international relations, and the source of wide-ranging patronage. The performance of these roles has prompted a long-running debate about the power of the Prime Minister between 'the presidential school' and 'the chairmanship school'.

One of the champions of the presidential school was the Labour politician and Cabinet Minister Richard Crossman, who in his introduction to Walter Bagehot's *The English Constitution* and in a series of lectures he gave at Harvard in 1970, set out the case for the presidential view.[1] In his introduction to Bagehot, published in 1964, Crossman stated that 'the post-war epoch has seen the final transformation of cabinet Government into Prime Ministerial Government'.[2] And while for Bagehot it was the Cabinet which played the critical co-ordinating role in British Government – 'a hyphen that joins, a buckle which fastens, the legislative part of the state to the executive part of the state'[3] – for Crossman that role had been taken over by a single office-holder, the Prime Minister. Crossman outlined the range of powers which were at a Prime Minister's disposal – the selection and dismissal of ministers, the control of Cabinet business, the leadership of the ruling party, and the control of the key posts of the civil service – and he believed that the increasing centralization of the party and of the government bureaucracy together with its increasing spread of activities had further enhanced the power of the premier. He argued that decisions were no longer taken by the Cabinet as an entity but either within the separate departments or by Cabinet committees. The Cabinet itself:

becomes the place where busy executives seek formal sanction for their actions from colleagues usually too busy – even if they do disagree – to do more than protest. Each of these executives, moreover, owes his allegiance not to the cabinet collectively but to the Prime Minister who gave him his job, and who may well have dictated the policy he must adopt.[4]

In that context the doctrine of collective responsibility has changed its meaning. For while the discipline implied in the doctrine is still scrupulously enforced, wrote Crossman, it has now been extended to cover ministers both inside and outside the Cabinet who may have had no part in the decisions. The overall result is that collective responsibility now 'means collective obedience by the whole administration, from the Foreign Secretary and the Chancellor downwards, to the will of the man at the apex of power'.[5] Furthermore, Crossman set the increased powers of the Prime Minister over the Cabinet within the broader context of declining parliamentary power. No longer, said Crossman, could it be described as a body of independently minded men, but rather as a body divided by and controlled by the party machine. These parties were subject to the control of their leader, who, in the case of the governing party, was the Prime Minister.

Crossman re-examined his views in a series of lectures he gave at Harvard in 1970. In the intervening period he had served for six years as a member of the Cabinet; an experience which largely confirmed his earlier findings. In the Harvard lectures Crossman started by rejecting the claim that an attempt to unseat Wilson as Prime Minister during a government crisis of 1969 had seriously challenged his earlier thesis. He accepted that any Prime Minister could by mismanagement or continuous lack of success so undermine his position that he became dispensable. Also he recognized, as he had in the introduction to Bagehot, that the Cabinet did have a reserve power which, when exerted, reduced the Prime Minister to a *primus inter pares*. Indeed, some Prime Ministers had voluntarily accepted such a role for themselves. But the Crossman thesis was that these situations are very rare – the exceptions that prove the rule. It is very unusual, he argued, to find a government in such a perilous state that the Prime Minister's position is threatened, and in those cases when a Prime Minister chooses the chairmanship role it is because he consciously refuses 'to make use of the powers which now constitutionally belong to his office'. He picked out Attlee as an example of a Prime Minister who had made such a conscious renunciation. Crossman also noted a particular example from Eden's premiership when the Prime Minister had been forced to accept the views of Harold Macmillan, the Chancellor of the Exchequer, because of the latter's threat to resign. However, according to Crossman, 'the moral of this story is not that a Prime Minister is not empowered to give orders to his Chancellor, but that on this occasion Mr Eden did not dare to use the power he undoubtedly possessed'.[6]

Crossman also reasserted his judgment that an underlying reason for the increase in the Prime Ministerial power is the increased activity of modern government. As the machinery increases in size so, according to Crossman, the man at the centre becomes more powerful. Prime Ministerial government is based on his unique integrating role in three fields – his control of the civil service, the party machine, and the Cabinet.[7]

Crossman recognized that in selecting a Cabinet the Prime Minister has to choose a party as well as governmental team, and so draws representatives from the main groups in the party. A major consideration is the need to counter potential rebellion and rivalry, but this can be done by offering places in the government to the most dangerous rivals. Furthermore, the Premier decides the portfolios ministers hold and he controls Cabinet business by deciding its agenda, chairing its discussions, summarizing the decisions and saying how they are to be implemented. As it is from these decisions that the whole of Whitehall operates, it is critical for departmental ministers that they win Cabinet battles to preserve their standing in the department and the government generally. To do that they need the Prime Minister's support. And finally, the premier can dismiss a minister without warning. The Prime Minister is therefore the centralizing figure in the Cabinet, who prevents it falling into departmental factions and gives it a general drive and tone.

In Parliament, Crossman argued that the Prime Minister's main concern, and indeed that of the government in general, is not with the opposition but his own supporters. The chief fear of the ministers is of organized rebellion in their own party ranks. This problem can largely be overcome by the Prime Minister's patronage, for many offices in addition to Cabinet posts are available for him to dispense, and a decision by the Cabinet binds the whole government, not just those who have participated directly in the decision.

Crossman believed that only the premier can prevent the civil service, because of its size, knowledge, and permanence, endangering ministerial control of policy-making. The Prime Minister has responsibility for the appointment of the most senior officials in each department, and he is the single overall authority recognized by the top mandarins – the Cabinet Secretary and the Permanent Secretary of the Treasury. According to Crossman, ministers are especially vulnerable to civil service domination during the settling-in period of a new government, but that is the most critical time to establish broad policy orientations. To achieve that early impetus the Prime Minister is compelled to concentrate power at the centre, because if anything new is to be achieved it has to be imposed with an authority which only he possesses.

Crossman cited the change over from Wilson to Heath in 1970 as an example of this. According to Crossman Heath affirmed his ascendency by altering the direction and style of government. He introduced radical change by using the mandate based upon the party's election programme and in so doing demonstrated 'that it is *after* the election in its effect on the civil service, not *during* the election in its effect on the voter that the mandate plays its most essential role.'[8] In the previous government Wilson had been trying to transform the Labour party from a party of protest to a party of government. He sought out the middle ground in British politics by aiming to please the broad electorate rather than his more extreme supporters. In contrast, Crossman argued that Heath wanted to show that the 'era of vague consensus and lazy compromise' was at an end. He was out to lead a counter-revolution, to reverse 'progress towards greater equality and the expansion of universal social services that has characterized Britain since 1945'.[9] For Crossman this change of direction and mood demonstrated the power of the Prime Minister.

Crossman's position did not go unchallenged. Among those who disputed it was G.W.Jones, who in an article published in 1965 presented the chairmanship view, in which the Prime Minister is surrounded by constraints and dependent on the support of others.[10] Jones said that the Prime Minister is not a figure set apart but the leader of a group without whose support he is ineffective. Jones believed that this is true both with government and the party, where the Prime Minister is surrounded by powerful interests and rivals so that he is only as strong as his colleagues and the party allow him to be. He must work continuously to retain the support of his colleagues, the most powerful and senior of whom are his rivals, eager if necessary to replace him. This extends both to the composition and behaviour within the Cabinet. In choosing a Cabinet, wrote Jones, the Prime Minister certainly does not have a free hand, for he has to satisfy powerful party interests and often give office to those with whom he has little sympathy either personally or in terms of policy. It is in fact often safer to have strong opponents inside the Cabinet than stirring up trouble outside. Given this situation, therefore, the Prime Minister's patronage is not a powerful weapon for it has to be used to satisfy the ambitions of other party interests rather than those of the Prime Minister.

Jones went on to state that although collective Cabinet responsibility still operates, the principle does not imply simple obedience to the Prime Minister, but rather implies reaching agreed views which the Prime Minister along with the other ministers has then to accept. Moreover, the strong constraints surrounding the Prime Minister extend to policy-making generally, where his ability to influence developments has, according to Jones, been greatly exaggerated. There are several sources which combined together to constitute these constraints. First, there is the huge scale and complexity of the government machine and the scope of government business, which means that the Prime Minister can be involved in only a very small part of it while the great bulk is conducted without any Prime Ministerial interference. Second, even when a Prime Minister does take an active part the other ministers and government departments involved always have their own interests and perception of the situation, and seek to ensure that these interests are protected and promoted. In doing that they often have the advantage of the Prime Minister for while the staff of the Prime Minister's office is small, many of the ministers are backed by the great departments of state with their hierarchical ranks of civil servants, and while the Prime Minister can give only limited time to any one section of government, the department can concentrate its attention there and develop a policy momentum which is difficult to shift.

Jones argued that similar constraints surround the Prime Minister within the party organizations, for again there are interests to be reconciled, an organization to be managed, and individuals to be accommodated. As party leader the Prime Minister can seek to guide and to point a way, not to dominate. And Jones challenged the assumption that elections were essentially a popularity contest between party leaders – rather, he argued, they turn on the broad party 'image' which is built on its record in office. Taking the public image question further, Jones stated that in relative terms the television age had enhanced the position of the other ministers rather than that of the Prime Minister. Before the days of television, said Jones, the Prime Minister had been the centre of attention whereas now he had to share it with the other ministers.

Because Jones was largely concerned with refuting the claim of the presidential school he tended to concentrate on the limits of the Prime Minister's power, but he did not argue that the Prime Minister was powerless. Rather, said Jones, both in the governmental and party setting, the Prime Minister is best seen as a chairman – the leader of a group rather than a presidential figure, removed and set apart from his colleagues.

The presidential/chairmanship debate continues. Sometimes it is confronted directly, as in Patrick Cosgrave's article 'The Weakness of the Prime Minister', published in 1972, in which he argued that although most Prime Ministers were of radical disposition, it has been impossible for them to achieve their ends in government because 'it has rarely been possible for any Prime Minister to exercise that broad, continuous and effective power over the government machine which alone can lead to the efficient and successful implementation of desired reforms'.[11] Cosgrave wrote of the punishing routine of office which exhausts even the most active of leaders, and called for a strengthening of the Prime Minister's office in relation to the departments.

Sometimes the comments on the Prime Minister's power come in an aside – in a general conclusion drawn from the premiership of a particular individual, as in the case of Douglas Jay writing about his time as Parliamentary Private Secretary to Clement Attlee. There was no all-powerful presidential figure to be seen in Jay's description. 'My vivid impression of all these months at No 10', wrote Jay,

> was the falsity of the illusion, harboured by journalists, academics and others that something called 'power' resides in the hands of the prime minister. The picture drawn, or imagined, is of a great man, sitting down in his office, pulling great levers, issuing edicts, and shaping events. Nothing could be further from the truth in real life of No.10 as I knew it. So far from pulling great levers the PM at this time found himself hemmed in by relentless economic or physical forces, and faced by problems which had to be solved but which could not be solved: unable to do this because Parliament had not yet legislated, or that because it cost too many

dollars, or the other because the Americans would not agree, or something else because an obstinate minister objected.

Jay recognized that there was a very limited range of options for the premier, but in his experience the position of Prime Minister was rather 'that of a cornered animal, or a climber on a rockface who cannot go up or down, than that of a general ordering his troops wherever he wished around the landscape'.[12]

Jay accused journalists and academics of harbouring the false illusion that the Prime Minister has great powers, but, as we have already seen, that accusation can be extended to include his own kind – politicians and ministers. To the name of Richard Crossman, whose comments we noted above, can be added that of Tony Benn. Benn gave his views on the premiership in a lecture at Bristol in 1979, and the views are interesting not only for the personal place Benn holds in British politics, but because he makes clear that he is arguing a case for reform – for what 'ought to be' rather than 'what is'. In contrast Crossman, Jones and Jay had presented their views largely as observations, with the emphasis on describing the situation rather than campaigning to change it, but behind the descriptions is some element of normative judgments, even if it is disguised. For instance, Jones concluded that good Prime Ministerial practice is to avoid interference in departmental work. That is not a description of what always happens – as Mrs Thatcher's period at No.10 has made abundantly clear – but of what Jones thinks should happen.

Tony Benn did not attempt to disguise his position. He was campaigning for reform. In outlining his case, Benn said that the powers exercised by the Prime Minister within the government and the party 'are now so great as to encroach upon the legitimate rights of the electorate, undermine the essential role of Parliament, usurp some of the functions of collective cabinet decision making, and neutralise much of the influence deriving from the internal democracy of the party'.[13] He said that many of the decisions that are thought to be made collectively 'actually reflect a more personal view of what should be done, by a Prime Minister who has the power to get his, or her, own way', and he concluded that the powers of the Prime Minister must be made more accountable, so that 'an Absolute Premiership' is transformed into 'a Constitutional Premiership'.[14]

In developing his view of the premier's powers, Benn made similar points to those of Crossman and was no less insistent about the dominance of the office. Benn spoke of the great powers of patronage – such as nomination for the peerage, together with the vast array of official and semi-official posts which are in the Prime Minister's gift, and which make all those who hope for such advancement deferential to him. The scale of the premier's patronage is, said Benn, breathtaking – 'no medieval monarch could compare with it, either in numbers, or in importance'.[15] Equally, within the government, the Prime Minister controlled much of the government's business through his dominance of ministers inside and outside the Cabinet. Benn spoke of a document which is handed to ministers on taking office which covers much of their conduct – from collective Cabinet responsibility to the authorization of all broadcasts and the banning of newspaper articles. By 1976 the document was 33 pages long, with 17 sections and 156 paragraphs. Within the party (and naturally he was mainly concerned with the Labour party), Benn noted the power of the Prime Minister to call elections even in opposition to colleagues' advice, and as party leader to have an overview of the party manifesto and to exercise a veto on what goes in it, and the power to decide when the manifesto is issued.

Benn said that he was not criticizing the individuals who had held the office but he argued, 'our history has taught us that even good Kings were not good enough to make an absolute Monarchy acceptable; and even good Prime Ministers can never be good enough to make the present concentration of power in their hands acceptable either'.[16] Benn finished by advocating the election of Cabinet ministers and the allocation of their portfolios by Labour M.P.s (he did not comment on the Tory party), parliamentary confirmation of public appointments, the end of peerages, a freedom of information act, and the further development of Commons select committees.

Having traced the presidential/chairmanship debate, the problem arises of evaluating the conflicting claims. Judgment is difficult because the evidence is limited and is often ambiguous and open to different interpretations. For instance, both Crossman and Jones noted that Prime Ministers often ask party rivals to join the Cabinet, but while Jones interpreted that as a substantial constraint on the Premier's powers because he had to buy off rivals and accept their presence in the government, Crossman saw the appointments as a weapon whereby the Prime Minister was able to suppress opposition by drawing rivals into a position of shared responsibility, and, by the distribution of portfolios, diverting them away from the main policy area.

There is a similar difference of interpretation over Cabinet committees. Much Cabinet business is conducted through committees which are formed by ministers, and sometimes civil servants, with shared interests in a particular sector of government activity. The number, nature and membership of these committees is decided by the Prime Minister. For reasons which are difficult to understand, the existence of these committees is treated as confidential by the government but they are well known and from time to time details are published in the press. According to *The Times* in February 1981, there were then 25 Cabinet committees. They ranged from a committee under the chairmanship of Angus Fraser which brought together Whitehall establishment officers to discuss personnel and industrial relations, to a committee chaired by Mrs Thatcher which covered foreign policy, defence and Northern Ireland.[17] Some committees are long-standing, covering a range of topics, whereas others are for specific items of immediate importance. That is clear from the other three committees that Mrs Thatcher was then chairing – in addition to the foreign policy committee noted above, they were (a) economic strategy, energy and the most important E.E.C. items, (b) the supervision of clandestine agencies, and (c) the replacement of Polaris with a new nuclear deterrent. While the work of all the committees is reported to the Cabinet, it is unusual to rediscuss the matter there unless the committee has failed to reach agreement. Wilson, during his premiership, laid down that agreements reached in committees should not be rediscussed in the Cabinet without the approval of the chairman of the committee and/or the Prime Minister.

In assessing the committees the presidential school stresses the premier's power to decide on the nature of the committees, who serves on them, who chairs them, the way their activities are handled in the Cabinet, and the fact that the Prime Minister chairs the most important of them. In contrast, the chairmanship school advances the view that the committees strengthen Cabinet government by extending the range of corporate decisions rather than the personal power of the Prime Minister. The outcome, according to that interpretation, is that Cabinet Ministers are able to play a more effective role. Also, although the Prime Minister decides on the committees there is in reality very little choice. There is, for instance, always a major committee to deal with foreign affairs and another with economic policy, and the Prime Minister has to have the minister dealing with these affairs on the committees.

Disputes about the interpretation extend to individual cases. For example, in the autumn of 1981 Mrs Thatcher moved James Prior from Secretary of State for Employment to Secretary of State for Northern Ireland, despite his very public stand against the move. A clear case, one might argue, of the 'presidential' power of the Prime Minister, but Prior was one of 'the wets' that Mrs Thatcher so disliked, and would have preferred to remove from office, and moreover in negotiating the change Prior successfully insisted that he should retain his seat on the economic strategy committee.

A final point to note about the evaluation of evidence is that both sides in the debate in trying to push their case sometimes go so far that they contradict themselves. For instance, it was noted earlier that Crossman in describing the relationship between Eden, the Prime Minister, and Macmillan, the Chancellor, claimed that Eden could not use the power he undoubtedly possessed. That is a very odd view of power. If Eden could not use it the presumption must be that he did not possess it. Power as a relationship is the capacity and ability to persuade or force others to behave in a way which is desired by the possessor of the power. As Eden dared not use it he must have lost that capacity. He had, in fact, become powerless in that particular situation. On his part, Jones may be questioned about his conclusions on the impact of television. At the end of the paragraph in which he dealt with the topic he states: 'Thus the case that the Prime Minister has been strengthened by television is not proven either way.' If that is the case, no firm conclusions can be drawn. It may or may not have strengthened the premier's powers, and yet earlier in the paragraph Jones had said that in relation to his colleagues the Prime Minister's position had been weakened because through the use of television the senior ministers 'have been strengthened in their relations *vis-à-vis* the Prime Minister'.

The advocates of the presidential and the chairmanship schools have sought to present broad pictures, and it is inevitable that in doing so exceptions can be found and many matters are subordinated to the general trend of the argument. The bold lines of the debate have clear advantages, but there is also the danger of distorting the situation by over-simplification, and of ignoring or undervaluing important factors and patterns of behaviour. In the remainder of this paper the argument is advanced that the lines cannot be drawn as clearly as the advocates of the two schools would have us believe – that a wider set of variables has to be considered which creates a more complex but more accurate picture.

Among the variables is change over time, even during the period of a premiership. A Prime Minister's powers and position are not static but can vary markedly during his time in office. Sometimes he appears as a dominating presidential figure, while at others as a chairman surrounded by constraints. In broad terms a Prime Minister is most likely to achieve a presidential aura either from a crisis which is successfully handled, or immediately after winning an election (especially if he has led his party from opposition to office). However, at any time a Prime Minister's position can fluctuate depending on success or failure, luck or misfortune, and whether his particular talents suit the situation. Examples of the enhancement of powers during crises include the wartime premierships of Lloyd George and Churchill, Baldwin's handling of the Abdication crisis, and Margaret Thatcher's position during and after the Falklands campaign. Yet other premiers have not flourished in crisis, as Asquith and Chamberlain discovered in wartime, and Anthony Eden during the Suez crisis.

Equally, although Prime Ministers are usually strong after an election the degree of strength varies. This was illustrated by the two elections Wilson won from opposition. The first was in 1964 when he was leading a party that had been in opposition for 13 years. Almost all the members of the previous Labour Cabinets had retired or died. Wilson therefore had the double personal advantage of electoral success and ministerial experience, and he was able to harness these to the energy built up in the party during the long, frustrating years of opposition. Wilson came to office claiming that he would effect dramatic quick change – the fabled 100 days. It was a very different situation in 1974 when he next led the party from opposition to government. As the party had been out of office for only four years, all its senior members had substantial ministerial experience. They went to their departments more conscious of the constraints of office than the opportunities. As individuals and as a group they had much greater experience and prestige than the raw enthusiastic Cabinet of a decade before, and therefore the Prime Minister's opportunity to dominate was that much less. Wilson's own public image, and even his self-image, had changed from that of a radical reformer to a cautious leader who offered continuity and stability. Using one of his favoured football images Wilson said that in 1964 he had been a striker, leading the team from the front, whereas in 1974 he had become the manager encouraging the others from the bench.

At other times fortunes can change dramatically, sometimes over relatively short periods. In the Wilson governments there were times when the Prime Minister seemed absolutely secure (none more so than when he resigned), but there were others, for instance during the crises over devaluation in 1967 and *In Place of Strife* in 1969, when his position seemed very vulnerable. He weathered these storms but for a time at least he was much less dominant than during his periods of relative success. During his premiership Harold Macmillan had similar changes of fortune, moving from the effortless superiority of 'Supermac', through the uncertainties that led to his dismissing a third of his Cabinet overnight, to the Profumo scandal when he seemed a pathetic figure who had lost control. In their successful periods Wilson and Macmillan had the presidential stamp upon them, but in their low moments they were no more than chairmen.

Mrs Thatcher's experience also supports the view of fluctuating power. Thatcher's early dominance of the government gave way to dissension as her economic policies ran into difficulties and the Cabinet split down the middle between 'the wets' and 'the dries'. Increasing opposition within the government meant that she failed to carry some of her most prized objectives – as is illustrated by the compromises that she and the Chancellor, Sir Geoffrey Howe, were forced to accept in their attempts to reduce public expenditure. However, the Prime Minister's dominance was reasserted during the Falklands campaign and persisted afterwards so that she was able to assert a distinctive and personal stamp on the government.

Although there will always be exceptions the following conclusions suggest themselves. (a) A Prime Minister's power is likely to be greatest when he handles a crisis well or at the beginning of a ministry, especially if he has led his party out of opposition. (b) The powers of the Prime Ministers fluctuate during his period of office. (c) Individual setbacks do not usually threaten the Prime Minister's position as the head of government, but they can reduce his powers within the government. (d) In exceptional circumstances a series of failures following one another can undermine a Prime Minister's position beyond recall, as happened with Eden.

Another factor which comes into play is the degree of commitment that a Prime Minister, or those who can exercise constraints on him, give to a particular policy. Some premiers have strong personal commitments – as Margaret Thatcher has to monetarism, and Harold Wilson had to trying to solve the Rhodesian crisis – and in such circumstances they may be able to carry their colleagues with them on that, but there is usually a price to be paid. By concentrating so much attention on one issue other areas of government business may pass by without Prime Ministerial involvement, and, even if done unconsciously, to gain support for top priorities the Prime Minister may be less insistent on having his way elsewhere. Moreover, if a Prime Minister fails to achieve objectives to which he is strongly committed, his status and power suffer.

On some policy matters the party may feel especially committed so that on these not only the Prime Minister but his ministerial colleagues will find little room for manoeuvre. Similar constraints may arise from the commitments of some leading ministers, or even a powerful and determined department. When there is a fairly even balance within the government the Prime Minister's intervention will usually settle the issue. Often a Prime Minister will try to avoid confrontation by anticipating the views of the party, colleagues' and departments' views, and the number of issues on which a Cabinet will be divided, or a section so committed that it will not accept a clear Prime Ministerial lead, will usually be small – if for no other reason than that there is insufficient time to handle more than a few controversies. And, of course, a government recognizes that internal Cabinet controversies can create major problems of confidence. An example of such concern came in 1976 when the Labour government was divided on the terms being asked for a large International Monetary Fund (I.M.F.) loan. The views of Denis Healey, the Chancellor, which gained the support of James Callaghan, the Prime Minister, were strongly challenged in Cabinet, but eventually the dangers of trying to overrule the Prime Minister and the Chancellor were thought by critics like Tony Crosland (the Foreign Secretary) to be so great to the government and the value of the pound, that they decided it was better to accept what they regarded as unsatisfactory terms rather than continue the conflict. This does not imply, however, that conflicts do not arise and that on occasions Prime Ministers are not overruled – they are.

The shifting pattern of relationships is documented in the diary which Richard Crossman kept during his period as a minister in Wilson's cabinets. Despite his commitment to the presidential school his keen eye recognized the peaks and troughs of Wilson's position.

The Prime Minister's strength was demonstrated in July 1965 when Crossman, who was then Minister of Housing, was called before a committee of five of his Cabinet colleagues: 'the five wise men' who had the responsibility for examining and reporting on government cuts that were to be made. Crossman knew that he had Harold Wilson's sympathy and support. After an hour-long argument Crossman recorded:

> Douglas Houghton said: 'I must say I don't like this at all. The others all came in here fearing their programmes will be cut. This fellow saunters into the room giving the impression that we dare not cut him for political reasons.' Of course, what Houghton said was the precise truth. I know I have the Prime Minister behind me. I also know that my housing programme is at the mercy not of any cuts they may wish to make but of economic forces which are threatening and pressuring and bullying this poor Government.[18]

In that instance Crossman was demonstrating the Prime Minister's power, but in contrast another example drawn from that same month illustrates the limitation of that power. Again public expenditure was involved and on this occasion both James Callaghan, as Chancellor, and George Brown, as Secretary of State for Economic Affairs, combined against Wilson to prevent the restoration of £20 million from cuts in the overseas aid budget, although Barbara Castle, the Minister of Overseas Development, had gained Wilson's support in attempting to restore the cuts. On previous occasions when Callaghan and Brown had opposed each other the Prime Minister's support had been decisive because he held the balance, but in this case when the two major 'economic ministers' were united, their combined weight left Wilson with no presidential-like powers. When Wilson showed sympathy for Barbara Castle a long argument ensued:

> The First Secretary and the Chancellor, clearly in some sense working together, leapt on Harold like wolfhounds in at the kill. . . . They tore him from both sides. They insulted him, tried to pull him down in the most violent way, obviously both feeling that Harold was evading his responsibilities as Prime Minister and trying to do an unseemly fix. And of course that is what he was doing. . . . When he was defeated he tried to pretend he hadn't made the proposal and had the whole story removed from Cabinet

minutes – historic proof that those minutes never tell you a damn thing of what goes on in Cabinet unless the P.M. and Cabinet Secretariat want to publish it.[19]

Another factor that bears investigation is the relationship between the Prime Minister and his party. The presidential/chairmanship debate plays little attention to party differences but that may be a mistake. A national party is a plurality in terms of (a) its supporters, with distinctions between the bulk of its voters and the much smaller and usually more extreme party activists; (b) its institutions from the constituency through regional and national organizations; and (c) its ideas and beliefs, for each party has to be a 'broad church' to embrace a spectrum of beliefs. The Prime Minister, as party leader, has the problem of trying to satisfy this plurality of interests at a time when he has little time for party matters. His office may give him an aura of authority within the party, but the problem of decision-making in government can distance him from party concerns and create tensions and disputes with party members; James Callaghan bluntly told the 1976 Labour Party conference that while the National Executive Committee (N.E.C.) produced no more than statements and resolutions the government was accountable for decisions and actions.

The expectations placed on the Prime Minister by his party are immense. Ideally his ideological stance should satisfy broad party views but also have a national electoral appeal; he should be a powerful parliamentary figure able to counter the thrust of the opposition; he ought to be an outstanding organizer, and so on. Plainly no Prime Minister can live up to all these expectations and while there may be broadly agreed views on who has or has not been a successful premier, a fertile field lies open for subjective judgments – which reflects as much about the observer as about the Prime Minister. Michael Foot's picture of Clement Attlee is one of a timid, 'small' character with no fire or zest, and whose only virtues were negative. Foot admitted, however, that Attlee's 'mind, however unadventurous, was usually open and unprejudiced', and, perhaps unconsciously foreseeing his own tribulations as leader, said of Attlee that 'perhaps a sphinx was the only emblem which *could* lead the Labour Party'.[20] In contrast Francis Williams saw Attlee as a brisk, competent, clear-minded man who knew how to organize a government.[21] In the same way, many Tories see Sir Alec Douglas-Home (Lord Home) as a splendid British gentleman full of conservative virtues and graces. For Enoch Powell he was a weak, naïve man who went wherever the wind would blow.[22]

Is there then a difference in the position and power of a Labour and a Tory Prime Minister? Robert McKenzie examined that question in his classic study of British political parties, which was first published in 1955 and revised in 1963.[23] (The timing of the publications is worth noting because the changes which McKenzie introduced in the revised edition underline that we are examining a dynamic process in which the party leader's position has changed and is changing.) McKenzie set out to contrast the formal position within the parties with their actual behaviour. In formal terms he argued that the Conservative leader has much more power than his Labour counterpart. For instance, when in opposition the Conservative leader selects the 'Shadow Cabinet'; the Labour leader does not. The Conservative leader has ultimate responsibility for the formulation of party policy, while the Labour leader shares this with the party conference and the N.E.C. McKenzie's view, however, was that this formal position created a very misleading picture. In practice their positions especially when in office were very similar; the party of origin made no observable difference to the Prime Minister's relationships or behaviour.

To support this view McKenzie examined a number of issues, including the premier's role in forming a government. Within the Labour party there have been suggestions that the leader should seek the party's approval before seeing the monarch, or certainly before accepting the invitation. Such opinions were heard in 1945 after Attlee had led the party to an election victory. Herbert Morrison urged Attlee to postpone seeing the King until a new leadership election had been held; although in this case Morrison may have been less interested in the general principle, than in advancing his own ambitions to replace Attlee. Attlee ignored such calls. As Labour leader he accepted the King's invitation to form a government, 'If you are invited by the King to form a Government', said Attlee, 'you don't say you can't reply for forty-eight hours.'[24] The Labour party quickly accepted Attlee's position, and thereby confirmed that, as with the Conservatives, the leader had the right to accept the invitation to form a government without reference back to the party. Equally, according to McKenzie, the two parties have behaved in the same way in the leader's right to appoint and dismiss ministers (despite the different arrangements over the Shadow Cabinet). McKenzie noted that despite all the attempts within the

Labour party to change this nothing had been achieved, but as is clear from Tony Benn's views that dispute is far from dead. Finally, in terms of policy-making, McKenzie found similar practice in both parties. While within the Labour ranks there are many who believe in, and continue to fight for, the right of the party through the N.E.C. and the Annual Conference to lay down the policy to be pursued by the government, this has not been accepted by Labour leaders. Equally, in the reverse case, the Conservative leadership has paid greater attention to the views advanced at conferences than the formal position might imply. The result, McKenzie argued, is that policy-making in both parties is very similar – the government and not the party outside makes the decisions although governments are conscious of the need to retain party support.

That last point 'the need to retain party support' is one on which McKenzie's view may be challenged. The challenge is that past experience shows that Labour leaders have had to pay more attention to party opinion than their Conservative opponents. In part, this can be explained by the different party organizations. The Labour party is much more complex than its Tory counterpart, with powerful organized interests forming a structure in which power is divided between the leader, the parliamentary party, the N.E.C., the Annual Conference and the trades unions. That structure imposes considerable constraints on the party leader and often absorbs much of his time and energy. Added to the organizational complexity the Labour party places greater emphasis on ideology which leads to persistent controversy about the path which should be followed. These organizational and ideological constraints are more effective on the leader when the party is in opposition but they do not disappear when it is in office. The result is that Labour Prime Ministers have usually had to spend more time and energy on managing the party than Tory premiers.

In office Labour leaders have often protested, as Harold Wilson did in 1976, that 'the Prime Minister and the cabinet cannot be instructed by the National Executive Committee or by the Conference'.[25] However, the very fact that he and other Labour Prime Ministers have been forced to make such statements indicates the tension that is there. On occasions the parliamentary leaders appear to have accepted the claims of extra-parliamentary right to dictate policy. For instance, in 1957 during the fierce debate about the retention of the H-bomb, Aneurin Bevan called on the Conference not to send a future Labour Foreign Secretary 'naked into the

International conference chamber' – thereby implying that a Conference decision on the matter was binding on a Labour government. That is not a view that has normally been accepted by Labour leaders, but the argument goes on, as the bitter battles of the early 1980s served to underline. Not only was the method of selecting the leadership changed, but, with the defection of so many Labour M.P.s to the Social Democratic party (S.D.P.), the wing of the party which supported the view of a leadership drawn from and responsible to the parliamentary section of the party was weakened. At the time of writing, Labour is not in power, the effect of this on a Labour Prime Minister is unknown, but it is clear that the recent party battles and divisions have challenged the parliamentary leadership. If men like Tony Benn have their way, the pressure will not stop, for as he told his Bristol audience,

> The real tension within the party does not only stem from left versus moderate, or from Labour M.P.s or the unions versus the N.E.C. and the Conference. It derives to a great extent from the tension that exists between the dominating power of the Party leader, especially when he is Prime Minister, and the rest of the Labour movement, Labour M.P.s, the N.E.C., Conference, and the trade unions.[26]

Conservative leaders have not faced such intense party pressures. Their position in an organization that has its predominant strength in the parliamentary group has given them more flexibility and, at least in the past, the Conservatives prided themselves on their pragmatism; on their concern with exercising power and responding to changing circumstances rather than pursuing precise ideological goals. Added to that, past Conservative leaders usually put considerable emphasis on achieving internal consensus, and that, together with a more hierarchical structure than the Labour party, gave them greater freedom and discretion. Within that context, there was less support than in the Labour party for adopting a comprehensive policy programme which it was committed to implement when in office. This is not to suggest that the party did not have broad programmes or that there were no internal party conflicts or challenges to the leadership. There were. But the emphasis was different from that in the Labour party, with the Tory leader having more discretion and flexibility. That situation seems to have been changing in recent years, and ironically the impetus for change has come as much from the party leadership as from the grass roots. The leaders have started to commit themselves to precise policy objectives, and in doing so have reduced their discretion within the party and their ability to seek internal consensus. There were signs of that happening in Edward Heath's time, but it has reached full fruition under Margaret Thatcher. Mrs Thatcher believes in 'commitment politics', in which the government seeks to achieve precise policy objectives, and she has the will and determination to push on whatever the opposition, including opposition within the party. The result has been greater tension and division in the Tory ranks than at any time since the war, with Mrs Thatcher openly stating that she is opposed to consensus politics and she has left no doubt about her disdain for 'the wets' who favour it.

Within this context of change, the mechanism for selecting the leaders of both the Labour and Conservative parties has been altered. In the past, the Tory leader 'emerged' after consultations among leading party figures, whereas the Labour leader has always been elected, but until recently only Labour M.P.s voted for the leader. All that has changed. Since 1965 the Conservative leader has been chosen by the party's M.P.s, while the Labour party now involves directly the trades unions and the constituency parties in the electoral process – indeed the Labour M.P.s are now in a minority position, for the voting powers are 40 per cent unions, and 30 per cent each for the constituencies and the M.P.s.

As the Labour party leader has always been elected it might be thought that his tenure and hold on the office was more uncertain than that of his Conservative counterpart. That has not been the case. Despite the tradition of elections, and the party's well-founded reputation for internal divisions and squabbles, Labour leaders have enjoyed greater security of office than their Tory rivals. If we take the period 1945 to 1981 there have been five Labour leaders and six Conservative. In the case of Labour – for all the tumult and shouting in the party – no leader has been voted out of office or been forced to resign under party pressure. Attlee resigned from old age, Gaitskell died in office and Haold Wilson and James Callaghan retired from choice when their leadership was secure. The contrast with the Conservatives is striking. A case can be made out that Eden, Macmillan, Douglas-Home, and even Churchill resigned earlier than they intended because of party pressure. When the first Conservative leadership election was held in 1965, Home did not stand. Heath, who did, was elected. Ten years later he was defeated by Margaret Thatcher, so that within two contests the Conservative party had achieved something never done by the Labour party. It had ousted a sitting leader by voting him out of office.

How do we explain this difference of behaviour? One possibility is that it is just a matter of chance; a combination of personality and circumstances, which cannot be explained in terms of party differences. This is possible but the pattern is fairly clear even if the explanation is not. One possibility is that the image and styles of the party have had the reverse effect on the leadership. Because in the past the Tories believed they ought to be united, that they should present a common front to the public, and because the leader felt that a major task was to sustain a clearly united body, pressures and criticisms directed at him from inside the party had greater effect. On the opposite side of the fence, divisions within the Labour party are more overt and are more easily absorbed. The party sees itself as one of controversy and endless debate in which the leader could never hope to satisfy all factions. Added to this may be the general tradition of loyalty to leaders which have revealed itself in the unions and working-class movements. There was therefore the apparent contradiction whereby the party in which every voice cried 'unity' has rejected its leaders regularly; the party which is noted for internal strife holds on to its leaders over long periods. Ironically the introduction of elections in the Conservative party may, despite Edward Heath's experience, start to make it more difficult to remove the leader – certainly one as determined as Mrs Thatcher. In the past when informal pressure was applied, the leader who resisted the pressure could be held as the one responsible for splitting the party by stubbornly holding on to office, but with formal elections the onus for making a challenge which is likely to split the party falls on those who put up a rival to the leader.

In concluding the discussion about the relationship between party and leader, what can be said is that the relationship is complex and dynamic. In the past there has been the apparent paradox of greater party constraints and tensions but greater security of office for the Labour leader, whereas the Conservative leader has had more discretion, but less security. That may be changing, but even greater changes may be ahead both from the increased use of electoral colleges outside parliament (with the possibility of a leader imposed on a reluctant set of M.P.s), and from the possibility of the break-up of the established two-party system. An S.D.P./Liberal Alliance might come into power and the relationship between Prime Minister and the party in that case is unknown. Moreover, other coalitions might have to be formed to gain a parliamentary majority. In the case of alliance and/or coalition, the relationship between leader and parties which support him could well be different from the single party situation of the past. What this speculation about the future underlines is that the relationship between the leader and his party is not one that can be taken for granted and varies according to the party and the circumstances. It certainly cannot be ignored as the presidential and chairmanship schools tend to do.

The relationship that he has with the party forms part of the Prime Minister's own interpretation of his office. In very broad terms the views of the Prime Ministers can be divided between those who have largely seen their task in terms of achieving specific goals, and those who have placed the greatest priority on team leadership, on holding the party and the government together to meet largely unforeseen problems and circumstances. Of course, the division is never that clear-cut but the difference of emphasis is there. In recent years the goal-seeking interpretation has become more prominent, with increasing attention to party manifestos in which specific claims are made about the future achievements of the government. Are such claims usually based on sound evaluations, or are the politicians deluding themselves, or perhaps trying to delude the electorate? Lord Hailsham has little faith in such manifestos. In 1976 he said: 'The actual situation with which a new government is confronted is often vastly different from what it was imagined to be in opposition, and the measures proposed in the manifesto often include the impossible, the irrelevant, and the inappropriate.'[27]
Nevertheless, there is a great appeal in a political leader who sets himself grand challenges. Who can fail to savour the scene in 1868 when Gladstone, on receiving the news that he was to form a ministry, paused in felling a tree to declare: 'My mission is to pacify Ireland'? A splendid scene, an admirable objective, but neither he nor any of his successors have been able to realize it. The same is true of more recent Prime Ministers – from Wilson's confidence that he could revolutionize British industrial practice through the use of modern technology, to Margaret Thatcher's claims for monetarism. If we compare the objectives Prime Ministers have set themselves with their achievements, a substantial gap appears. Perhaps the gap seems unduly wide because the failures tend to be emphasized by the media and critics inside and outside the governing party. James Callaghan told the 1976 Labour Conference that: 'Sometimes I

think those who ask us to stick to the manifesto are rather selective in their reading. The remarkable thing is not what we have failed to do, but how much has been carried out.' Later he said that the Labour party 'has already put many of the aspirations of the pioneers on to the statute book as law of the land'.[28]

Despite such protests the gap exists, and is difficult to bridge; governments have become involved in an ever-increasing range of responsibilities, and those responsibilities may be one of the reasons for the difficulty in achieving precise goals. The powers of the Prime Minister and other ministers may even be diminished with the continued extension of government activities. For one thing the ministers, however conscientiously they work, can only touch a small part of the great range of government business. Furthermore, a vast bureaucratic machine has been built up with an almost irresistible inertia. Hugh Stephenson, in assessing Mrs Thatcher's first year in office, said that while she had given the civil service a culture shock by refusing to compromise, and by refusing to abandon her novel views about how the economy worked and how social policy should be conducted, she made the mistake of failing to overhaul the civil service structure, and, added to that, she accepted 'the Whitehall rules' on relations between ministers and civil servants, 'which reduced the impact of the policies she was trying to get across'. According to Stephenson, Keith Joseph, Mrs Thatcher's close ally, failed even more to impress himself on his civil servants. Joseph started by giving them a reading list of 'right wing' books on the economy. For the civil servants 'it was an unnerving start, but it was not to last for long. By the middle of June his senior civil servants were confident that they had got the guru under control.'[29]

There are other possibile explanations for the Prime Minister's difficulties in achieving objectives. He is usually drawn into the goverment's most intractable problems – whether they are industrial relations, Northern Ireland, or negotiating refunds from the E.E.C.'s agricultural policy – and he often finds himself surrounded by constraints from outside Britain which are beyond his control. Jay noted that in his assessment of Attlee's position, as did Crossman in recognizing that while he might be able to bluff his way past the committee of fellow ministers, he could not overcome the 'economic forces' that were holding back the housing programme. One of the clearest examples of the strength of external constraints came in 1976 when the Labour government turned to the I.M.F. for help. After a fierce Cabinet debate the I.M.F. terms were accepted despite the strong doubts of many ministers.

The constraints – both domestic and external – which surround a Prime Minister and his government serve to underline an aspect of 'power' which is often neglected in the debate on the Prime Minister's position. Usually the discussion concentrates on the Prime Minister's power in relation to those with whom he works closely – the ministers, civil servants, and leading party members – but 'power' can also be interpreted as the ability to achieve defined goals. In that sense fortunes are mixed because the Prime Minister's power is hedged about by constraints. Yet is is often sympathy with or opposition to the aims of a Prime Minister that influences judgment about how much power he should have. According to Gavyn Davies, who had served in the Prime Minister's policy unit and who in 1980 was a member of a Fabian committee which looked into the powers of the Prime Minister: 'How much power you want to give to the Prime Minister depends on how much you like what he or she intends to do.'[30]

Sympathy with or opposition to the aims of a particular Prime Minister raises the question of personality. So far the personality of the premier has only been mentioned in passing, and yet for some scholars, and for some Prime Ministers, it is the single most important determinant of a Prime Minister's power. For them the emphasis is on the person not the role, on the man and not the office. In Asquith's words: 'The office of Prime Minister is what the holder chooses and is able to make of it.'[31]

In the presidential chairmanship debate the emphasis is different. Crossman made some mention of personality in contrasting the different commitments of Wilson and Heath, but he did not labour the point, and Jones scarcely mentions personality at all. A very different approach is adopted by Lord Blake. He states that certain personal qualities are required for the job (which make up a 'Prime Ministerial temperament') but not all premiers have possessed them. A temperament is difficult to define but for Blake the ideal would include 'courage, tenacity, determination, firm nerves, . . . clarity of mind, toughness of skin and lack of great sensitivity', with tact and the ability to manage men as valuable additions. Blake believes that 'Possession of the right temperament is not a guarantee of success but lack of it is a firm guarantee of failure.' Further, Blake stated that Prime Ministers are not usually men of original mind, although of recent premiers he excepted Lloyd George and Churchill, who both came to office during wars. In less critical times perhaps a Prime Minister is best equipped with the characteristics Bagehot attributed to Peel: 'A man of common opinion and uncommon abilities'.[32]

One of Blake's doubts about Crossman's views was their lack of historical perspective. For Blake, premiers of earlier generations often enjoyed greater power and authority than Crossman was prepared to recognize. Nobody, in Blake's opinion, had come nearer to exercising presidential-like powers than Lloyd George, and yet the principal features of government which Crossman said had so enhanced the Prime Minister's powers did not then exist. Also Blake believes that modern Prime Ministers have been more 'correct' than earlier holders of the office in consulting and checking with their colleagues. He challenged the two examples that Crossman had quoted to support the view that Prime Ministers acted without consultation – Attlee's decision to go ahead with the building of the atomic bomb, and Eden's to invade Suez in 1956. 'Although', wrote Blake, 'one or two of the ministers may have felt they had been "bounced", the correct constitutional procedures were followed. No doubt much more was known by some than others, but that is common form.'[33]

Blake would probably point to Mrs Thatcher's premiership as further evidence of the importance of personality; underlining her distinctive style, her determination to have her way against friend and foe alike, her strengthening of the Prime Minister's office with rumours that she intends to form a separate Prime Minister's Department, and the way she uses the powers of patronage more widely than ever before in such areas as the nationalized industries. Yet, as previously noted, Thatcher's powers have fluctuated during her premiership, although her personality remains constant. Whether she was at her most powerful following the Falklands campaign, or being forced to modify her demands for public spending cuts, there was no doubting her determination and willingness to try to browbeat her ministers into submission, but her success varies according to the circumstances. Blake would probably endorse that view, for he does not lay the full burden of explanation on personality, rather he recognizes the importance of 'particular circumstances', and how institutions develop over time. For Blake, however, the institutional development is not nearly as dramatic as Crossman envisaged. Blake traces relationships in government through the evolution of the electorate, parliament and the parties.

The result of this, according to Blake, is that the leader has become more dependent on the party machine, especially in periods of opposition, because of the need to organize for elections. While, at the time he wrote, the selection of all the party leaders was still in the hands of the parliamentary parties, Blake foresaw the time when the leader might be elected at a party conference, preceded by primaries.

The chief significance of these institutional developments for Blake was that they created the framework for the inter-play of personality and circumstances. 'The truth is', he wrote, 'that the powers of the Prime Minister have varied with the personality of the Prime Minister, or with the particular political circumstances of his tenure.'[34] In terms of relationships within government the balance has altered only slowly over long periods. 'The differences, if we are to take any half century, or even more, are largely between personalities – the way in which this or that occupant of 10 Downing Street in the light of his own circumstances feels that he should or can or wants to behave.'[35]

Blake probably pays too much attention to personality over role, but it is another of the factors that has to be taken into account, and the differences of personality are very striking – from the taciturn Attlee to the loquacious Churchill, from the assurance of Macmillan to the busyness of Wilson, from the mildness of Douglas-Home to the abrasive Margaret Thatcher.

One way to draw conclusions about the variety of factors that operate to make up the Prime Minister's powers, is to take a number of decisions and examine the role played by the Prime Minister within them. This method was employed by Jock Bruce-Gardyne and Nigel Lawson in 1976. They concentrated on four decisions – the early development of Concorde, the abortive approaches to the Common Market in 1961 and 1967, the abolition of resale price maintenance in 1963–4, and the decisions not to devalue the pound between 1964 and 1967.[36]

In their conclusions they noted that during the 1960s and 1970s the presidential thesis had taken a few knocks, for Wilson had been coerced by his colleagues to abandon trade union legislation, while Heath who was 'arguably the most dominant Prime Minister within his own administration since the war, was eventually persuaded to seek a dissolution [of Parliament] in the spring of 1974 against his own inclination'.[37] Of the four cases they studied, the authors concluded that it was only the 'non decision' about devaluation which was truly dominated by the personality and policy of the Prime Minister (Harold Wilson). He was so opposed to it that he would not allow the subject to be discussed and had papers destroyed in which reference was made to the possibility. Yet even in this case, while Wilson could have forced Callaghan, the Chancellor, into devaluation against his (Callaghan's) wishes, Wilson himself, they believed, could have been overruled if Callaghan and George Brown (the Minister of Economic Affairs) had combined against him. However Bruce-Gardyne and Lawson argue that during this same administration the decision to apply for membership of the E.E.C. in 1967 could not have gone ahead, despite the enthusiasm of ministers like Brown and Jenkins, had not the Prime Minister been converted. His support tipped the balance when the Cabinet was divided.

Bruce-Gardyne and Lawson's conclusion is that balances of forces exist between ministers and within the government generally. The strength of any side in a division of views rests on such factors as the number of ministers supporting a cause, their status within the government, the efficiency of the departments which are backing them and the amount of commitment involved. The effectiveness of the Prime Minister often depends on recognizing where the balance lies and in a sense of timing. For example, they explained that during the debate about Concorde in Macmillan's Government the Prime Minister played very little part, but as the forces and arguments were fairly evenly balanced the Prime Minister made a small but crucial intervention in the final stages. It also provided a piece of vintage Macmillan. Following differences between ministers he had deferred the decision to let passions cool down. At the following Cabinet meeting he was in reminiscent mood. He told his colleagues about his great-aunt's Daimler, which had travelled at 'the sensible speed of thirty miles an hour', and was sufficiently spacious to enable one to descend from it without removing one's top hat. Nowadays, alas! people had a mania for dashing around. But that being so, Britain ought to 'cater for this profitable modern eccentricity'. He thought they all really agreed. No one seriously dissented. It was all over in a few minutes.[38]

According to Bruce-Gardyne and Lawson, Macmillan was in a very different situation over the first applicaion for membership of the E.E.C. The public picture that has been presented is one of Macmillan, by skilful persuasion and timing, dragging reluctant colleagues behind him. This was not so, said Bruce-Gardyne and

Lawson. Macmillan doubted the success of the venture and feared the effect of its failure on the party. His instinct was for a bilateral agreement with the French but he did not have the resolution to overcome the combined efforts of the Foreign Office and the United States. The Prime Minister may initially have mobilized support for the idea of membership, but he could not then check its momentum. The application of 1961 should be seen as an example of the limitations, and not the extensive powers of the Prime Minister's position.

From the particular decisions they had examined, Bruce-Gardyne and Lawson concluded that the common theme which emerges is of the Prime Minister 'as an arbiter of choice in government, rather than the preselector of decisions. His acquiescence is a necessary (though not a sufficient) condition for decisions on major policy issues – even if that acquiescence has sometimes to be extracted by something akin to *force majeure*.' They concluded that a strong Prime Minister is not indispensable for decisive government – citing the example of government activity continuing unabated under Alec Douglas-Home – and suggesting that the relaxed style of Wilson in his second term of office may well have been more rewarding than the frantic activity of the first. They also recognized the shifting pattern of relations over time. All Prime Ministers, they argued, come to office with a stock of political capital on which they can call, especially if their appointment follows on election success. Yet this wears with use and even more of it is abused. 'So long as a Prime Minister delivers the goods of electoral esteem his power, uninhibited by a written constitution, is indeed greater than that of Presidential counterparts overseas – if he wishes it to be. But let his government run into serious electoral trouble and he will swiftly discover, as Mr Nigel Birch icily informed Harold Macmillan in the Profumo debate in the summer of 1963, that it is "never glad confident morning again".'[39]

The approach adopted by Bruce-Gardyne and Lawson provides a nice contrast to that employed by the presidential and chairmanship schools. While Crossman and Jones were making broad sweeps across their canvases, Bruce-Gardyne and Lawson built up their picture point by point, examining particular decisions. This latter, 'micro' approach, has the merit of taking account of a wider set of variables and illustrating the mixed fortunes that every premier experiences, but it too has its limitations. Although it appears to build its case on more specific 'harder' evidence, like the other approaches it cannot escape subjective judgments. For example, the authors conclude that a strong premier is not indispensable for decisive government, but it is not difficult to imagine other writers reaching the opposite conclusion. Another obvious limitation is that it is impossible to examine all the decisions in which a Prime Minister is involved and therefore the selection may be untypical or based on less important decisions. It also leaves open the question of why the Prime Minister becomes involved in some decisions and not others. Finally there is the danger that by concentrating on particular decisions the broad picture of the Prime Minister's position may be missed by standing too close and failing to appreciate the overall picture.

In conclusion it can be said that no single approach is entirely satisfactory, but what is clear is that both the presidential and chairmanship schools give too fixed a view of the Prime Minister's power and position by failing to recognize many of the variables that affect his position. A Prime minister is neither a dominant presidential figure nor merely a chairman – a *primus inter pares* – although traces of both can be found in his office. A Prime Minister has a great range of powers but he is also surrounded by many constraints. The balance shifts according to the factors which have been discussed earlier – such as success or failure in achieving objectives, personality, relations with the party, and the experience and strength of fellow ministers. Introducing these variable factors creates a more complex but a more accurate and flexible picture than that offered by the presidential and chairmanship schools.

NOTES

1. W.Bagehot, *The English Constitution* with introduction by R.H.S.Crossman (1963) and R.H.S.Crossman, *Inside View* (1972). Crossman's views were strongly influenced by those of J.P.Mackintosh, *The British Cabinet* (1968).
2. Bagehot, introduction, 51.
3. Bagehot, 68.
4. Bagehot, introduction, 52.
5. *Ibid.*, 53.
6. Crossman, 8.
7. *Ibid.*, 18.
8. *Ibid.*, 19.
9. *Ibid.*, 20.

10. G.W.Jones, 'The Prime Minister's Power', *Parliamentary Affairs*, XVIII (1964–5), 167–85.
11. P.Cosgrave, 'The Weakness of the Prime Minister', *Spectator*, 2 Sep. 1972.
12. D.Jay, *Change and Fortune* (1980).
13. T.Benn, *The Case for a Constitutional Premiership* (Text of lecture delivered in Bristol, 14 July 1979 – published by Institute for Workers' Control, Nottingham, 1979), 5.
14. *Ibid.*, 5.
15. *Ibid.*, 12.
16. *Ibid.*, 20.
17. *The Times*, 10 Feb. 1981.
18. R.H.S. Crossman, *The Diaries of a Cabinet Minister* (1975), I, 268.
19. *Ibid.*, 282.
20. M.Foot, *Aneurin Bevan 1945–60* (1975), 22.
21. F.Williams, *A Prime Minister Remembers* (1960).
22. Enoch Powell – book review, *Spectator*, 9 Oct. 1976.
23. R.McKenzie, *British Political Parties* (1955 and 1963).
24. Williams, *op.cit.*, 4.
25. *The Times*, 15 Oct. 1976.
26. *Op.cit.*, 19.
27. Lord Hailsham, *Listener*, 21 Oct. 1976, 497.
28. *The Times*, 29 Sep. 1976.
29. H.Stephenson, *Mrs Thatcher's First Year* (1980).
30. Quoted by M.Dean in 'Putting the grist in the oyster of government', *Guardian*, 26 Nov. 1980.
31. Quoted by H.Wilson, *The Governance of Britain* (1976), 1.
32. R.Blake, *The Office of Prime Minister*, (1975), 20.
33. R.Blake, 'The Key to number 10', *Sunday Times*, 30 Nov. 1975.
34. *The Office of Prime Minister*, *op.cit.*, 51.
35. *Ibid.*, 66.
36. J.Bruce-Gardyne and N.Lawson, *The Power Game: An Examination of Decision Making in Government* (1976).
37. *Ibid.*, 151.
38. *Ibid.*, 28.
39. *Ibid.*, 158.

5 THE EVOLUTION OF THE POLITICAL PARTIES

H.M.Drucker

DURING that delightful Indian summer of British self-confidence
between the advent of the Macmillan government in 1957 and the
devaluation of the pound in 1967, Professor S.H.Beer concluded his
description of British politics with these words:

> . . . a peaceful and orderly political process does require as an
> essential condition the presence of substantial consensus on values
> and beliefs in the political culture. . . . After experiencing the
> ravages of ideological passion in the recent past, however, we are
> hardly inclined to deny that, for good or ill, for peace or war,
> men's visions of legitimate authority and the common good have a
> dynamic and sometimes terrible power over their behaviour.
> Happy the country in which consensus and conflict are ordered in
> a dialectic that makes of the political arena at once a market of
> interests and a forum for debate of fundamental moral concerns.[1]

Beer's main argument in *Modern British Politics* was with those who
believed that the competition between the parties had little or
nothing to do with ideas, for the parties agreed on most important
issues. Whatever one thinks on the point of issue, few would have
denied in 1965 that British politics was dominated by two parties
each of which sought to govern within a consensus which included
the leaders of both parties as well as all other political opinion that
mattered. No one would argue this today.

Today, commentators compete with one another to produce the

most convincing analysis of our parties' failure. Professor John Lucas speaks for many when he says:

> Elective autocracy although not necessarily the worst form of government, is not good enough. It is a guarantee against bloody revolution and effective in preventing the government from systematically ignoring the interests and flouting the interests of the governed. It avoids the worst abuses and makes the government responsible to large shifts of opinion. But it cannot discriminate finely enough to take account of the individual, to remedy his grievances or carry out his ideas.[2]

Britain used to have a strong responsible moderate two-party system. After each general election the party with a majority of seats in the House of Commons formed a government without help from any other party. That party's leader became the Prime Minister and he chose his Cabinet of about 20, and his government of about 100, entirely from his own side. The government thus formed had the undivided loyalty of the civil service who could be depended to carry out the new government's policies regardless of whether it or the present Opposition had formed the government before the election. At the election both sides would have stood on both their previous records and their promises for the future. Each would have interpreted the needs of the country according to his own general philosophical principles, Labour being collectivist and Conservative individualist. But in power each would have accepted the legislation and policies of its predecessors as part of the inheritance of the nation and not changed them wilfully.

The electorate was, roughly, over a period of time, evenly divided in its support for the two parties and, as it happens, both parties were strong in some parts of the country so that each major party was sure of the support of about a third of the seats, and a third was seriously contested between them. No part of the country, such as Scotland or South-East England, was so heavily weighted in favour of either party that the other party had no interest in this area. There was one major social divide, class, which affected how electors voted. The position in some European countries where religion, language and region found political expression was not paralleled in Britain. This being so, the party leaders believed that the way to gain and keep office was to compete for the middle ground (and not for the preference of some special interest group such as, say, Welsh nationalists).

This competition for the votes of the centre on the one hand, combined with the party's divergent philosophies on the other, to produce the happy result Beer celebrated. The parties occupied much the same ground. Each argued that it could continue the nation's heritage best. Each pursued slightly different versions of the same policies. Each avoided moving to its own extreme (Labour to the Left, Conservatives to the Right). Together they excluded the few extremists from any important say in the nation's politics without recourse to formal proscriptions. Communists were welcome to put up candidates at parliamentary or local elections. There was nothing like the proscription in Germany of Fascists. The extremists formed so small a group that they gained few votes and failed to influence the major parties.

Once a party gained a parliamentary majority it enjoyed the plenitude of power until the next general election. The parliamentary Opposition was free to use the forum of the House of Commons to attempt to embarrass the Government – and it did succeed in embarrassing the government often enough to make the game worth playing. But aside from using the parliamentary timetable to stall government legislation, the Opposition had little other power. M.P.s, mindful on the one hand of the patronage of their party leaders, and on the other of the certainty of electoral defeat if they were denied the right to stand as the candidate of their party, rarely rebelled.

The parliamentary power of the government was augmented by the authority of Parliament in the country. Interest groups such as the trade unions, industry and others accepted the authority of the government and especially of a government of their favourite colour, and bowed to its wishes after being consulted on subjects relevant to the interest group's activities. This was a much more satisfactory situation than that which obtained in many other European countries where general strikes were known, if not common, and private firms did what they could to get their capital out of the country.

Local authorities were not as proud as they had been between the wars, let alone at the end of the nineteenth century, but they still exercised considerable autonomy and were happy to do so within the law.

The national economy was growing. Most people were better off than they had been before and were confident of becoming increasingly so. For much of this period the Conservative party was in office and it was happy to preside over this increase in the national wealth, confident that it could avoid any potential trouble.

The parties differed over matters of principle. Labour wanted the wealth of the country to be controlled collectively and distributed more equitably, while the Conservatives would have liked to see more economic power in private hands because they believed that it would grow more quickly were that the case. Neither party pursued their principles very vigorously, however, because the leaders of each were conscious of the need to win votes from the centre of the political spectrum and both thought the way to do this was to minimize their ideological commitments.

The parties, though similar, did differ in this period. The most important difference is summed up in the fact that the Conservatives ruled during this period. The Conservative party considered itself to be the normal party of rule. The Labour party, though it hardly admitted the truth of this belief to itself, contained a large and powerful section – broadly, its Left – which tacitly accepted the minority role of its party. This section of the Labour party thought of Labour as the normal critic of government and did not expect to come to power until Conservative, capitalist rule had failed. This failure, the left of the Labour party believed, would come inevitably.

The parties differed in their organization in ways which reflected this Conservative dominance. The Conservative party was a leader-dominated party. The leader of the party had considerable power to do as he wished. He chose his Cabinet, his policy, his central office and – since he was Prime Minister – the time for the subsequent election – with little complaint from the rest of his party. Certainly there was nothing in the Conservative party organization like the Annual Conference of the Labour party which might try to hold the leader accountable to it.

Labour, on the other hand, paid lip service and, occasionally, actual heed, to the wishes of its local activists and trade unionists as these wishes were marshalled at its annual conference. Labour was a more factional party than Conservative. It was more difficult to control and it was openly divided into right and left wings. Labour's Left, a minority overall, were nevertheless well entrenched in the constituency parties and were better able to manipulate the rhetoric of the party's ideology against the Right than vice versa. The Labour Right for its part was secure in power within the party because it had the loyal support of the major trade unions and the overwhelmingly larger number of M.P.s. These divisions within the Labour party embarrassed the party's leaders and delighted the Conservatives.

The major parties were also unequal in that the Conservative party enjoyed a predominance of support from the major social institutions of the land. The Church of England, caricatured as the 'Tory party at prayer', the House of Lords, overwhelmingly Tory, the armed services, and to a lesser but no less considerable extent, the universities, the majority of the press, and the B.B.C. were all institutions where Conservative values held sway. The support of these institutions made it possible for the Conservative party to portray itself convincingly as the party of the nation. Labour, on the other hand, was in the less fortunate position of being the party of a class. That Labour was the party of the larger class (about 2/3 of Britons were working class) was a threat to the position of the Conservative party but the threat was never successfully deployed because about a third of working-class people voted Conservative while only 10 per cent of middle-class people voted Labour.

But the differences between the major parties, while they were emphasized by the leaders of these parties in public, were offset to a considerable extent by the fact that the country had a two-party system and that each of the major parties' leaders was aware of this fact and of the considerable advantages the system brought to this party. Liberals used to complain that canvassers for each of the major parties would urge their (temporarily) disaffected voters to vote for the other major party rather than for the Liberals or any other third party. Their complaint, whatever the truth behind it, pointed to a real feature of British politics in this halcyon period. Minor parties were squeezed out.

Minor parties did not, however, completely die away. In Northern Ireland neither of the major British parties contested elections. The battle there was between the Unionist party which won the Protestant vote and various parties which competed for the Catholic vote. Most of the seats regularly went to the Unionists and when they went to Westminster they voted as docile members of the Conservative lobby. In Scotland the S.N.P. fought by-elections from the mid-1960s on and began to do well at the end of this period, but for most of it they were simply eccentric. In Wales the Plaid Cymru fared no better. Neither of these nationalist parties did as well in its country as the Liberals. The Liberals were much the most considerable of the minor parties. They always retained a handful of seats in the House of Commons and, though few noticed the fact at the time, their vote tended to rise steadily under Conservative governments. None of these minor parties was able substantially to intrude into the political *pas de deux*. On the contrary British voters chose between the two major parties. What was more they tended to swing in small numbers from one to the other of the major parties in remarkably similar numbers across the entire country at general elections. The vagaries of the plurality electoral system magnified the slight shifts in votes into sizeable shifts in seats and this exaggeration ensured that either of the two major parties could form a government unaided after each successive general election.

Since the mid 1960s the party system and the parties have been changing. The foundations of the old system have been weakening and something remarkably like a new system has been emerging. The simplest way to summarize the change is to say that it is no longer the case that the leaders of the two major parties can assume that either will be able to form a government unaided by another party after the next general election. In this important sense Britain no longer enjoys two-party politics. It is tempting to take our earlier description of the party system: strong, responsible, moderate two-party and suggest that each feature has been negated, that the system is now weak, irresponsible, extremist and multi-party. But this would be to take matters too far. Nevertheless, the system of party competition which Britain now employs has moved closer to the later description and further from the earlier description with the passage of time.

Let us look first at what has changed, then at why the changes have occurred and finally at the implications of the changes for the government of Britain.

Electoral support for the two-party system has been declining. The decline has not been even or steady but since the peak of two-party competition in the early 1950s the decline is noticeable, important and unlikely to be reversed. In 1951, when Britain was as politically bi-polar as it had ever been, 96 per cent of those who voted, voted for one or other of the two major parties. At the general election of 1979, 80.8 per cent of those who voted opted for one of the two major parties. At the previous general election, October 1974, support for the major parties reached its lowest so far, of 74.8 per cent. While support from those who vote for either of the major parties has been falling, the proportion of the electorate who do not vote at all has been rising. In 1951, 17.4 per cent of those on the electoral register did not vote. The figure was never so low again; having reached a peak of 28 per cent in 1970 it fell back to 23.8 per cent in 1979.

These figures add up to falling authority for the two parties. In 1951, 79.9 per cent of the electorate voted for the major parties; in 1979 the figure was 61.3 per cent. Part of the reason for the drop has been the rise in popularity of the other parties. Only 2.1 per cent of the electorate voted Liberal in 1951 or 1955 – in the elections of 1974 and 1979 the Liberals never had less than 10.5 per cent (in 1979) and reached a peak in February 1974 of 15.2 per cent. The smaller minor parties won a mere 0.6 per cent in 1951 but never failed to win less than 4.4 per cent in the 1974 and 1979 elections.

The movement of voters away from the major two parties has not been either even or steady. In general, the movement tends to occur after periods of Conservative government. The peaks of minor party support occurred after the second 1974 general election. On the other hand, after a period of Labour government the voters tend to return to their old political homes. But they do not return after Labour governments in such numbers as at the end of the previous Labour government. Thus the 1979 general election which occurred after a spell of Labour government saw a reassertion of two-party voting compared to the previous (i.e. the October 1974) election. But the return still produced more minor party votes than the general election of June 1970 after the previous spell of Labour government.

This phenomenon can be expressed differently. We may say that the voters are increasingly willing to vote for a party other than Labour or Conservative, but the two major parties, both of whom tend to lose votes after spells in office, do so in different ways. Labour loses votes after a spell in office which, on the whole, it does not regain. Its vote has been going down almost steadily so that at the 1979 general election Labour were reduced to the smallest percentage – 28 per cent – it had won since the débâcle of 1931. The Conservative party also tends to lose votes after a period in office. Indeed, its percentage of 26 per cent in October 1974 was smaller than Labour's 1979 total. But the Conservative votes tend to rise as well as fall.

Perhaps this is because people who leave the Labour party tend to go over to the Tory party, but voters who are disenchanted with the Conservative party tend to move to a minor party. The Conservative total resembles the action of an ebbing tide, first in, then out – but the overall tide is falling. Labour, on the other hand, is a slowly melting iceberg.

The declining electoral support for the major parties has not been fully reflected in the House of Commons. The number of M.P.s which the major parties win is greater than the proportion of the votes they win. This is possible because the plurality electoral system makes it extremely difficult for minor parties to win seats. Liberals can win large numbers of honourable seconds across the country in a good year. This is little use in the House of Commons. Nevertheless, the number of non-major party M.P.s has been rising since the early 1950s. In 1951 there were nine minor party M.P.s, in 1955 eight. In the 1974 and 1979 elections the minor parties had never less than 28 and reached a peak of 39 in October 1974.

Even if the minor parties do not get anything like proportionate justice from the electoral system, the cracks in the two-party dominance are now so big that no party had a majority of seats after the February 1974 election and Labour had only a tiny majority after the October election. Thus, after those two elections the minor parties had a role to play at Westminster even if strict proportionality would have given them an even larger role. It is true that the Conservatives won a comfortable overall majority of seats in the House of Commons after the 1979 general election, but the frightening thing about this for the major parties is that the Tories needed a massive two million advantage over Labour to win this parliamentary majority.

At the same time as support for the two major parties is weakening, the country is also seeing the rise of geographically based parties. The Conservatives are overwhelmingly strong in the South and East of Britain; Labour are predominant in the North and West of the country. This movement has been accompanied by a rural-urban shift. No longer is it the case that both parties have substantial interests in the inner cities and the country. Labour holds the cities. Conservative holds the surrounding countryside.

Along with this shift has come the rise of the national parties. The Conservative party never did particularly well in Wales. It won some seats there in the 1979 election it had not dared hope for before and yet it was still a minority party in the Principality despite its overall Commons majority. The Conservative Party used to trade advantages with Labour in Scotland. That country's 71 seats were nearly evenly divided. But not since 1955 has the Conservative party won a majority in Scotland and in the 1979 election won less than half the number of seats north of the Border held by Labour – and this was after a considerable recovery of fortunes for the party from its 1977 trough in Scotland.

Neither party can count on automatic support from any Ulster party. To be sure, the majority of the seats in the Province, now increased from 11 to 17, are in Protestant hands and most of them are held by men who normally vote with the Conservatives. But the support of the Ulster parties is conditional. It can be, and was, bargained for by the major parties during the 1974–9 Parliament. The number of seats held by the Welsh and Scottish national parties has varied. But they both managed to hold on to at least some seats even after the unfavourable (for them) election of 1979 and both remain formidable threats to the major parties.

At the same time as electoral support for the major parties has been declining, the loyalty of the parties' M.P.s is also no longer as automatic as once it was. During the 1970–4 Parliament the Heath goverment suffered a number of defeats on whipped votes, especially on its European Communities Bill and in the following Parliament the Labour government which never had a secure parliamentary majority lost numerous votes, especially on devolution.

These defeats are not particularly remarkable unless they are seen in their historical context. It used to be assumed in the House of Commons that an M.P. who voted against his party risked almost certain destruction. He would be denied the whip and would face an official candidate from his party at the subsequent general election. This threat is no longer credible. Neither, and this second may be more significant, do M.P.s any longer tremble at the thought that their rebellion might lead the government to fall. The Labour governments of 1974–9 suffered numerous major defeats. On one occasion they even lost a vote on a budget proposal – in the historic phrase that had 'failed to secure supply'. The heavens did not fall. No election was called as a result. The Government simply carried on. The following Conservative Government also suffered a defeat on a budget proposal as the result of a rebellion of its backbench M.P.s. In that case too the heavens remained in place. Rebellions are still not common. The case must not be overstated. Neither are they likely to become common, for the people who become M.P.s are likely to be loyal to their party. But it now realized that an M.P. can survive rebellion and, if he has taken the precaution of acting in concert with his constituency party or association, need suffer no ill effects at all.

Here, as ever, the parties are on different footings. Rebellion is a more common feature of Labour M.P.s' behaviour than of Conservative M.P.s'. Nevertheless, Conservative M.P.s are not so dependable as they used to be. Rebellions of backbench M.P.s have been paralleled by indiscipline within governments. Previously the doctrine of the collective responsibility of the government secured the total loyalty of that part of the House. This loyalty extended not merely to voting with the government on all occasions, it also involved not speaking out in opposition to government policy. Collective responsibility was the apotheosis of party discipline. Cabinet rank was a reward to some of the party M.P.s who had been disciplined all their political life. Cabinet posts are still handed only to party members in the Parliament, but these posts no longer prevent their holders from speaking and on occasion voting against the government.

Once again it has been Labour which has led the way in the breakdown of the old system. Tony Benn carried his opposition to the Common Market to campaigning against the Cabinet's recommendation of a 'yes' vote in the referendum on continued membership of the Market. But his action had an echo in the subsequent Conservative government. That Cabinet was openly divided into 'wets' and (pro-Prime Minister) 'dries'. The former did not hesitate to attack the latter in speeches and on radio and television and their criticism was publicly returned. When two-party politics was at its peak, such indiscipline would have led to an immediate sacking. Alternatively, if a substantial number – let alone a majority – of a Cabinet disagreed with a Prime Minister they would unseat that Prime Minister. None of these consequences has followed from the Cabinet indiscipline of recent years.

The most dramatic form of indiscipline is the formation of a breakaway party. This has now happened three times to sitting M.P.s in recent years. In October 1972 Dick Taverne left the Labour Party in Lincoln, formed his own Democratic Labour party and resigned his seat to force a by-election (which he won) over the Common Market issue. In July 1976 two Scottish Labour M.P.s, Jim Sillars and John Robertson, also resigned the Labour whip and formed their own breakaway party because of policy differences with Labour (in their case over devolution). Neither of these two parties, despite the considerable and overwhelmingly flattering receptions both received from their local press, amounted to much. Taverne lost his seat after a short spell and even though his party held on to power in Lincoln at local government level it had no effect else-where. The Scottish Labour party formed by the Scottish rebels did not fight by-elections nor hold any seats at the 1979 general election and later disappeared.

But the most spectacular and more important breakaway occurred in the spring of 1981. Eleven Labour M.P.s and one Conservative M.P. as well as two prominent ex-Labour M.P.s broke away to form the Social Democratic party. It is too early to assess the success of that party. But its creation was greeted by flattering results in the opinion polls; within the first year of its life the party was the second party in the polls more than once. It won its first three parliamentary by-elections. More important, the creation of this new party, apparently so popular with the voters, has frightened the major parties' leaders.

The leaders of the new breakaway S.D.P. have taken their plunge convinced that the two major parties have each moved so far to its own political extreme – Labour to the Left, Conservative to the Right – as to leave the centre of the political stage free for a new force. This is another dimension of the changes in the parties. In the mid-1960s the two parties competed for the political middle ground. Each hoped to win the next election by winning more of the uncommitted voters in the centre. Since then the parties have each moved in the opposite direction. Labour has become more definitely socialist, Conservative has become more determinately individualist and monetarist. Each has abandoned consensus politics for ideological politics. The Right of the Labour party and the Left of the Conservative party have been increasingly uncomfortable at these changes brought about as the local activists of the two major parties come to exert increasing influence over the leadership, and finally the politicians in the centre have formed a new party to protect themselves.

So far we have observed the evolution of the parties as these have affected the voters and the politicians. This is the public face of politics. But politics has private faces too and these are not less important even if they are less well known. Politics is about policy-making and governing as well as winning votes and forming Cabinets.

Increasingly as the post-war consensus evolved the nature of government policy-making changed. The institutions and practices of the welfare state came to be increasingly important and along with the management of the economy these institutions and practices came to dominate the politics of Britain. Policy-making for the welfare state and for the management of the economy is different in kind from the older politics which dominated Britain – and the rest of the world – until the end of the Second World War. It used to be sufficient for a government to have a majority in its legislature and have the ability to raise taxes. Any régime which had these two powers could do much as it wished. British governments certainly had both these powers in abundance and the high repute of British politics in the eyes of foreign commentators owed much to the way the party system delivered this power into the hands of the governments of the day.

In a welfare state the government needs support from a variety of interest groups and individuals which it is not able to command by law or by tax. To run a health service you need doctors, to run an education service you need teachers; to run an incomes policy you need trade unions and industrialists. In each of these cases the co-operation of the private group named in its professional capacity is needed. Governments cannot order teachers, doctors and trade unions to behave to suit the government. They need to achieve a consensus. This consensus might once have been achieved by the parties but no longer.

Doctors, teachers, farmers, miners, bankers, all require government to come to them and court them on each occasion the government wants their co-operation. These groups are now public powers even if they have only private bases. No one elects the President of the British Medical Association other than doctors, but this does not prevent him treating with governments as an equal when government wants to change some aspect of the National Health Service.

Parties have become increasingly irrelevant to the bargaining which now takes place between governments and these powerful private pressure groups. They are not quite totally irrelevant. The trade unions, who are collectively a considerable power in the country, deal more happily and more moderately with a Labour government than with a Conservative government. But most of the large pressure groups deal equally with governments of either party just as they would, presumably, deal quite happily with coalition governments. The rise in the welfare state and the governments' increasing need to manage the economy have resulted in diminished status for some of the traditional tools of government: the law, the power to tax, and the army; and for some of the traditional supports of government such as parties. In this way we can see that the parties are less responsible for they have come to lack the power to deliver their promises. That power can only be gained by negotiation with outside bodies.

Finally, the parties' relationship with the civil service has changed. When the two-party system worked its way most happily the civil service was assumed to be a politically neutral tool. At the time the public face of the civil service was of a somewhat bumbling, ineffective, dense group of men; now it is of a shrewd, machiavellian cabal of highly intelligent manipulators.

The service probably has not changed very much – indeed, that is one of the most frequently heard complaints against it – but politicians of both major parties criticize the service in public. Amongst Conservatives the service has the reputation of being part of the Socialist government machine. Tories see that Labour's plans for greater state-run programmes are in the interests of the civil service for such programmes inevitably mean more jobs for civil servants. Amongst Labour politicians the service has the reputation of being a league of upper-class Oxbridge-educated classicists determined to thwart the democratically elected Labour politicians in order to protect the *status quo*. Since the smooth flow of government policy depends crucially on trust between government and civil service, neither of these images helps.

If party politics in Britain is moving with some speed from being strong, responsible, moderate two-party government to its opposite we need to try to understand why the change has occurred. Many of the causes of the change in party behaviour are to be found in changes in Britain. Since the end of the Second World War, Britain has lost much industry, become multi-racial, acquired a large public sector and a large private service sector to its economy, ceased to be so divided by class and become relatively less prosperous than its European neighbours. Britain has also lost an Empire and joined the Common Market.

The loosening of class feeling has had a fundamental impact on the parties. Class was the heart of British party politics. This is much less so than in the past. Fewer people are willing to ascribe themselves to a class when asked to do so by pollsters and still fewer identify with the party of 'their' class. At the 1979 general election Labour only just succeeded in gaining a majority of the votes of trade unionists. The middle class at the same time is changing. Nearly a third of people whom sociologists call middle class voted Labour in 1979.

The weakening of 'class' as a political focus has opened the way for other sorts of identity to acquire political force and for people to vote for and against parties because they agree or disagree with them on issues or because they like or dislike their performance in government. This has produced two changes. It has made possible the emergence of the nationalist parties in the non-English parts of Britain – where 'nation' provides an alternative source of identification available for political exploitation. It has also produced considerable shifts of support between elections and at by-elections. It is estimated that at the 1979 election something approaching a third of the voters made up their minds in the 24 hours before they voted.

The old world when people voted for their grandfathers' party has passed. In the new world there is room for new parties and for considerable shifts of votes between the parties. Labour, whose vote had come to be heavily dependent on class ascriptive voting is more threatened by this change than the Conservative party; but other changes in the social composition of the population have helped Labour. Labour does well from the newly educated, and from highly educated groups of voters who now run the services which Labour's policies have been aimed at extending. Its vote amongst teachers, social workers, public service employees in general is higher than amongst the traditional middle class and these new groups are growing rapidly. Labour also wins a plurality of the votes of people from the 'new Commonwealth'. It wins the Black vote. But opinion polls suggest that both of these groups are precisely the people who are willing to support the new Social Democratic party.

Another reason why the parties have evolved is that governments have failed. Being in power used to be a great political asset. The party in power could provide jobs for its well-placed friends and give favourable legislative treatment to the groups which had supported it. Most important, in the mid-1960s it was widely believed that governments could manipulate the economy on the eve of an election – much as the Conservatives did in 1959 – to create a general euphoria which would carry the government party back into office for another five years. All this has changed.

Government is now a handicap for a party. To be the government party is to be blamed for everything that goes wrong. Between 1959 and 1983 no party won re-election after a full term of office. The central failures of the governments of the past 20 years have been economic. Increasingly British politics has become about the economy and repeatedly governments have left office having disappointed all their supporters by their inability to regenerate British industry and revive economic growth. Increasingly throughout this period the problems of the economy worsened. The rate of inflation rose and the number of unemployed remained above levels which were thought inconceivable only five or ten years before.

There remain differences between the major parties on this issue. Labour remains more concerned about the rate of unemployment; Conservative about the rate of inflation. But at least it used to be thought that there was a trade-off between the two. There would either be a high rate of inflation and a low rate of unemployment or a low rate of inflation and a high rate of unemployment. Both Conservative and Labour governments in recent years contrived to produce both high unemployment and high inflation. Voter disillusion has a deep root here.

So, paradoxically, does party ideological rigidity. Given the falling class identification of Britons and the passing of many of the industrial and social conditions which led to the creation of the individualism and socialism in the first place, one might have expected the ideologies to have waned. But the reverse has occurred. The notion that ideology was dead was, paradoxically, most popular at the peak of British prosperity in the end of the 1950s and early 1960s. With the increasingly economic troubles of the late 1960s, 1970s and 1980s, the old ideologies are back in fashion.

One reason for this has been the failure of centrist government. So long as the party of government produced much of what it had promised the politicians in the centre had no trouble in keeping the ideologists in their party at bay. Now the tables are turned. As each nostrum is tried and rejected the alternatives of ideological extremist remedies are resorted to in desperation.

In addition the parties have been losing local activists. This loss is probably the result of decreasing class tension and class identification with party. One result is to increase the authority of the remaining activists, who tend to be the more committed. The effect of these changes at local level have been noticed and appreciated in the parliamentary centre of the parties. Each of the last three leaders chosen by the Conservative party was more right-wing than his opponent: Home over Butler (1963), Heath over Maudling (1965), and Thatcher over Heath (1975); and two of the three recent Labour leadership contests have resulted in victories for left over right-wing candidates: Wilson over Brown and Callaghan (1963) and Foot over Healey (1980) – the exception was Callaghan over Foot

(1976). At the same time both parties have become more sensitive to the opinion of their local activists. The Leader of the Conservative party now actually attends her party conference. This practice was begun by Edward Heath. Previously the conventional wisdom about party conferences in the Tory party was summed up in a remark often attributed to Balfour that he would sooner consult his valet than a party conference. At the same time Labour has been convulsed since the mid–1970s by the campaign of the party's Left to impose three constitutional changes on the party which are designed to undercut parliamentary sovereignty: Labour M.P.s must now face re-selection conferences each parliament; the party leader is now chosen by the entire party; and the party manifesto may soon be written by a group which includes National Executive Committee members.

The opportunity for the Liberal and other minority parties in these changes arises from the fact that the major parties' leaders now seem more concerned to placate their local activists than to win support from the electorate. The minor parties, unsullied by spells in office, can move into the middle groups where the voters are.

The decreasing economic success of British governments has posed particular problems for the Conservative party. Once the party of the nation which could proudly wrap itself in the flag at convenient moments such as the Falkland crisis, the party is now rather at a loss since so many of the institutions of the state are either lost – such, most importantly, as the empire – or discredited (British industry) or a skeleton of its former self (the armed services or the Church of England). Since so much of the growth that does exist in British society comes from the investment of foreign firms who act on the encouragement of central government, the role and value of indigenous capital is falling. The Conservative party's decision to take the country into the E.E.C. is emblematic of the changes. The argument for accession to the treaty of Rome was medicinal. Britain needed a sharp dose of Continental competition to wake it from its slumbers. The Conservative party, in taking Britain into the Market completed the process whereby it weakened its right to call itself the national party. This chauvinist role is now the property of the left of the Labour Party which is delighted to urge withdrawal from Europe.

The E.E.C. and the resulting legislation became a whipping boy within the Labour party for the ills of the nation. Other people had other ideas about the cause of the ills. Outside the Labour party a popular view blamed the country's problems on the trade unions. These complaints had one important feature in common: they, like most of the rest of the party and public debate in Britain in the 1970s, were about the cause of the troubles. British public debate had become negative and critical. The parties could hardly escape this mood even if they tried to harness it to their own electoral ends. And the cogency of the criticism of the parties gained credibility from the wider mood and did the existing parties little good.

Nevertheless, we are still talking about a party system and a series of parties which has evolved. The changes we have observed do not amount to a revolution. Britain still has only two parties likely to form a government unaided. The two major parties are still more weighty than their opponents. Only a change in the electoral system – from the plurality system to a form of proportional representation – could ensure that two-party politics had been replaced by multi-party politics and that change is still just a gleam in the S.D.P.-Liberal Alliance's eye.

What are the implications of these changes?

The first question must be whether the emerging party system will be better able to cope with the problems of economic management and welfare politics than its predecessor. At first glance it ought to be able to avoid the ideological rigidity of the major parties and recent governments and the consequent rapid shifts of policy. If a third party or coalition of minor parties acquires enough seats in the House of Commons to prevent either major party forming a government unaided – and all the trends suggest that this is more than possible – this coalition ought to be able to avoid the worst extremism of the past.

On the other hand there will be a price to be paid for coalition government. The first is likely to be deadlock, immobility of policy and indecisive government. Single-party governments elected on even impractical manifestos are able to put together something like a coherent series of policies. For the first few years of their rule, at least, the population, the pressure groups and the civil service know where each stands and what the government is likely to try to do. None of these advantages will be forthcoming from coalition. At every twist and turn the party leaders will have to consult one another more than their parties. Coping with the problems of the economy may well require decisive government action backed by popular approval. Government in a more nearly multi-party Britain may lack this ability much more than the now decaying two-party system.

The second question is whether the new competition will improve the quality of public life. In the first instance we can give an unqualified 'yes' to this question. Recent British governments have been elected with too small popular support. The Liberal party, on the other hand, has been getting too many votes for the paltry number of seats it collects. In February 1974 – the worst case – the Liberals won 19 per cent of the vote but only 2 per cent of the seats. The usual political scientists' comment that this reflects the thin spread of the Liberal vote across the country is beside the point. The February 1974 result was a formidable, universally recognized injustice. Its perpetuation creates a sense of unfairness which does the authority of the country's politics no good. A multi-party system in which the Liberals occasionally had a share in government – whether or not they something approximating to proportional justice in the share of House of Commons seats – would help re-establish the legitimacy of the democratic institution of state.

But there is another side to this arrangement. Within a more nearly multi-party politics the important pacts might often be concluded after the election between the leaders of the major parties. The people's voice would hardly be heard. In addition, democracy might be thwarted in that multi-party politics might too easily lead to similar governnments emerging after a whole series of elections. One time we would have Lib-Right wing Lab-S.D.P government; the next time Lib-S.D.P.-Left wing Tory government. It is not simply that the extremes are excluded – though that would occur – but that almost no shift of popular opinion would shift the Liberals and Social Democrats out of office. This may be an appealing thought to them but it is hardly a more democratic mechanism than the waning two-party system. A poll of 19 per cent of the votes for the Liberals may be poorly rewarded with 2 per cent of the seats, but it is over-rewarded if it always gets, say, 20 per cent of the Cabinet seats.

The old system may have exaggerated shifts in popular support, and given the ideologies in the parties more power than was their due – but at least it allowed for firm government and for change of government. In its place we may get the same sort of ineffective muddle each time. This kind of system would be fun for the leaders of the 'middle of the road' parties, for the powerful pressure groups and for the more political parts of the civil service. It could, also, too easily lead to cynicism amongst the electorate, which cynicism would be particularly dangerous after a prolonged period of – inevitably ineffective – government during a difficult crisis.

NOTES

1. S.H.Beer, *Modern British Politics* (1965), 390.
2. J.Lucas, *Democracy and Political Participation* (1976), 200, quoted in S.E.Finer, *The Changing British Party System* (1980), 230.

6 THE ROLE AND POWER OF PRESSURE GROUPS

Wyn Grant

THE POST-WAR period has seen a change in the relative importance of pressure groups and political parties in the British political process. The number of groups has greatly increased, particularly 'cause' groups such as those campaigning for environmental protection; older groups, such as those representing private industry, have consolidated and reorganized; and new trends have been discerned in the relationship between pressure groups and the state. Political parties, on the other hand, have suffered from declining memberships, declining staffs, and a declining proportion of the electorate prepared to identify with them.

This pattern of change has deep historical roots in a tradition of 'corporate bias',[1] but it also reflects both the increasing importance of state intervention in economic and social policy in the post-war period and an increasing disillusionment among the politically active with the possibilities of achieving change through the political parties. One attempt to understand this pattern of change has been often exaggerated speculations about the existence of a 'corporate state' in Britain, despite the fact that specifically corporatist governing institutions are weakly developed.

1. The problem of definition

There has been considerable academic debate about the definition of the term 'pressure group', but a widely shared definition has not emerged. Three elements are common to a number of definitions: (a) pressure groups are organized; (b) their range of concern is narrower than that of political parties; (c) they seek to exert influence on government, rather than taking control of, or a share in, government themselves. Each of these elements raises a number of problems. First, although pressure groups as such are formal organizations, there are important interests which are not organized in an associational form. The financial services sector of the economy, generally referred to geographically as the City of London, is regarded as having a considerable influence on the making of economic policy. However, although there are a growing number of associations representing financial interests, there is no all-embracing organization representing the City as a whole. Indeed, traditionally, the views of the City have been expressed to government through a *person* – the Governor of the Bank of England. Second, although the range of concern of pressure groups is generally narrower than that of political parties, this is not always the case. In the late 1970s, the Confederation of British Industry (C.B.I.) produced a series of policy programmes which were as comprehensive as any of the manifestos produced by the political parties. In these documents, the C.B.I. did not confine itself to economic issues, but also covered policy areas such as housing and education. It is true that the C.B.I. did not express an opinion on such subjects as abortion and capital punishment, but the political parties generally regard these matters as ones of individual conscience. Third, although pressure groups usually seek to exert influence by lobbying ministers, civil servants and Members of Parliament, they may contest elections as a tactic to gain publicity or embarrass politicians. One also has to take account of the special relationship between the trade unions and the Labour party which, in effect, allows individual unions to nominate Parliamentary candidates.

Nevertheless, most politically literate people would agree that the Conservative party and the Scottish National party (S.N.P.) are political parties and that the C.B.I. and the Conservation Society are pressure groups. The common-sense definition that applies in most cases is that political parties exist primarily to contest elections to pursue their political objectives, whether it is forming a U.K. government in the case of the Conservatives or working for a separate Scottish government in the case of the S.N.P. For most pressure groups, contesting elections is, at best, an ancillary tactic. Even the trade union movement does not see its sponsored M.P.s as its main channel of influence on government.

In many ways, it is more difficult to distinguish between a pressure group and other kinds of voluntary organization than it is to distinguish between a pressure group and a political party. For example, is the Stockport Odd Feet Association which exists 'for people with odd-sized feet, to match up shoes with a "partner" or by negotiations with manufacturers'[2] primarily a welfare organization seeking to ease the problems of its 42 members, or a pressure group whose efforts to influence the production policies of manufacturers may benefit all those with odd feet? At the local level, there are a large number of organizations which normally take no part in politics, but suddenly become politically active or a base for political activity when their interests are threatened: for example, water-skiers whose sport may be restricted by a new council by-law. In addition to these 'sporadic interventionists'[3] at the local level, professional associations at the national level may primarily be concerned with setting standards, training, examining etc., but may also act as pressure groups on matters of interest to them.

2. Pressure groups and the state

Whatever form it takes, the pressure group habit has undoubtedly become more popular in the post-war period, and particularly in the last 20 years. Higher standards of education, increased leisure and imitation of the apparent success of other groups have probably all contributed to this trend. One illustration of this trend of a growth in the number of pressure groups, particularly cause groups, is provided by the increase in the number of environmental groups. A survey by Barker in 1974 showed that 37 per cent of local amenity societies had been founded between 1970 and 1974 and another 20 per cent between 1966 and 1969.[4] Recently, however, there have been indications that the environmental movement has passed its peak and is in decline.

In any case, it is not so much the growing number of groups that matters as their changing relationship with the state. There is an increasing recognition of the importance of the state as a regulator of the pressure group system. The state gives groups the political equivalent of a licence, it mediates between them, in some cases it even creates them, yet at the same time it often seems powerless in the grip of groups that appear to have acquired the status of 'governing institutions'.[5] Certainly, the picture is different from the classical pluralist one of autonomous groups seeking to exert influence on a state apparatus which acts as a neutral umpire between competing groups.

Why should the modern state, with its organizational and coercive resources, need to develop a close relationship with pressure groups at all? One answer that is frequently given is that the state needs access to the specialized expertise that the groups possess. However, it should be emphasized that the civil service employs every conceivable kind of expert: doctors abound in the Department of Health and Social Security, the Department of Industry can draw on the specialized knowledge of the scientists in its research establishments, and the Department of Transport has the services of the Road Research Laboratory. There may also be occasions when the civil service needs to draw on outside expertise, although it could and does use consultants rather than pressure group specialists. It may be cheaper or more efficient to 'sub-contract' certain tasks to pressure groups, e.g., collection of data relating to an industry, but this represents a judgment about cost-effectiveness rather than being evidence of an irreversible reliance on pressure group expertise.

Rather more important is the fact that the groups aggregate (or at least appear to aggregate) the opinions of their members. Instead of consulting every farmer in Britain about agricultural policy, which would be impossible, the Ministry of Agriculture can go to the National Farmers' Union (N.F.U.) for a collective opinion. The groups can also be used to communicate government policy to their members and secure their adherence to the implementation of government policies, although it is doubtful whether more than a handful of groups work in such an ideal way. Above all, groups are seen as possessing democratic legitimacy. By talking to a pressure group, government can claim that the interests affected by a proposed measure have been consulted. Indeed, consultation with pressure groups is a civil service habit, aided by the fact that many directors of pressure groups are former civil servants who have moved 'round the table', but it is a habit reinforced and legitimized by the widely held view that those particularly affected by a decision should have the right to be consulted about it. The habit of group consultation is also underpinned by a recognition that many pressure groups have the ability to frustrate a policy through obstruction, non-cooperation or even simple indifference.

3. Corporatism

Much of the recent writing on pressure groups has been concerned with the topic of whether Britain is, or is becoming, a corporate state. Indeed, this revival of interest in corporatism is not confined to Britain, but is to be found throughout the Western world. What is being talked about is not the old-fashioned corporatism of the medieval guilds, nineteenth-century Catholic thought or Fascist Italy, but a new form of corporatism which is compatible with liberal democracy – indeed some writers on the subject see the development of liberal corporatism as the best way forward for the western democracies.

There is little agreement on the definition of corporatism, but most definitions include the following three elements. First, corporatism involves the development of a new relationship between government, employers and the unions in which they take together major decisions about economic policy. One consequence is that Parliamentary institutions may be bypassed. Second, in return for their increased participation in decision-making about the economy, the employers and the unions enter into a new relationship with the state – in short, they are incorporated. Having reached an economic policy agreement with the state, they are required to discipline their own members to adhere to it. Third, these relationships may lead to the development of new corporatist institutions of government, although informal meetings in fact play an important role in the running of many liberal democracies which display corporatist tendencies.

Apart from the analytical work of Schmitter which is discussed more fully below, the body of writing about whether modern Western democracies may be characterized as neo-corporatist can be divided into four main categories. First, there is a sociological variant represented by Pahl and Winkler[6] which attempts to set out a general account of societal development in terms of a model of state corporatism rather than focusing primarily on interest group interaction. Second, there is a Marxist literature – exemplified by the work of Panitch[7] and Jessop[8] – which attempts to expose what is seen as the use of corporatism as a mode of class rule and to assess the implications of corporatism for working-class political action. Third, there is a literature by academics and practitioners which is well disposed to corporatist arrangements and sees them as perhaps the best way of overcoming the problems faced by contemporary British society. This strand is best exemplified by the work of Colin Crouch[9] who sees what he calls 'bargained corporatism' as having much to offer the unions and the nation as a whole and, among practitioners, by Michael Shanks[10] who places considerable faith in the educative value of tripartite discussions. Fourth, there are a number of political scientists who have expressed scepticism about the value of corporatist solutions, either because they are seen as inimical to Parliamentary democracy (Gordon Smith[11]) or on the pragmatic grounds that they do not and cannot work in Britain (Marsh and Grant[12]).

However, perhaps the most influential writer on the subject of the 'osmotic process whereby the modern state and modern interest associations seek each other out'[13] has been Philippe Schmitter. He erects an analytical distinction between corporatist and pluralist systems of interest representation which can best be understood in tabular form (see table 8).[14]

The constituent units of the British system of interest representation – the pressure groups – look remarkably pluralist using Schmitter's schema. For example, the system of industrial representation is made up of hundreds of organizations, often serving broadly similar interests, and defining their own scope of operation. However, when one turns to their relationship with the state, one detects at least what Schmitter calls 'emergent properties'[15] of corporatism, although it should be stressed that the connection of groups with public policy in Britain would be characterized as pluralist rather than corporatist using Schmitter's schema.

It is, then, in the area of the relation of pressure groups to public authority that corporatist tendencies are most apparent in Britain. Although pressure groups are not actually set up by the state, their formation is often deliberately encouraged, for example, by seconding civil servants to staff the organization or even by providing Crown premises at a low rent. For example, the formation of the Federation of British Industries in 1916 was actively encouraged by the Government and the first two chief staff members of the new organization were seconded from the Foreign Office. On a more prosaic level, the formation of the Scottish Woodland Owners' Association resulted from a recommendation by an official committee set up by the Scottish Office that there should be a 'strong and effective association of private owners, the purpose of which would be . . . first, to stimulate each private owner of woodland to fulfil his obligations as a producer or potential producer of timber'.[16]

Table 8: Schmitter's ideal typical systems of interest representation

PLURALISM	CORPORATISM

Organization of constituent units

Unspecified number	Limited
Multiple	Singular
Voluntary	Compulsory
Competitive	Non-competitive
Non-hierarchically ordered	Hierarchically ordered
Self-determined (as to type or scope of interest)	Functionally differentiated

Relation to public authority

Passive, multiple recognition	Active singular recognition
Inclusion of irregular contacts	Exclusion of irregular contacts
Not specially licensed, recognized, subsidized or created by the state	Recognized, subsidized or licensed (if not created by the state)

Connection with public policy

Pressure	Concertation
Refusal to accept authority	Devolution of authority
Not responsible for policy	Co-responsible for policies
External role in influencing policy choice	Internal role in implementation

Although the British government does not confer representational monopolies on particular organizations, it can show a preference for consulting one organization more than others. Thus, government has much more intensive consultations with the C.B.I. than it does with other organizations representing business interests such as the Association of British Chambers of Commerce or the Institute of Directors. Moreover, groups admitted to the consultative process are supposed to adhere to an unwritten code of conduct which requires them, for example, not to leak confidential information or engage in unorthodox pressure tactics. Groups who do not adhere to this code may be punished by exclusion from the consultation process. Thus, when a pressure group called the Standing Committee on National Parks was too forceful in its criticism at a meeting chaired by the responsible minister, they did not receive copies of the Consultation Paper which the department eventually prepared.[17]

However, one must not exaggerate the extent to which the state regulates pressure groups in Britain. Groups can, of course, exist without state approval, settle their mutual quarrels without state mediation, and generally come into existence without state assistance. Moreover, the attempts of the state to reorganize the system of interest representation often seem to have failed. Thus, a civil servant was seconded as secretary to the Devlin Commission which devised a blueprint for reforming the chaotic system of industrial representation, but few changes resulted from this initiative. An attempt to produce a more cohesive representative body for the mechanical engineering industry failed with the collapse of BRIMEC (British Mechanical Engineering Confederation), despite the backing that the new organization received from the Government and the C.B.I.

Nevertheless, there have been a number of signs of the development of an embryonic corporate state in recent years. As Schmitter has pointed out, 'the origins of societal corporatism lie in the slow, almost imperceptible, decay of advanced pluralism'[18] and such a process may be observed in Britain so that one has a weakly developed system of corporatist interaction between the state and pressure groups coexisting with a still healthy and important pluralist system of representation. A number of tripartite institutions, bringing together the government, the C.B.I. and the T.U.C. have been created to provide a neutral ground for discussion and action one step away from the central machinery of government itself. The National Economic Development Council and its economic development committee provide a forum for discussion of economic and industrial policy, although they fall far short of the 'Industrial Parliament' which has been a recurrent theme of prescriptive corporatist writing in Britain. Agencies like the Manpower Services Commission and the Health and Safety Commission provide a framework for tripartite action on important areas of policy, with the government effectively delegating its executive responsibilities to the C.B.I. and T.U.C.

Above all, one has seen repeated attempts by different governments to agree a framework for the conduct of economic policy with the C.B.I. and T.U.C., a practice often referred to as 'tripartism'. Such consultations have particularly been conducted in association with attempts to implement prices and incomes policies, although students of corporatism disagree whether it is the pursuit of such policies that leads to corporatism or whether corporatism makes the pursuit of such policies possible.

However, all this activity amounts to much less than a corporate state. First, it excludes possibly the most important source of economic power in Britain, the City of London, apart from some rather tenuous links between the City and the N.E.D.C. Second, Lehmbruch has stressed the importance of direct links between the major economic interest groups, as distinct from links between them and the state, as crucial to the success of a system of liberal corporatism, but such links along the base of the corporatist triangle – that is, links between the C.B.I. and T.U.C. – are weakly developed in Britain.[19] Third, corporatism in Britain is not a permanent feature of the political system, but has been associated with particular periods in British political life. It acquired a new vitality after Edward Heath's 'U turn' in 1972 and reached its highest stage of development under the Labour government of 1974–9 when major White Papers and even the Queen's Speech were replete with references to the government's consultations with the C.B.I. and T.U.C. However, corporatism has waned under Margaret Thatcher's government.

A graphic illustration of this shift away from corporatism is provided by the fate of the Retail Consortium. Under Edward Heath and under the Labour government, this organization representing the retail trade had access right up to Prime Ministerial and Chancellor level to the extent that there was speculation whether Britain's version of corporatism should be termed 'quadripartite' rather than 'tripartite'.[20] In part, this level of access reflected the interest of both Edward Heath's government and his successors in voluntary price control, as exemplified by Shirley Williams's 'red triangle' scheme to limit prices on certain groceries operated with the co-operation of the Retail Consortium. When the Retail Consortium asked to meet Sir Geoffrey Howe, the Chancellor in 1981, to discuss the problems of the retail trade, they were told that he could not find the time to see them.[21]

Insofar as it exists at all, corporatism in Britain seems to have been not so much an immutable feature of the operations of the state as a style of government, reflecting choices by politicians in power. The literature on neo-corporatism does draw our attention to the growing importance of the tripartite relationship between the Government, C.B.I. and T.U.C. However, even if one adopts a minimal definition of corporatism as a set of tripartite arrangements which

bring about a 'practical working relationship between the three
estates of the realm: organized labour, organized employers and the
government',[22] it is doubtful whether anything resembling corporatism has ever existed in Britain except in the special conditions of
wartime. In times of war, the additional coercive resources available
to the state and the shared pursuit of a single goal make it possible to
submerge sectional differences, although they do not disappear even
then.

Cox has argued that the recent writing on corporatism 'does not
enable any fuller understanding of the forces shaping government
actions than the "pluralist" and "parliamentarian" theses which it has
questioned'.[23] This is too harsh a judgment; at least the corporatist
literature does try to grapple, however inadequately, with the
complex relationship between state and pressure groups. However,
if we are to understand fully the complex pattern of interaction
between the state and pressure groups, then we need a 'typology of
pressure groups and their legitimacy, and relationships to the
state'.[24]

4. Insider and outsider groups

It is suggested that a fundamental distinction can be made between
insider groups and outsider groups, which can be elaborated into a
six-fold typology which helps us to understand the range of
strategies open to a pressure group. All groups enjoying a corporatist
relationship with government are insider groups according to this
typology, but not all insider groups can be termed corporatist. Thus,
the Chemical Industries Association (C.I.A.) is an insider group,
but is not involved in the kind of tripartite relationship with
government and the unions that the C.B.I. has enjoyed. The way in
which an insider group exerts influence is well illustrated by a
quotation from a C.I.A. report:

> Over the years, in regular communication and consultation,
> C.I.A. has welcomed the opportunity of consultation with various
> branches of government. This has been helped by monitoring and
> anticipating trends in public opinion; through informing politi-
> cians, civil servants and commissions; through trying to influence
> the course of legislation from early principles to final drafts;
> through co-operating with government departments and bodies in
> the detailed implementation of legislation . . . Relationships are

close with the Department of Industry, C.I.A.'s sponsoring Ministry, and there are good working arrangements with the Departments of Environment, Trade, Energy and with N.E.D.O. as well as through MAFF [Ministry of Agriculture, Fisheries and Food] and D.H.S.S.[25]

It must be emphasized that the acquisition of insider group status by a pressure group involves *both* a decision by government and a decision by the group concerned. Some groups may want insider status and be granted it; others may want it, but may not be able to attain it; yet others may wish to avoid becoming enmeshed in the political-administrative system and may therefore prefer to remain as outsider groups. Although 'the criteria used by individual departments in the selection of those organizations whose views are to be solicited are somewhat obscure',[26] it is argued that a useful distinction can be made between those pressure groups that are accepted by central government departments (or other public authorities) as legitimate spokesmen which have to be consulted on a continuous basis and those groups which are not consulted on a regular basis. The crucial distinction is between those groups which are invited by central government departments to submit their views on topics relevant to their concerns and those groups which are at best tolerated to the extent that they are allowed to send occasional deputations to the relevant department. Thus, for example, although the National Federation of Old Age Pensioners Associations was reassured by a junior minister at the D.H.S.S. that 'the Department's doors were always open to the Federation's officers',[27] it is clear that this access has been confined to the occasional deputation.

The length of time that a group has been in existence has little to do with the way in which it is treated by government. For example, the Committee of Directors of Polytechnics quickly won recognition from the Department of Education and Science when it was established in 1970, whereas the National Union of Ratepayers' Associations (founded in 1921) has been 'sending telegrams to the Treasury'[28] for 20 years, but its only channel of access is still through the Post Office. From time to time, groups will be upgraded as happened with the recognition of the Farmers' Union of Wales by the Labour government in 1978.

It must be stressed that the distinction being made is not based on any measurement of effectiveness or perceived effectiveness. Outsider groups can be effective and insider groups can be ineffective. Whereas insider groups enjoy access to key decision-makers, outsider groups can escape the constraints which such access often imposes. Czech Conroy, Campaign Director of Friends of the Earth (F.o.E.), has argued that traditional pressure group tactics are 'particularly useful for . . . groups which have fairly high level political or civil servant contacts, and are able to activate an "old-boy network"'.[29] Groups that are pressing for radical changes in policy may find that they are regarded as cranks or that they lack 'clout' in terms of their technical credibility or political muscle. Conroy argues that 'F.o.E.'s "clout" was directly proportional to the amount of public concern which it could generate'.[30] The 'controlled event' was a most effective way for generating that public concern: spontaneous bottle-dumping to encourage the use of returnable bottles, funeral processions for whales – each in their way a form of street theatre with a particular emotional theme, calculated to induce anger, humour or sorrow.

Some forms of demonstration, e.g., the lobby of Parliament, are accepted as a legitimate means by which an interest group may draw attention to its grievances. However, less conventional forms of protest may endanger a group's relationship with government. A civil servant responding to Conroy's arguments suggested that demonstrations of the type favoured by F.o.E. could give an organization a frivolous appearance, and another civil servant argued that demonstrations could lead government to defer policy changes.[31] In particular, there is a risk that the support of key influentials within government may be lost by the pursuit of certain forms of protest. For example, Crossman notes in his diaries that a series of farmers' demonstrations lost them Cabinet support: 'Those of us in the Cabinet who want to give the farmers something realise that they are trying to force our hands and that whatever we do, they won't be grateful, so this time we will probably be really tough.'[32]

In contrast to the unconventional tactics often used by outsider groups, insider groups place considerable emphasis on adhering to what might be called a 'strategy of responsibility'. Thus, a President of the C.B.I. has commented, 'The growing influence we can . . . exert carries with it a corresponding responsibility. Whilst our first responsibility is to represent the views of our members as forcefully and effectively as we can, we must also be prepared to give advice and guidance to our members as to the right policies for industry itself to pursue based on our experience and all the information available to us.'[33] A similar case for responsible behaviour in the pursuit of insider status has been put by much smaller groups. Thus, an article in the journal of the Conservation Society states: 'The Society must not be, or seem to be, merely a vehicle for anti-establishment agitation . . . the Society must beware of even appearing to be associated with those who are simply agitators or protesters. A reputation for obstructionism will inevitably prevent the Society's case from being considered.'[34] Cause groups can seek insider status just as eagerly as groups representing socio-economic interests.

Insider groups may be subdivided into three categories: prisoner groups; low profile insider groups; high profile insider groups. 'Prisoner groups' are those groups which find it particularly difficult to break away from an insider relationship with government, either because they are dependent on government for assistance of various kinds or because they represent parts of the public service (e.g., the chairmen of nationalized industries). However, such groups are not necessarily condemned to a lifetime of servitude. Desperation at lack of success by acting through the normal channels may lead them to make a risky attempt to 'break out', e.g., threats by the members of a nationalized industry board to resign *en bloc* unless they receive a salary increase. However, such groups gain their cohesion from their common experience as 'prisoners of the state' and, unless they have exceptional resources, cannot survive 'on the outside' for very long.

Insider groups may choose between a 'low profile' and a 'high profile' strategy, with the use made of the media being the distinguishing factor. In its most extreme form, the 'low profile' strategy would involve concentrating on behind-the-scenes contacts with government and not making even routine statements to the mass media (e.g., the former British Employers' Confederation). A 'high profile' strategy involves a considerable emphasis on cultivating public opinion to reinforce contacts with government. For example, the C.B.I. has shifted towards a 'high profile' strategy in recent years. The staging of a televised conference of members, largely as a platform to gain publicity for the C.B.I.'s policies rather than as a contribution to the organization's decision-making procedures, is one sign of this shift of strategy.

It should not be assumed that insider groups will always adopt a strategy of responsibility and that they will always remain insider groups. Pressures for a change of strategy may emanate from the leadership, the membership or from a new leadership responding to a change in the mood of the membership. If the membership of a pressure group perceives that the effectiveness of their organization is declining, they may threaten to resign or otherwise agitate within the organization to bring about a change of strategy (as happened in the C.B.I. after 1974).

However, although the identification of the internal sources of pressure for a change of strategy is important, these internal pressures are often a reflection of some change in the group's external environment. One such change would be an alteration in the distribution of influence between government departments, particularly away from a department with which a pressure group has good contacts. For example, Coates makes the point that the behaviour of teachers' associations in Britain in the 1960s was affected by the fact that they 'lacked access individually to centres of government decision-making other than the Department of Education and Science'.[35] One response to access 'only on certain terms' in accordance with 'the code'[36] was increased militancy.

Outsider groups as a category are by their nature more disparate than insider groups. The very fact of being an insider group imposes certain constraints and patterns of behaviour on a group. Outsider groups are not committed to a strategy of responsibility and therefore have a greater range of strategies open to them. They may be subdivided into three categories: potential insider groups; outsider groups by necessity; and ideological outsider groups.

Potential insider groups are those outsider groups that would like to become insider groups but face the problem of gaining government's attention as a prelude to their being accepted as a group which should be consulted in relation to a particular policy area. Unlike the high profile insider group, for which the use of the media is a supplementary strategy, securing media attention can be the main force of an outsider group's activity in its early years of existence. For example, the Forestry Action Group was formed to challenge existing forestry policy, largely on environmental grounds. However, as it did not own or manage any forests, it had to try and publicize its cause through the media so as to gain the attention of politicians.

Outsider groups by necessity may also wish to become insider groups, but may be prevented from doing so by a lack of political sophistication. One reflection of such a lack of political sophistication may be an absence of understanding about the way in which the political system works and the importance of gaining access to senior civil servants. The group has to show civil servants that it can (and is prepared to) talk 'their language'; that it knows how to present a case and how to bargain and accept the outcomes of the bargaining process. As the professional journal for pressure group executives, *Association Management*, has stressed in an editorial: 'We have to learn the language and procedures of government and blend our work with it where necessary.'[37] If anything, the language of the British civil service is a language of veiled understatement and it is characteristic of politically unsophisticated outsider groups that their demands are presented in strident terms. Their lack of understanding of the political system leads them to make demands which are constitutionally impossible. For example, the National Association of Ratepayer Action Groups which spearheaded the 'ratepayers' revolt' of 1974 told the Layfield Committee that 'NARAG very seriously requests that, in any future Parliamentary debates on this subject, a free and open vote be taken; and that an amendment be added, that, no alteration of the agreed method be permitted at any time in the future without a similar free and open vote.'[38]

The demarcation line between being an outsider group by necessity and a potential insider group is not an insurmountable one and groups may cross it as a result of acquiring political knowledge and skills, although the consequent change in the character of the group itself may lead to strains within the organization. Bechhoffer and Elliott have traced how the National Federation of the Self-Employed (N.F.S.E.) began to change from an outsider organization to an insider one. An early emphasis on protest and direct action was replaced by more emphasis on contacts with government. Bechhoffer and Elliott conclude that 'N.F.S.E. as an organization has shifted away from the kinds of direct action which gained it much publicity in its earliest phase to more conventional and, from the point of view of ministers and civil servants, more acceptable forms of representation. The game has changed from protest to persuasion.'[39]

Ideological outsider groups are careful not to become too closely entangled with the political-administrative system because they wish to challenge accepted authority and institutions. Rather than becoming part of the existing system, they wish to replace it or alter it in some fundamental way. They may pursue this objective of fundamental change by attempting to alter public attitudes towards certain problems; or they may adopt more militant strategies such as occupations of government offices or attacks on the property of individuals. For example, Welsh language demonstrators have damaged television transmitters and occupied television studios. Radical anti-vivisectionists have daubed slogans on the homes of scientists who use animals for experimental purposes. Many such organizations feel that they have to resort to illegal tactics because no notice is taken of them when they use conventional channels to exert pressure.

In a critique of the typology outlined here, Buksti and Johansen argue that it underestimates the importance of organizational resources as a determinant of pressure group activity. They stress 'the importance of the size of the secretariat or the bureaucracy of organizations in relation to their ability to join corporate structures' and term 'organizations with less than six people employed on their staff' as 'weak insiders'.[40] However, the Retail Consortium which was granted high level access by the 1974–9 Labour government had only five executive staff. Admittedly, the Retail Consortium had something to 'offer' the Government in the form of co-operation with voluntary price restraint schemes, but one can find cause groups with very small staffs and insider status. For example, the law reform group, Justice, has a staff of only four, but has been the mainspring behind the development of the Ombudsman system in Britain. It has gained attention from government because of the prestige of its governing council, made up of M.P.s and senior lawyers; and because of the quality of its reports, based on a blend of the experience of practising lawyers and research conducted by academics. Nevertheless, association permanent staff – a job increasingly seen as a career – are often the most enthusiastic advocates within pressure groups of developing and maintaining an insider role. The larger the association bureaucracy becomes, the more close relationships with politicians and civil servants may be cherished and defended.

It is not denied that the possession of substantial organizational resources can help an insider group to become more effective. However, the grant and retention of insider status ultimately depends on government. Such a status depends on many factors, but among the most important are whether the group can help the government to implement its policies; whether it is seen as representing a significant interest or strand of opinion; and, perhaps most important of all, whether it is prepared to abide by the unwritten code of insider group behaviour.

5. How pressure groups exert influence

In the preceding section on pressure group strategies, reference has already been made to the importance of contacts with civil servants involved in the formulation and implementation of policy. As the Devlin Commission on Industrial Representation stressed, 'All executive policy and most legislation is conceived, drafted and all but enacted in Whitehall.'[41] The first point of contact for an industrial pressure group is usually its sponsoring division in the Department of Industry or another ministry. The sponsoring division will act to some extent as a spokesman for its industry within the government machine, although always weighing the industry's representations against current Government policy and prevalent conceptions of the public interest. These arrangements do not change very much from one government to the next. Thus, although the 1979 Conservative government initiated a significant change of direction in economic and social policy, it did not 'change the basic procedural relationships which the T.U.C. has with governmental and public bodies'.[42] The T.U.C. has stressed 'the importance of influencing the policies of different Government Departments, and considerable detailed consultation takes place with Government across Whitehall.'[43]

The relationships between pressure groups and government are largely conducted with civil servants: ministers are, after all, busy men and civil servants advise them on what they see as the credible policy options. However, a group which feels that it is not making progress with the responsible civil servants may ask to see the minister. Gerald Kaufman, a minister in the 1974–9 Labour government recalls, 'When delegations write in asking to see you without the support of a sponsoring Member of Parliament, your Private Secretary will send the letter down to the appropriate policy division for advice. It will then come up in a case folder, with a minutely detailed and generally very acute assessment of the qualities and merits of the applicants, followed by a recommendation.'[44] Kaufman notes that such meetings 'proceed according to a ritualistic scenario'.[45] That is not to say that they are never negotiations, although that is most common in situations where government is effectively the employer and what is happening is really collective bargaining rather than pressure politics. More typically, a meeting between a minister and a pressure group will consist of the minister explaining the government's policy and the group saying why they disagree with it. The group can then go away and tell their members and the press that 'We told him', and the minister can tell his colleagues that he has defended government policy.

Although most pressure group contacts are with the executive, one should not ignore the importance of contacts with Parliament. Some groups can, of course, attain their objectives through the passage of a Private Member's Bill, e.g., the abortion law reform lobby. Other groups which still rely principally on contacts with the executive have displayed an increasing interest in Parliament in recent years. For example, the C.B.I. has always used contacts in the House of Lords to try to delete clauses in technical legislation to which it objects. However, in recent years it has developed a systematic set of arrangements for lobbying M.P.s modelled on the system used by the N.F.U. In part, this greater interest in Parliamentary lobbying is a response to the experience of the 1974–9 Parliament when the government had at first a very small majority, and then no majority at all, and it was possible to defeat legislation by winning support from the Liberals, Nationalists or Ulster Unionists.

The post-war period has seen a considerable expansion in the number of public agencies or 'quangos' as they are sometimes called. Despite recent attempts at 'quangocide', most of these bodies look like remaining a permanent feature of modern government. Some of these agencies were set up with the explicit duty of acting as spokesmen for what were seen as insufficiently well-represented interests, such as the National Consumer Council, or were given the task of co-ordinating and representing the views of a range of disparate but related interests, e.g., the Countryside Commission and the Cooperative Development Agency. Yet others were required to mediate between competing groups, e.g., the Red Deer Commission which was, among other things, given the task of reconciling the conflict of interest between those who wanted to ensure that there were suffficient deer for them to hunt and farmers who resented the damage done by the deer. Those agencies which have a regulatory function, such as the Health and Safety Commission, are more difficult for pressure groups to influence, perhaps because they may see attempts at influence as a means of diverting them from their task.

Some pressure groups attempt to promote their interests by developing relationships with political parties. There are, for example, pressure groups within the political parties such as Conservative

Action for Electoral Reform. More importantly, the trade union movement clearly sees its symbiotic relationship with the Labour party as an important means of securing the economic and social advances it regards as desirable, although not to the exclusion of developing links with Conservative governments. Links between business and the Conservative party are more tenuous than is often assumed, although the C.B.I. and the Conservative party evolved broadly similar policies in the run-up to the 1979 general election, however much they may have disagreed since then. In many respects, pressure groups and political parties live separate, if parallel, lives, with the fact that individuals are members of both types of organization being the most important conduit for the exchange of ideas between them.

Public opinion is a fiction which exists perhaps only as a set of aggregate statistics in the opinion polls, but it is important because people believe that it exists. However, much pressure group effort is directed towards specialized publics or the informed public of decision-makers and those who write about decision-making, rather than any generalized public opinion. A civil servant has criticized F.o.E.'s demonstration strategy on the grounds that the type of audience influenced is 'the concerned middle class rather than public opinion generally'.[46] However, given that members of the middle class have a greater propensity to engage in political activity, and are more likely to possess relevant political skills, an opinion-forming strategy which concentrates on the middle class, whether intentionally or not, may be more efficacious than a strategy with a more diffuse appeal.

Whatever the target group chosen, access to the media is of key importance to a pressure group that wants to put its message across to a particular segment of opinion in the hope of establishing the correctness of its case or winning further support for its point of view. Some groups have even been established as a result of a newspaper article (Amnesty International) or a television programme (Shelter). Environmental pressure groups regarded media coverage as so important that they formed a co-ordinating organization known as Environmental Communicators Organization to gain greater coverage for environmentalist topics.[47] However, although media campaigns can secure recognition for a hitherto unrecognized group, it should also be remembered that media coverage 'is a fragile and transient resource'.[48]

Membership of the European Community has had surprisingly

little impact on British pressure groups, even those major economic groups that count as 'social partners' in the E.E.C.'s corporatist terminology. Most groups have joined their appropriate European organization and one or two (e.g., the C.B.I. and N.F.U.) have established offices in Brussels. However, even groups operating in areas where Community decisions are a major determinant of policy, such as the farming unions, often prefer to press their case with the British government who can then represent their views in the negotiations in Brussels. In part, this nationally oriented approach reflects a preference for using familiar and well-established channels of access. In part, it reflects the relative weakness of the European pressure groups which were supposed to be one of the driving forces behind integration. Even the farming organization, COPA, has a staff of only about 35 to cope with a Community which, even if it has a much smaller bureaucracy than is generally supposed, is still capable of producing prodigious amounts of paper for representative organizations to digest.

6. Conclusions

The modern state cannot ignore pressure groups because, without their active consent, it is difficult to govern effectively. A situation in which a dense network of groups can offer enough resistance to frustrate the policy intentions of government may seem to offer both a recipe for ineffective government and to be essentially anti-democratic. However, pressure groups at least offer a means, which the ballot box does not, for the expression of the intensity of opinions about an issue. Vested interests may have axes to grind, but they also have something of interest and importance to say about the issue under discussion. There is nothing anti-democratic in paying particular attention to those who stand to lose from a government decision.

The experience of the first two years of the 1979 Conservative government shows that governments can, in the medium term at any rate, ignore a wide range of political pressures if they want to. Not only was the government prepared to disregard the advice of the trade unions, but it was also prepared to ride roughshod over such traditional Conservative interests as those of the rural areas, house purchasers and small businessmen. One cannot understand British politics without a knowledge of the pattern of pressure group activity, but British politics amounts to far more than the activity of pressure groups.

NOTES

1. For an analysis of this concept, see K.Middlemas, *Politics in Industrial Society* (1979).
2. *Directory of British Associations, Edition 6* (1980), 361.
3. R.E.Dowse and J.Hughes, 'Sporadic interventionists', *Political Studies*, XXV (1977), 84–92.
4. A.Barker, 'Local amenity societies' in Civic Trust, *The Local Amenity Movement* (1976), 21–31, 22.
5. For an analysis of this concept, see Middlemas, *op.cit.*, 20–1.
6. R.E.Pahl and J.T.Winkler, 'The coming corporatism', *New Society*, X, Oct. 1974, 72–6.
7. L.Panitch, 'The development of corporatism in liberal democracies' in *Trends Towards Corporatist Intermediation*, ed. P.C.Schmitter and G.Lehmbruch (1979), 119–46.
8. B.Jessop, 'Corporatism, parliamentarianism and social democracy' in Schmitter and Lehmbruch, *op.cit.*, 185–212.
9. C.Crouch, *The Politics of Industrial Relations* (1979).
10. M.Shanks, Planning and Politics (1977).
11. G.Smith, 'The reintegration of the state in Western Europe', in *Divided Loyalties: British regional assertion and European integration*, ed. M.Kolinsky (1978), 172–94.
12. D.Marsh and W.Grant, 'Tripartism: reality or myth?', *Government and Opposition*, XXII (1977), 194–211.
13. P.C.Schmitter, 'Still the century of corporatism?', in Schmitter and Lehmbruch, *op.cit.*, 7–52, 27.
14. Based on personal communication from P.C.Schmitter, Berlin, 20 Feb. 1981.
15. P.C.Schmitter, 'Still the century of corporatism?', 21.
16. House of Commons Select Committee on Scottish Affairs, 1971–2, *Land Resource Use in Scotland*, 362.
17. J.Richardson, 'The environmental issue and the public', in *Decision Making in Britain, Block V, Pollution and Environment* (1975), 15–34, 24.
18. P.C.Schmitter, 'Still the century of corporatism?', 23.
19. G.Lehmbruch, 'Liberal corporatism and party government' in Schmitter and Lehmbruch, *op.cit.*, 147–83.
20. W.P.Grant and D.Marsh, 'The representation of retail interests in Britain', *Political Studies*, XXII (1974), 168–77.
21. 'Retailers feel snubbed by Howe', *Financial Times*, 28 Jan. 1981.
22. Viscount Watkinson, *Blueprint for Industrial Survival* (1976), 81.
23. A.Cox, 'Corporatism as reductionism: the analytic limits of the corporatist thesis', *Government and Opposition*, XVI (1981), 78–95.
24. Middlemas, *op.cit.*, 381.

25. Chemical Industries Association, *Activities Report 1978*, 12.
26. J.Richardson, 'The environmental issue and the public', 23.
27. *Pensioners' Voice*, J. of National Federation of Old Age Pensioners' Associations, Dec. 1974, 5.
28. *Committee of Inquiry into Local Government Finance (Layfield Report)*, evidence of the National Union of Ratepayers' Associations (1976), 104.
29. C.Conroy, 'Public demonstrations – a Friends of the Earth view', paper presented at the Royal Institute of Public Administration conference on 'Public Influence and Public Policy', April 1981, 1.
30. C.Conroy, 'Public demonstrations – a Friends of the Earth view', 2.
31. 'F.O.E.'s "street theatre" alerts public to issues', *R.I.P.A. Report*, 2 (1981), 10–11, 11.
32. R.Crossman, *The Diaries of a Cabinet Minister* (1977), III, 798.
33. *C.B.I. Annual Report 1967*, 5.
34. R.D.Harrison, 'Who do we think we are?', *Conservation News*, Winter 1977–8, 3–4, 3.
35. D.Coates, *Teachers' Unions and Interest Group Politics* (1972), 120.
36. D.Coates, *Teachers' Unions and Interest Group Politics*, 121.
37. 'Associations and government', *Association Management*, II (1980), 5.
38. *Committee of Inquiry into Local Government Finance*, evidence of the National Association of Ratepayer Action Groups, 103.
39. F. Bechhofer and B. Elliott, 'Pathways of protest: bourgeois social movements in Britain', paper presented to the conference on 'Capital, Ideology and Politics', Sheffield, Jan. 1981, 13.
40. J.A.Buksti and L.N.Johansen, 'Variations in organizational participation in government: the case of Denmark', *Scandinavian Political Studies*, N.S. 2 (1979), 197–220, 209–10.
41. *Report of the Commission of Inquiry into Industrial and Commercial Representation (Devlin Report)* (1972), 5.
42. 'The organisation, structure and services of the TUC', a TUC consultative document (1980), 9.
43. 'The organisation, structure and services of the TUC', 9.
44. G.Kaufman, *How to be a Minister* (1980), 140.
45. Kaufman, *op.cit.*, 144.
46. 'FOE's "street theatre" alerts public to issues', *R.I.P.A. Report*, 2 (1981), 10–11, 11.
47. S.K.Brookes, A.G.Jordan, R.H.Kimber and J.J.Richardson, 'The growth of the environment as a political issue in Britain', *British J. of Political Science*, VI (1976), 245–55, 254.
48. J.Richardson, 'The environmental issue and the public', 17.

7 FISCAL CRISIS AND PARLIAMENTARY DEMOCRACY

Peter M. Jackson

Budgets are not merely affairs of arithmetic. In a thousand ways they go
to the root of prosperity of individuals, the relations of classes, and the
strength of Kingdoms.

William Gladstone

PUBLIC expenditure over the past 15 years has tended to dominate much political discussion. The poor economic performance
of the U.K. and the attendant increase in the relative size of
the public sector have brought forth debate about the needs for
stricter control over public spending. The U.K. does not stand
alone in this respect. Cries of fiscal stress and fiscal crisis are to be
heard emanating from the central, state and local governments
of the major industrialized countries following the increase in the
world price of oil in the mid-1970s and the decline in world
economic growth which came in its wake. The last five years have
seen dramatic changes in politicians' attitudes to the role of
public expenditure in the general economic strategy. Although
these changes are not confined to any single political party they do
tend to be more concentrated amongst those to the right of the
political spectrum. Whereas public expenditure was once regarded
as a means through which governments could spend their way
out of a recession, these Keynesian ideas have reached their zenith
and have now given way to monetarist demands for public expenditure control. Public expenditure is now regarded as a destabil-

izing influence on the economy and, moreover, one which promotes inflation.[1]

This change in attitude has ushered in demands for reforms of the way in which public expenditure is managed. Activities which were at one time organized within the public sector are now being 'privatized'[2] in an attempt to roll back the frontiers of the state, increase individual freedom of choice, reduce the burden of taxation and run down the 'army' of public sector employees. Requests are made for a greater use of referendums to make decisions on specific changes in the government's budget or its tax system. Efficiency gains, productivity improvements and value for money are sought in public sector programmes. There is a demand for changes to be made in the fiscal constitutions of governments requiring them to balance their budgets and to abandon the Keynesian principles of demand management through budget deficits. Professionals and bureaucrats employed in the public sector should, it is argued, be made to be more accountable for their decisions which often affect the welfare of millions of individuals.

Responses to the fiscal crisis have been varied. In the U.K. there have been cutbacks in real spending since 1979. Stricter controls over local government spending have introduced a greater degree of centralism into central-local government relations. These centralizing tendencies are in evidence with the nationalized industries also. Such movements pose a threat to the federalist principles of local democracy. Moreover, fiscal stress brings with it an increase in political lobbying and special pleading from those who wish to protect their own programmes. Strategies of budgetary politics of this kind can weaken both the control and planning of public spending since the final outcome depends upon how resilient controllers are to special pleading. Budget decline and the pressures placed upon public sector pay restraint can have an adverse impact upon the morale of public employees. Such a reaction insofar as it influences morale and productivity can be counter-productive.

The impact of the fiscal crisis upon society generally and the machinery of government in particular is not neutral. First, reactions to the fiscal crisis can promote, in a subtle and covert way, a redistribution of both economic and political power amongst groups and individuals in society.[3] Second, to the extent that these reactions and changes take place outwith the business of

Parliament then the power of one of the most fundamental institutions of democracy is weakened. Public expenditure control lies at the heart of parliamentary democracy. To have control over public expenditure is to have power over the business of government, its activities, its outputs, and the services which it provides. Control over public expenditure represents authority over the resources which are necessary to make the bureaucracy function.

This perspective has characterized much of the *a priori* thinking about the role of parliament in the process of public expenditure control. It must, however, be recognized that this is a purist or idealized view. Whilst the control of public expenditure is a necessary condition for the control of the activities of government it is not sufficient. Effective control demands power *de facto* over the use of resources by government. Do modern Parliaments have such power? An examination of Parliamentary control over government must look beyond the institutions and processes of public expenditure control *de jure*. Instead it must deal with the complex interactions between the various political agencies which characterize modern governments: Parliament and government (central and local); Parliament and the nationalized industries and public corporations; Parliament and the quangos (quasi non-governmental organizations); and finally, Parliament and the bureaucracy which is comprised of professional and specialist interests.

Over the post-war period the size and the scope of government has expanded enormously both in absolute and relative terms. Public expenditure in 1981 accounted for 48 per cent of G.N.P. About 20 per cent of those in employment were employed in the public sector[4] and much of socio-economic life was regulated by government. Given these far-reaching changes in economic and social philosophy and given the sense of crisis which surrounds public sector budgets, a natural question to ask is how much influence does Parliament in the U.K. have? Has Parliament adapted sufficiently, in piecemeal fashion, by producing an optimal committee system which will handle the issues of the last quarter of the twentieth century? More specifically, does Parliament have power over economic policy-making and changes in the underlying philosophy upon which policies are formulated? Does Parliament have effective control over public spending, its size and composition? Those questions naturally lead into a set of supplementary questions about Parliament's relationships with

central government, local government, the nationalized industries and the quangos. Are the present arrangements for the accountability of government to Parliament wide enough and do
they embrace sufficiently notions of efficiency and effectiveness? Is
the public sector organized in the interests of those whom it *ought*
to serve? Whom does it serve in practice? Is it sufficiently representative? How are competing interests reconciled? Who benefits
from government policies? Is it the public sector unions through
high public sector wages? Is it the consumers of public services
and if so, which particular groups of consumers?[5] Do groups outside Parliament, such as the trade unions and organized industrial
interests, play a more active role in the formulation of policy than
do elected backbench M.P.s? Is the business of government and
the operation of the bureaucracy too well hidden behind an unnecessary veil of secrecy so that neither those whom it serves nor
Parliament itself are capable of finding satisfactory answers to
these questions?

1. Parliament and economic affairs

The traditonal functions of Parliament evolved during the nineteenth century from an economic and political philosophy of
liberalism and *laissez-faire* which emphasized notions such as
social harmony and the self-adjusting and equilibrating tendencies
of the economy. Because society and the economy were able to adjust
to a natural order of things the role of the state was minimal. Political parties were essentially agreed upon the fundamental principles
of government, which were to maintain law and order, to minimize
the role of government and to secure Parliamentary accountability
by the executive. Thus in the nineteenth century there were no
active socio-economic policies pursued by governments as they
are known today and public spending as a proportion of G.N.P.
was, during peacetime, of the order of 11 per cent.[6] Parliament's
function was to 'mobilize the widest degree of popular consent
possible behind the activities of government in order to make its
decisions as authoritative and binding as the nature of the democratic process permits, and to ensure a degree of popular accountability of the executive processes involved'.[7] It performed this
function through its legislative and budgetary powers by providing
support or otherwise to the government's new legislation and by
voting an annual budget to the government.

Socio-economic life has, however, changed over the last 150 years. Realization that the economy will only come into equilibrium after a very long period of social hardship, unemployment and perhaps even civil war created strong demands for governments to intervene in economic affairs by designing policies which would minimize unemployment and the attendant misery which it caused. At the same time there was also the realization that even if the economy was in equilibrium the distribution of income and welfare which would be associated with that state of the world might be totally unacceptable on ethical and political grounds. As the franchise was extended during the first quarter of the twentieth century to include the lower-income groups, political demands were made to expand the activities of government into the generation of social policies that would transfer income and wealth in the direction of the least well-off members of society.[8] This has been described as the transition from the 'guardian state' to the 'welfare state' and has meant a shift in emphasis from collective security to social and individual security.

Public sector budgets after 1950 have grown, in both absolute and relative terms, reflecting the new functions of government. At the same time the business of government has become increasingly more complex. In their attempts to fine-tune the economy and to implement their social policies, successive governments have had to confront a constantly changing socio-economic system which has been moving at increasing speed towards greater degrees of complexity and uncertainty. The economy is no longer a set of domestic relationships. Expansions in world trade make the U.K. domestic economy extremely sensitive to changes in the international economy so that the economic and foreign policies of governments become intertwined.[9] The rise of the trade unions during the post-war period has meant that governments which once relied upon a sense of deference from the populace for the implementation of their economic policies could no longer do so. The relative power of organized labour lies at the heart of the success of any government's economic policy. Alongside these institutional changes in the labour market other institutional changes were taking place. The opening-up of the economy to world trade, the floating of the exchange rate, the abolition of controls over the export of capital, the power of the U.K. in world financial markets all added up to increasing the complexity of economic life and making the U.K. economy more sensitive to changes taking place outside the government's sphere of economic influence.[10]

What do these changes have to do with the business of Parliament in a democracy? The answer is straightforward: the emergence of the technocratic corporatist state based upon its complex web of national and international economic relationships has moved the locus of decision-making away from Parliament to a set of agencies outside Parliament which include the trade unions, the E.E.C., the I.M.F. and organized industrial and commercial interests. Coombes and Walkland in a recent study of parliaments' roles in economic affairs have put the case clearly as 'there is at first sight very little connection, either theoretical or practical between the fact of parliamentary government and the practice of national economic management . . . parliamentary involvement in economic policy tends to be episodic and occasional, tactical and not strategic and very late in the day'.[11] The reason for this state of affairs is that much economic legislation is enabling, and only comes about when existing powers are inadequate. It gives discretionary powers to ministers to legislate by statutory instrument, and new departments and functions can be set up without Parliament's consent. Examples include the setting up of the National Economic Development Council, the Monopolies and Restrictive Practices Commission, the Manpower Services Commission, and the Prices Commission. Each of these, and there are many more examples, removed significant economic functions from their sponsoring departments and were placed outside direct parliamentary control. During the past 30 years there has been an explosion in the economic powers of these non-departmental agencies and no corresponding matching of watchdog powers by Parliament despite the fact that the recommendations and decisions made by these agencies can influence the welfare of very many individuals. To whom are such agencies accountable and whose interests do they represent? These questions, fundamental as they are, remain unanswered, leaving Parliament with the problem of keeping a watch on the discretionary powers of departments and their agencies.

Another problem with economic legislation is that the formulation of most bills which have an economic content is carried out after consultation with groups which lie outside Parliament, such as trade unions, social pressure groups or industrial interest groups. Whilst this is a perfectly reasonable course of action to pursue, especially if policies are to be targeted towards specific groups and if they are to be implemented in a smooth way, it does nevertheless have consequences for the authority of Parliament. First, political influence now comes from sources outside of Parliament. The rise of corporatism (i.e. functional representation) can mean that the success or failure of policies does not depend upon whether or not Parliament gives its approval but instead whether or not powerful groups outside of Parliament will give their co-operation when the policies come to be implemented.[12] It is this power rather than that of Parliament which is now decisive. Second, having struck bargains with these outside groups, a government, when it presents a bill to Parliament, will not wish to make concessions. To do so could imply that the whole bill would have to go back to the bargaining stage. Third, co-operation can promote an expansion in public expenditure to the extent that each bargain has a price tag in terms of public funds. One of the consequences of obtaining the cooperation of a diverse set of interests groups is therefore to increase public expenditure.[13]

Because there is no specific Department of Economic Affairs,[14] because there is very little specific 'economic' legislation and because radical changes in economic philosophy such as the conversion to monetarism in the 1970s can take place within the existing system and do not require new legislation, Parliament's power to control the executive in this sphere is greatly reduced. Parliament is not required to give approval. There is, however, much debate about the likely consequences and the desirability of policies. Parliament, therefore, becomes a debating chamber in which party politics are played out in the drama on the floor of the House whilst the real business of government takes place behind a veil of secrecy hidden from the view of Parliament. Political careers, it has often been argued, are made on the floor of the House, not from the diligence and hard work of being a Committee member. But how well informed is Parliamentary debate? This in large measure depends upon the work on the House of Commons Committees, a subject which is considered in greater detail below. Until recently, the select committees did not concern themselves specifically with economic management. Such matters tended to be treated indirectly as, for example, the examination of regional incentives and hence regional policies or macro-economic policies in the context of the terms of reference of the Expenditure Select Committee.[15] There is no evidence to suggest that the output of select committees has much impact upon Parliamentary debates.[16] With the establishment of the new select committees in 1979 this was changed. The new committees were intended to shadow the work of individual departments. By far the most powerful of these committees has been the Treasury and Civil Service Committee under the Chairmanship of Edward du Cann. This committee has concentrated much of its time upon examining the underlying rationale for the government's macro-economic policy, in particular its monetary policy. The reports produced have been of an extremely high level of technical competence and have opened up discussion for the first time into matters relating to the macro-economic management of the economy. Much, however, remains to be done. Given the key role played by monetary policy in the current economic strategy the time is ripe for a select committee of the House to penetrate the veils of the Old Lady of Threadneedle Street and to bring into the open some of the workings of the Bank of England in the sphere of economic policy. Attempts have been made in the past but without success as select committees have been denied access. This is surely a classic example of how power has shifted away from Parliament to a body which lies outside its control. The conduct of monetary policy, which is the province of the Bank of England working in conjunction with the Treasury, affects the fortunes and welfares of millions of U.K. citizens. Without a detailed examination of the conduct of the Bank of England's business it is impossible for Parliament to know if the Bank organizes its affairs in such a way that it is the general public which benefits or if it benefits those who work in the City. Whom does the Bank of England serve? Whilst the Treasury ministers were exposed to answering questions in the House relating to the control of the money supply, the production of the consultative document *Competition and Credit Control*[17] by the Bank of England was not debated by Parliament although it formed the basis of new, far-reaching policies.

Parliament's function is not to make economic policy; that is the business of government. It is, however, Parliament's role to monitor and to be critical of government policy and when necessary to prepare and present alternative strategies. In performing these functions it should provide a sufficiently strong check or balance so that the executive does feel accountable for the consequences of its decisions. However, the reality of Parliamentary life, as was demonstrated above, is far removed from this ideal. The rise of corporatism has brought with it a situation in which the formation and implementation of economic policy involves negotiation and bargaining with groups outside Parliament. The countervailing power lies outside and not within Parliament. Whilst Parliament gives its consent, the details of policy analysis are worked out elsewhere.

Economic planning, even in its weakest form as portrayed in monetarism, implies a transference of power to the bureaucrats and planners. In a democracy a constant source of concern must be who controls the planners; to whom are they accountable? Parliamentary control of economic planning in the U.K. is totally inadequate. How might Parliament regain its power in the making of economic policy? To anyone who believes strongly in representative government the role of Parliament must be to ask questions about the government's proposed strategies for fiscal and monetary policies. It has the demanding responsibility of examining the proposed strategies carefully and considering alternatives to them. If Parliament believes that the government's strategy is wrong-minded or unworkable then it must put together an alternative and be prepared to argue the case.

To examine the Chancellor's economic strategy and to be in a position to propose an alternative, Parliament requires a committee which will marshal the expertise equivalent to that at the Chancellor's disposal through the Treasury. For years, Parliament's effective power in the realm of economic policy-making has been constrained through a lack of technical information and expertise which are necessary to bring to account modern governments operating in complex environments.[18] Prior to the 1979 abolition of the Expenditure Select Committee much of the business of parliamentarians was taken up in the scrutiny of the details of expenditure figures in the Supply Estimates or the public expenditure White Papers. There was explicit analysis of the budget and the public expenditure White Paper but no analysis of how they related to the government's overall economic strategy. Any discussion which might have taken place in committee was *ad hoc* and piecemeal. The 1979 reforms with the establishment of the Treasury and Civil Service Committee introduced changes which had long been advocated by, amongst others, the late John Mackintosh.[19] But they did not go far enough.

There can be no doubt that since 1979 the level of Parliamentary debate on economic affairs has benefited enormously from the deep and searching analysis of the Chancellor's macro-economic strategy carried out by the Treasury and Civil Service Committee. The evidence obtained on the role of monetary policy and the underlying assumptions of monetarism is an excellent example of how a select committee can carry out penetrating examinations of highly technical issues. But to be an effective countervailing force Parliament needs additional information and more especially needs to present alternative proposals if, from its own analysis of an issue, it is of the

strong belief that a better alternative exists. To proceed in this way
Parliamentary committees need to be supplied with many more
resources than they currently have at their disposal. If Parliament is
to provide a forum for debating alternative fiscal and budgetary
strategies then it requires a team which will:

(a)   provide its own economic forecasts and challenge the validity
       of the assumptions upon which government forecasts are
       based;
(b)   monitor the implementation of existing programmes from
       the point of view of their effectiveness in achieving stated
       objectives;
(c)   carry out policy analyses upon specific micro-programmes to
       consider their effectiveness and efficiency and to propose
       alternatives which have been independently costed;
(d)   examine the whole package of macro-economic strategies
       and social spending policies.

To a limited extent some of these activities are already carried out
by the specialist select committees which shadow individual departments. Policies and programmes are monitored and judged but
well-articulated and costed alternatives are never presented for
debate. Nor is the whole package considered and analysed to see if its
constituent elements are incompatible. If the Treasury and Civil
Service Committee was to produce its own policy options rather than
to ask questions of government policy it would be forced to consider,
in much greater detail than it does, the way in which taxation, public
spending plans, monetary policy, incomes policies, industrial policy
etc. fit (or do not fit) together. At the same time, if there was some
'mega' committee drawing together the findings of the specialist
select committees then it would be possible to consider whether
housing policy was compatible with policies in the field of social
security or if education and industrial policies were compatible.

Many will, of course, shy clear of any suggestion of giving select
committees more resources. This is a somewhat curious and short-
sighted view. In today's society when so much effective power lies in
the hands of the professional and the bureaucrat, when it is their
unchallenged decisions that will decide who will gain and who will
lose as a result of public policies, then Parliament, and thus
democracy, is totally weakened unless it has equally good professional expertise and information at its disposal. Compared to the U.S.
Congress the U.K. Parliament's resources are paltry. Strengthening

Parliament's power can, of course, also strengthen that of the government. Thus, if Parliament is convinced of the correctness of the government's economic strategy this can give the government the resolve to pursue its programme with vigour and challenge the power of extra-parliamentary groups.

2. Parliament and public spending

Whilst Parliament has ultimate control over public spending in the sense that it can refuse to vote supply it has, in practice, little effective control. In recent discussions on this issue two leading Members of Parliament had the following comments to make:

> I strongly agree with the now widely held view that the present position, whereby huge sums of money are granted to the Government virtually without debate, is quite intolerable in a democratically elected Parliament.
>
> *Joel Barnett*[20]

> . . . our systems are complex, archaic and are a denial of democracy. There is not the opportunity to look at or discuss money that there should be. We who have the honour to be the people's representatives in the Parliament are not carrying out the work which the electorate believes and trusts us to do. . . . The way in which we fail to examine expenditure is in my opinion a disgrace in a modern Parliament . . . the sooner we make a start on getting better control of expenditure the healthier our democracy will be.
>
> *Edward du Cann*[21]

The concept of Parliamentary control over public expenditure is not unambiguous and it is necessary to be more precise and to define clearly the decisions over which Parliament should hold the executive accountable. Should Parliament have control over both the level and the composition of public spending? At what level of detail should control apply: at the aggregate level of spending by Departments or at the micro-level of spending on specific programmes within Departments? Furthermore, there is the question of the type of control which is required. What is the purpose of control of public spending? Against which set of criteria are spending programmes to be judged?

There are three general areas in which Parliament might wish to have control over public spending. First, there is the ex-post-audit exercise in which Departments' expenditures are scrutinized to ensure that resources have been allocated to the purposes which Parliament voted them. Second, there is the question of the overall level of public spending which is consistent with the government's macroeconomic strategy. Third, do public spending programmes give value for money and are public funds efficiently allocated?

The audit function is quite straightforward. It is purely an accounting and legal exercise and is a check upon financial propriety. Where debate exists is in the area of the scope of the Comptroller and Auditor General's powers to examine the accounts of all areas of the public sector. At present about 60 per cent of total public spending is scrutinized by the office of the C.A.G. Those areas which escape are the accounts of the local authorities, the nationalized industries and the health authorities. That is not to say that the accounts of these organizations are not audited; they are. However, because the audits are not carried out by the C.A.G. the accounts are never laid before Parliament and its committees for more detailed examination.[22]

Ensuring financial regularity is an extremely limited kind of control. Parliament is much more concerned to establish whether or not public funds have been used efficiently and if value for money has been obtained. To assist Parliament in this activity the Public Accounts Committee (P.A.C.), one of the oldest select committees of the House, examines a selection of the audited accounts and reports which are brought to its attention by the C.A.G. Because the effectiveness of the P.A.C. depends upon the quality of the information it is provided with, recent debate has centred around the work of the office of the C.A.G. and the information which it provides.[23] In particular, it is now generally recognized that the information which is necesssary for Parliamentary accountability should take the form of 'value for money audits' rather than the existing financial audits.

Value for money audits provide management information about resource use.[24] Faced with tight budgets and cash limits placed on public spending it becomes necessary for governments to become more efficient. The Policy Analysis and Review (P.A.R.) exercises which were discussed during the 1970s never really became established as serious management exercises to promote efficiency.[25] However, recent attempts to improve Civil Service efficiency, 'Raynerism' and the value for money audit have produced immediate results.[26] Each exercise involves a scrutiny of a particular public sector programme or department with a view to reducing inputs, especially manpower. One of the stated objectives of the 1979 Conservative government was to cut back on civil service manpower by one job in seven by May 1984. To achieve this each department was allocated a manpower target. To assist departments to achieve these targets Rayner and value for money audits search out possible input savings through detailed cost accounting and O. & M.-type exercises.[27] In the case of the Department of the Environment an elaborate management information system for ministers (MINIS) has been introduced.[28]

Whilst it is too early to judge the total impact of these systems, a number of initial conclusions can be drawn. No one could argue in favour of inefficiency or waste in public spending programmes. However, by concentrating purely on the input side these new management techniques, which are really old ones with new names, quickly run into many difficulties. To judge efficiency purely in terms of a reduction in inputs is one-sided since it ignores completely what is happening to the output side. An efficiency gain is achieved only if the reduction in inputs is accompanied by a maintenance or an improvement in the level of output. Unless this happens efficiency will, in fact, be reduced. But as is well known, output measurement for public services is extremely difficult and requires a much more sophisticated level of analysis. Thus whilst crude input budgeting and value for money studies of the Rayner kind appear to be serving a useful function they need to be balanced up against measures of the cost-effectiveness of programmes and this requires the introduction of output measures, however crude these might be. The public's interest is not served if wild assertions of gains in efficiency as measured by input reductions end up in the decline of service output and quality.

Moreover, from Parliament's perspective, whilst it wishes to ensure that public funds are not being wasted in the sense that for a given level of output fewer inputs could be employed, there are other more subtle dimensions of efficiency to which it could direct its attention. First, are resources being allocated to programmes in accordance with voters' preferences? This point refers to the balance of resources as between departments. To the extent that there is an imbalance of resources then there exists an 'allocative inefficiency', i.e. a re-allocation of resources would improve welfare. Second, is public sector pay out of line with that of the private sector? It could be that the civil service does not hire too many employees but that they are paid too much.

Both of these dimensions of efficiency raise important issues which are the subject of current discussion. Both Barnett and du Cann, whilst recognizing that Parliament does not have the power to increase an estimate did, nevertheless, see the case for a select committee recommending to Parliament that within a department's total spending more should be spent on programme X and correspondingly less on programme Y. But to be in a position to do this the select committees would need much more information about the details of spending programmes and hence more resources at their disposal.[29] Again, as in the discussion of the scrutiny of economic policy, if Pariament is to have a role in proposing its own alternatives to government policies then its committees must be adequately resourced.

The issue of public sector pay lies at the heart of much of the debate on public expenditure control. If Parliament were to suggest that public sector capital spending should be increased in order to promote economic growth whilst maintaining the total level of public spending it must also take a view on public sector employment and pay. Moreover, scrutiny of the estimates without some comment or observation on public sector pay is quite bizarre. To make such comments would, however, require Parliament to have the equivalent of its own pay research unit. Such a unit might also monitor and examine trends in public employment. Given the importance of payroll expenses in total departmental expenditures (up to 80 per cent in some cases) and given the political signals which are carried by information about public employment and remuneration (including pensions), Parliament's ability to understand the dynamic of public spending and the problems of reconciling cash plans with public spending White Paper plans would be greatly enhanced by such a unit. Furthermore, if Parliament is to take a view about who benefits from public spending it must be in a position to know if public sector employees are enjoying substantial economic rents, in the form of overmanning and excessive remuneration levels, at the expense of the taxpayer whose real disposable income is thereby reduced.

Auditing, value for money studies, and the elimination of waste are all traditional functions of Parliamentary accountability and control. The challenge presented to Parliament in this sphere arises from the size and complexity of the business of government in the 1980s. But Parliament faces other challenges which are more crucial. During periods of economic growth, which characterized most of the period 1950–75, the harsh realities of making allocative decisions were softened. Political conflict was minimized by allocating additional resources to most public programmes. Stagflation, a situation of zero or declining real growth which is eroded by rapid rates of inflation, has changed this completely and places political conflict at the centre of the stage as each department fights to maintain its resource base by minimizing the size of its spending cuts. In order to cope with the problems that stagflation and fiscal limitation pose, public budgets need to be much more flexible than they are at the moment. The problem is, however, compounded because public sector budgets in the U.K. typically do not possess the degree of flexibility which is required. Robinson and Ysander in recognizing this problem state it as:

> welfare strategies and planning methods hitherto used have entrapped them (i.e. governments) into a rather rigid system of commitments and responsibilities with little leeway for intra-marginal adjustments and reorientations. This has intensified the search for new ways to create flexibility, new strategies and planning methods that are better designed for the needed adjustment to a changing environment.[30]

These rigidities or inertiae within public budgets exist both on the input and the output side. With respect to outputs the transition from the guardian to the welfare state[31] has brought with it a series of social contracts which entitle individuals to the benefits accruing from collective insurance schemes such as old age pensions, sickness benefits and unemployment benefits. These commitments which must be honoured place an upward pressure upon budgets during times of inflation and recession since not only do the number of entitlements increase but the total cost of honouring them also rises. Moreover, political representation in the sense of politicians representing the interests of a general set of voters has given way to interest group politics. Thus, any attempt to reduce benefits or to break the contractual obligation becomes a centralized political issue and is viewed as discrimination against a particular group of individuals. This upward flexibility and downward stickiness in social spending programmes is further sustained by bureaucratic interests. The demand for welfare services is in large measure registered by professionals and bureaucrats who simultaneously regulate and supply the service.[32]

Inflexibility on the input side arises from the nature of public sector contracts, especially labour contracts, which tend to be written in such a way that making staff redundant quickly is both difficult and extremely costly.

To overcome these inflexibilities and to give both governments and Parliament the power to respond to changing environments the institutions of entitlement to social services and the practices of public production need to change. It is meaningless to ask Parliamentary committees to propose and to cost alternative policies if the institutions are so rigid that implementation of changes is impossible. First, the time-scale applying to entitlements could be made shorter and subject to revision after a period of five years at which time the case for the continuation of the entitlement in its present form would have to compete against revisions to its form and against demands for new entitlements. Parliamentary committees of the kind discussed above would play an important role in monitoring the performance of existing social welfare programmes, articulating the demands for new programmes and costing them. Second, longer-term contracts could be written in terms of the contingencies which would apply. Third, public resource use would need to become multi-functional in order to respond to changing demands. Thus, public employees could expect to be transferred between tasks and be retrained rapidly; buildings and capital equipment could be designed for multiple use.

The introduction of flexibility clearly requires a change in attitudes, innovative thinking on the part of public sector management and the co-operation of public employees and voters alike. The demand for flexibility does cut across intra-organizational politics and will be attained only after some internal conflict. If, however, the public sector is to respond to the changing demands of a complex environment and face up to the challenge of declining real budgets because of stagnation and inflation then flexibility must be assured.

3. Conclusions

The power of Parliament to hold the executive accountable for its decisions has been systematically eroded in the U.K. over the past three decades. The origins of this shift in power are varied. They include an expansion of the functions of government into more complex and uncertain environments, especially the economic and the social: the concomitant rise in the role of the specialist and the professional whose power originates in contextual knowledge: the constraints placed upon the implementation of policies by extra-Parliamentary agents such as trade unions and international organizations: the inflexibility of public budgets but most especially the inability of Parliament itself to organize its committees and to resource them properly so that Parliament is presented with information of the quality necessary to engage in informed debate and to present alternative strategies to be placed on the agenda for discussion. Unless Parliament breaks down these entry barriers to informed debate, power will continue to reside with the executive, with professional bureaucratic groups and with interest groups outside of Parliament. To the extent that the present system is perpetuated, democracy will be weakened.

NOTES

1. 'Public expenditure is at the heart of Britain's present economic problem.' This statement was made by Sir Geoffrey Howe in his first budget speech of June 1979. For a more detailed discussion of this change in philosophy see P.M.Jackson, 'The new economic order' in P.M.Jackson (ed.), *Government Policy Initiatives 1979–80: Some Case Studies in Public Administration* (1981), and 'The impact of economic theories in local government finance', *Local Government Studies*, VIII (1982).

2. I.e. allocated and distribuuted via markets. Such a programme, it is thought, will improve the efficient production of these services through the discipline of the market place.

3. Those most likely to suffer are the ethnic groups, the low-paid, females and the old.

4. See G.Wilkinson and P.M.Jackson, *Public Sector Employment in the U.K.* (1981).

5. J.Le Grand, *The Strategy of Equality* (1982), shows that it is essentially the middle classes who gain from public services. His evidence supports 'Director's Law'.

6. See C.V.Brown and P.M.Jackson, *Public Sector Economics* (1978), table 6.6, 121.

7. D.Coombes and S.A.Walkland, *Parliaments and Economic Affairs* (1980).

8. This was the birth of the welfare state and post-war Keynesian economic policies.

9. Examples include the changes in OPEC oil prices during the 1970s and the impact of the Reagan budgets of 1981–2 upon U.K. interest rates.

10. For example, changes in the U.K. inflation rate, exchange rate or interest rates can precipitate rapid movements of short-term finance into and out of the U.K. banking system with highly significant consequences for the money supply, interest rates, exchange rates etc.

Also the impact of cheap imported goods has contributed to the 'deindustrialisation' of the U.K. and increased unemployment; see F.Blackaby (ed.), *De-industrialisation* (1979).

11.   Coombes and Walkland, *op.cit.*, 27.

12.   The collapse of the Callaghan government in 1979 was essentially due to the failure to gain the co-operation of the trade union movement in implementing a 5 per cent incomes policy. The incomes policy (social contract) introduced by the 1974–9 Labour government was bought at the expense of increasing trade union power over economic decisions.

13.   This point is well known from the 'public choice school'; see J.Buchanan and G.Tullock, *The Calculus of Consent* (1965), and also A.M.Rivlin, 'The political economy of budget choices: a view from congress', *American Economic Review*, LXXII (1982).

14.   The Treasury is not strictly a Ministry of Economic Affairs.

15.   See Second Report, Expenditure Committee 1973–4, *Regional Development Incentives*, H.E.P. 85 and 85-I, H.M.S.O., December 1973; Ninth Report from the Expenditure Committee Session 1974, *Public Expenditure, Inflation and the Balance of Payments*, H.C. 328, H.M.S.O., July 1974; First Report, Expenditure Committee 1975–76, *The Financing of Public Expenditure*, H.E.P. 69I and II, H.M.S.O. December 1975. A notable exception is the *Report* from the Committee on Policy Optimisation, Cmnd.7148, H.M.S.O., March 1978.

16.   See A.Robinson, *Parliament and Public Spending* (1978).

17.   Bank of England, 'Competition and Credit Control: Text of a Consultative Document issued on 14th May 1971', *Quarterly Bulletin*, June 1971.

18.   Similar arguments have been advanced by A.Wildavsky, *Budgeting: A Comparative Theory of Budget Processes* (1975), when discussing budget decision-making; see also P.M.Jackson, *The Political Economy of Bureaucracy* (1982).

19.   J.Mackintosh 'The House of Commons and Taxation', *Political Q.*, XLIII (1972), reprinted in B.Crick and W.A.Robson (eds.), *Taxation Policy* (1973). Similar ideas were advanced by Winston Churchill in his Romanes lecture (1930) – see W.Churchill, *Thoughts and Adventures* (1932).

20.   *Memorandum* submitted by the Rt. Hon. Joel Barnett, M.P., Chairman of the Public Accounts Committee to the *Select Committee on Procedure (Supply)*; Session 1980–81, H.M.S.O., April 1981, H.C. 118–viii.

21.   Du Cann's evidence, para. 592, to the *Select Committee on Procedure (Supply)*; Session 1980–81, H.M.S.O., March 1981, HC 117–vi.

22.   For an extended discussion of this point see J.Barnett. 'Accounting to Parliament', *Public Money*, I (1981).

23.   See the Green Paper, *The Role of the Comptroller and Auditor General*, H.M.S.O., Cmnd.7845; Report of the Public Accounts Committee,

Session 1980–81, *Comptroller and Auditor General*, H.M.S.O., HC 115, March 1981.
24. See the papers presented to the 1982 Annual Conference of the Chartered Institute of Public Finance and Accountancy, Harrogate; especially, M.Shanks, *Accountability in the Public Sector,* A.Likierman, *Accountability – Do the Report and The Accounts Really Matter?*
25. See W.Plowden, 'Budgetary procedures and administrative change', in *Strategies for Change and Reform in Public Management* (1980).
26. See D.Allen, 'Raynerism: strengthening civil service management', *Royal Institute of Public Administration Report* 2 (1981), and C.Christie, 'The real Raynes targets', *Royal Institute of Public Administration Report* 3 (1982).
27. See Third Report from the Treasury and Civil Service Committee, Session 1981–82, *Efficiency and Effectiveness in the Civil Service*, H.C. 236, vols. I, II, and III, H.M.S.O., March 1982.
28. See A.Likierman, 'Management information for Ministers: The MINIS system in the Department of the Environment', *Public Administration* LX (1982).
29. Both Barnett and du Cann played down the need for additional full-time staff as in the U.S. case and preferred to rely more upon expert witnesses. In this respect they probably underestimate the resources which they require.
30. See A.Robinson and B.C.Ysander, *Flexibility in Budget Policy: The Changing Problems and Requirements of Public Budgetary* (1981).
31. *Ibid.*
32. P.M.Jackson, *The Political Economy of Bureaucracy* (1982).

8 BRITAIN AND THE E.E.C.

Michael Shackleton

IT IS NOW more than a decade since the Heath government finalized negotiations with the original six members of the European Economic Community (E.E.C.) and the Prime Minister signed the Treaty of Accession in Brussels on 22 January 1972. It is also well over half a decade since the issue of membership appeared to be settled by the referendum of 5 June 1975, when the British electorate gave a 67 per cent vote in favour of the re-negotiated terms presented by the Labour government of Harold Wilson. And yet for those who thought that the passage of time would by itself bring about convergence between Britain and her continental neighbours, with the emergence of a suitable mixture of active enthusiasm for and passive acceptance of the Community, the intervening years have proved a source of continuing disappointment.

Public support in Britain for the E.E.C. dropped consistently in the years following the referendum to a level and at a rate not found in any other Community country. By 1981, less than a quarter of British respondents expressed the belief that belonging to the E.E.C. was a good thing and nearly a half thought that it was a bad thing. In most of the other countries, the level of disenchantment was still under ten per cent: even in Denmark, the country with the widest public opposition to membership after Britain, those considering membershp to be a bad thing were nearly 20 per cent fewer than those with the same view in Britain.[1] Perhaps even more serious has been the breakdown of any kind of consensus on the issue of membership at the level of political elites. Most notably, the attitude of the Labour party changed from one of acceptance of the result of the referendum to that of outright rejection of continued membership. At its 1981 Annual Conference, the party committed itself by a massive majority to withdrawal without another referendum as a major plank in its manifesto for the next general election. Whatever their reservations about the Community, no other major party in the ten member states has assumed such a firm and apparently irrevocable stance.

What though, are the sources of this high level of public disenchantment and party disagreement? Why is it that after all these years, Britain's membership of the E.E.C. remains a live political issue? Was General de Gaulle right to argue back in 1963, when the Macmillan government applied to join, that Britain was structurally unsuited for membership of the Community? This chapter will suggest that answers to these questions need to be sought by examining the relationship between the E.E.C. and Britain at two levels: the institutional level and the policy level. It will argue that the *institutions* of the Community have posed major problems of adaptation for Britain and that the *policies* of the Community tended to come into conflict with certain important British interests and that both difficulties still remain to be resolved.

The argument is not that Britain is alone in facing such difficulties: the nature of the institutions and policies of the Community have posed problems for every member. Nevertheless, in the British case, the two elements have combined in a particularly potent way to prevent this country from becoming more firmly integrated into the E.E.C. and more fully engaged in debates about how it should evolve. Nor is it argued that the difficulties are necessarily permanent, that relations between Britain and the E.E.C. are set in a permanent mould. As to how they might evolve, we shall return in the conclusion.

1. The character of the institutions

It is almost a commonplace to suggest that knowledge of the Community institutions in Britain lies at a very low level. It is no surprise if people mix up the institutions or fail to distinguish them from non-Community institutions.[2] Thus the E.E.C. Court, the European Court of Justice in Luxembourg, can be easily confused with the European Court of Human Rights in Strasbourg, while the Council of Europe bears a marked similarity in name to the European Council, the latter referring to the thrice-yearly meetings of Heads of State and Government of the Community, the former to the inter-governmental body of European states, within and outside the E.E.C., which established the Court of Human Rights. Such ignorance of what and where Community institutions are can be seen as lying at the heart of the hostility in Britain towards the E.E.C. but it is surely only a part of the problem. More important than the ability to distinguish between the various Courts and Councils that dominate the European scene has been the difficulty for people in Britain – whether well-informed or not – of establishing any kind of clear perception as to what kind of an animal the Community is and what is involved in being a member.

Despite a decade of formal membership of the institutions, they have remained essentially unfamiliar to broad sections of British opinion, even at the governmental level. Moreover, that unfamiliarity, that feeling of strangeness has cut across the division between supporters and opponents of membership and for that very reason has had an important impact on the nature of the debate between them. For supporters of membership the problem has been one of not appearing to set Community institutions against or above national institutions: to opponents of membership, this very problem has provided a marked psychological advantage in that they have been able to use the unusual nature of the Community as the base for arguing that it does indeed constitute a threat to national powers and prerogatives. As Shonfield put it at the time of accession:

> One side was saying that the whole operation was a disgraceful and unnecesssary surrender of national power to conduct our own affairs . . . And the other side . . . told us authoritatively not to worry because the Community really had remarkably little power in practice to change the way in which its member states ran their national affairs. Well, which is it? Feeble or powerful? Historic or a dead bore?[3]

These questions remain without an answer in British discussion of the Community to this day. Indeed the debate is still cast in a very similar mould with no kind of consensus emerging as to the kind of relationship that does or should exist between Community and national institutions.

Above all, there has been continuing uncertainty and disagreement about the implications of E.E.C. arrangements for the basic principle of British government, namely, the 'sovereignty of Parliament'. According to this principle, not only does Parliament enjoy an unlimited legislative authority but also any law that it passes cannot be challenged by any other body or court.[4] Membership of the Community has involved a re-assessment of these rights of Parliament, not for the simple reason that accession meant subscribing to a written constitution, i.e. the Treaty of Rome, but because that constitution contains three elements which are unmatched in the rules of any other international organization: first, the 'direct applicability' of E.E.C. legislation; second, the 'institutional independence' enjoyed by organs of the Community; and third, the 'open-endedness' of the commitment involved in membership. Whatever the legal implications of these features of the Community system for the sovereignty of Parliament,[5] there is no doubt about their political importance in that they establish a supplementary source of law, set of institutions and policy-making process. The nature of the British response to them has revealed a high level of sensitivity to any idea that national powers are being superseded, combined with a marked uncertainty as to how to adopt national practices to the E.E.C. and its institutions.

2. Direct applicability

It is a fundamental feature of the E.E.C. that its institutions are able to make laws which apply directly within all the member states, without national authorities having to or being able to intervene. Article 189 of the Treaty of Rome specifies this clearly in outlining the character of the various kinds of legislative act available to the institutions.

> In order to carry out their tasks the Council and the Commission shall, in accordance with the provisions of the Treaty, make regulations, issue directives, take decisions, make recommendations or deliver opinions.
> A regulation shall have general application. It shall be binding in its entirety and directly applicable in all Member States.
> A directive shall be binding, as to the result to be achieved, upon each Member State to which it is addressed, but shall leave to the national authorities the choice of form and method.
> A decision shall be binding in its entirety upon those to whom it is addressed.
> Recommendations and opinions shall have no binding force.

In other words, once a regulation has been agreed upon in Brussels, it takes effect automatically in all Community countries: a price rise for a particular agricultural product, for example, has to be paid to all E.E.C. farmers as soon as all the agriculture ministers have accepted it in the Council of Ministers. A directive, by contrast, allows a measure of discretion as to how to implement an agreed aim: to decide, for example, that energy dependence on imported oil should be reduced to a certain level by a certain date would not involve specifying the balance between conservation measures and the development of new energy sources. As for recommendations and opinions, these correspond more closely to the kind of statement that emerges from the traditional international organization, where members are free to determine their response in the light of their own national interest.

The importance of this range of instruments became clear at an early moment in the Community's development. In a case which came before the Court of Justice in 1962, commonly called Van Gend en Loos, the judges ruled that the Dutch government did not have the right to introduce a change in the description of a particular product, thus altering the rate of duty payable by a Dutch importer, even though Article 12 of the Treaty of Rome only prohibits member states from introducing new custom duties between themselves. They argued that because of the character of the Community and its concept of 'direct applicability', Article 12 applied to individuals as well as governments. 'The Community', they said, 'constitutes a new legal order in international law, in favour of which the States have limited, albeit in restricted fields, their sovereign rights and of which the subjects are not only member states but also their citizens.'[6]

The idea of a 'new legal order' is one that has been reinforced in a whole series of judgments since then. In 1964 in Costa v. E.N.E.L. (Case 6 64), the Court ruled that no law, unilaterally passed by a member state after joining, could take precedence over Community legislation: indeed a state would be obliged to denounce the Treaty if it did not amend such a law. In 1977 in Administrazione delle Finanze Simmenthal S.p.A. (Case 106/77) the obligations of national courts in this context were made clear: 'every national court must, in a case within its jurisdiction, apply Community law in its entirety and protect rights which the latter confers on individuals and must accordingly set aside any provision of national law which may conflict with it, whether prior or subsequent to the Community rule'.[7]

The response of the British Parliament has revealed the political difficulty of integrating this doctrine of 'direct applicability' into the British political system. In a formal sense, an answer was given in October 1971 when the House of Commons voted in favour of joining the Community on the terms negotiated, terms embodied in the Treaty of Accession. Within that Treaty Article 2 laid down that 'the provisions of the original Treaties and the acts adopted by the institutions of the Communities shall be binding on the new Member States'. Hence signature involved explicit acceptance of Article 189 as well as of the judgments of the European Court based upon it.

However, practically speaking, Parliament proved dissatisfied with the role that it saw itself as having in the Community process. In the Treaties, national parliaments receive no direct mention, except as the bodies responsible for designating members of the Assembly or Parliament of the Community – a task which lapsed following the holding of direct elections for the first time in June 1979. And unlike its German counterpart, the British government made no special provisions for Parliament, though Geoffrey Rippon, who had negotiated the terms of entry, did express deep concern that it 'should play its full part when future Community policies are being formulated, and in particular that Parliament should be informed about and have an opportunity to consider at the formative stage those Community instruments which, when made by the Council, will be binding in this country'.[8]

To examine what kind of a role Parliament should play, select committees were set up in the Commons and the Lords. The Commons Committee, chaired by Sir John Foster, came to a conclusion which underlined the uneasiness of all sections of opinion, whatever their view on membership. It clearly perceived the sovereignty of Parliament as threatened by Community membership and thought it necessary to find ways of repairing the damage:

> It remains central to the United Kingdom concept and structure of Parliamentary Democracy that control of the law making processes lies with Parliament – and ultimately with the elected members of it. It follows therefore that new and special procedures are necessary to make good so far as may be done the inroad made into that concept and structure by these new methods of making law.[9]

The implication was that Parliament had indeed 'lost' certain powers – it no longer had 'unlimited legislative authority' – and that efforts had to be made at the national level to retrieve the situation. Its main proposal to that end was that of establishing a scrutiny committee and it was a committee of this kind which was set up in May 1974, under the title 'Select Committee on European Secondary Legislation'. This committee of 16 members was given the job of categorizing documents coming from the Commission in Brussels in terms of their political importance and of recommending certain items for debate by the whole house, making their choice with the help of explanatory memoranda from individual government departments.

Since its establishment the work of the Committee has generated a number of criticisms of the way in which E.E.C. proposals are handled and these highlight the continuing problem of adaptation to the new arrangements that has been faced by Parliament. Much of the criticism has, however, tended to overlook the fact that whatever Parliament's view on a particular matter, it cannot alter the legality of enactment from the Community institutions and it cannot change the way in which those institutions operate. This is not to say that Parliament is totally irrelevant to the Community process – after all, British ministers are members of that Parliament and are aware of its views – but it is to argue that national parliaments can play no formal part in the creation of Community legislation.

An example of the difficulty of coming to terms with this situation was obvious in the criticism directed at the government in 1976 when as part of the Community's annual setting of farm prices, the Council of Ministers agreed to get rid of surplus skimmed milk powder by making its use compulsory in the feeding of animals.[10] The House of Commons had explicitly disagreed with the original proposal to this effect and though the Commission had amended it, the House had had no time to consider the amended proposal. The response of the select committee was to seek ways of tightening up procedures to avoid this kind of problem but it was, in a sense, a misdirected response. However well such a committee operates and however much time the government is prepared to allow it, there is little that a national parliament can do directly to influence the outcome of the discussions in the Council.[11] Thus it is a feature of the Community process for 'package deals' to be constructed, in which national ministers can establish a trade-off of advantages. Inevitably, any such deal, set up behind closed doors in Brussels, cannot be directly monitored by Parliament nor can it expect to be able to unravel the deal after the event. Once the agreement has been made, the governments are obliged to keep to it. Thus to argue for better scrutiny procedures is, in part at least, to fail to acknowledge the way in which the Community operates.

What has been largely absent from the political debate about the effects of direct applicability has been the suggestion that the inherent difficulty of a national parliament controlling Community legislation should be corrected by encouraging greater scrutiny of Commission proposals at the European level. The attitude of the British Parliament to the European Parliament, for example, has been generally rather reticent in terms of encouraging it to press for greater control over Community legislation. When the Commons voted the bill to hold direct elections to the European Parliament, it was made an explicit condition of acceptance – as it was in France – that the powers of the directly-elected Parliament could only be increased following an agreement incorporated into national legislation and voted on within the national Parliament. And yet it is at least arguable that proposals of the Community cannot possibly be adequately scrutinized before they become law, unless that scrutiny is formalized within the Community process. For the moment, however, the British Parliament is obliged to put its faith in the work of its select committee, the debates that it provokes and the influence that it can exercise over the behaviour of British ministers attending the Council.

3. Institutional independence

The second problematical aspect of the Community for Britain is that of being obliged to adapt to a whole new series of institutions, which are independent and not accountable directly to national authorities. And of the four institutions designated in the Treaty of Rome to fulfil the tasks of the Community – the Assembly (or Parliament), Council, Commission and Court of Justice – there is little doubt that it is the Commission that has posed the most severe problems. The Assembly's limited powers, the Council's inclusion of national ministers and the Court's technicality have helped to direct the gaze of British opinion away from them and to concentrate on the fourth institution.

The Commission's role is quite unlike that of the central body of any other international organization in spirit and in content. The Treaties specifically lay down the way in which it should approach its task:

> The members of the Commission shall, in the general interest of the Communities, be completely independent in the performance of their duties.

In the performance of these duties, they shall neither seek nor take instructions from any Government or from any other body, They shall refrain from any action incompatible with their duties. Each Member State undertakes to respect this principle and not to seek to influence the members of the Commission in the performance of their tasks.[12]

The tasks themselves can be divided into three main categories. First of all, it has the job of initiating all Community legislation, by presenting legislative proposals to the Council of Ministers. It may have been asked to present a proposal by the Council or by the Heads of State and government; it may be acting upon its own initiative in putting forward a proposal; either way, no legislation can come into being without an initial draft from the Commission. Second, it acts as a mediator between the member states. If the national representatives, whether at the ministerial or civil servant level, are unable to reach agreement, they will look to the Commission representatives to present a compromise proposal to overcome the difficulty. Third, it is up to the Commission to implement the policy agreed by the Council of Ministers. Within the limits of that policy, it can itself make binding regulations, covering, for example, the operation of the agricultural market. It can also ensure that Community law is being followed – whether by governments or by firms – and refer a case to the Court of Justice in the event of contravention of the law.

The consequences of having these tasks, embodied in Article 155 of the Treaty of Rome, is to give the Commission considerable political prominence. It attracts a whole range of interest groups who are eager to influence the shape of its initial proposals. The farmers, for example, have in COPA (Comité des Organisations Professionnelles Agricoles) a Brussels-based organization which is widely regarded as extremely successful in formulating a common position on agricultural questions and in pressing that position in consultations with the Commission. The latter also attracts substantial criticism for the kind of decisions that it takes in implementing policy. On a whole series of occasions, concern has been expressed at the Commission's willingness to dispose of surplus butter by agreeing to subsidize its sale to the Soviet Union, an act which it has regularly defended as flowing from the decisions of the Council of Ministers as to the level of export restitutions for agricultural products.

Within Britain such a politically prominent body has again posed problems of adaptation in the context of the doctrine of the sovereignty of Parliament. The idea of giving an independent political role to officials, who are appointed and not elected, is one that sits uneasily in the British context, where ministers are formally responsible to Parliament and civil servants to their ministers. To argue that in Britain the process may in reality be quite different from the way in which it is supposed to work is to overlook the importance of constitutional doctrine in providing an image of how various institutions should be linked. The appearance of the Commission on the British political scene has meant the upsetting of this image and an uncertainty as to the way in which its behaviour should be viewed. Should it be regarded as an overbearing bureaucracy beyond political control? Should it be seen as severely limiting the sovereign decision of national governments? They are questions which have exercised the British political mind without any clear view emerging.

Control over the Commission is an issue much affected by where the observer places stress on Community activity. It is true that the Commissioners that head the Commission in Brussels are assisted by over 10,000 civil servants but this information alone reveals little about the character of the bureaucracy in Brussels. The Commission itself is very eager to underline its comparative weakness compared with national administration. It points to the fact that its staff represent only 0.0045 per cent of the population of the member states, whereas national bureaucracies average 2.9 per cent within each of their communities.[13] At the same time, it is important not to underestimate the force of national views at the level of the Commission. Thus despite the insistence of the Treaty on 'independence', the Commissioners themselves are appointed for their four-year terms by their own governments and are dependent upon them, if they seek re-appointment. And in pursuing their aims, they are aware of the need to anticipate the responses of government and not to take rash action in, for example, taking governments to the Court of Justice, without exhausting all other avenues to a settlement first. In the final analysis, the Commission does not have the means to enforce a decision of its own or of the Court and relies very heavily on the willingness of national authorities to 'play along'.

Nevertheless, the point remains that there is no direct national mechanism for keeping the Commission in check during its period of office and this has inevitably increased sensitivity in Britain to the possibility of bureaucratic meddling. One result has been a tendency to exaggerate the degree to which the E.E.C. can limit the sovereign decisions of a national government. A classic example arose in 1974–5, when there was widespread discussion of the possibility that the Community might deprive Britain of the right to take the decisions it chose on the development and use of its North Sea oil reserves. In Parliament the Commission's proposals were discusssed in a lengthy seven hour debate in February 1975 and in the referendum campaign of that spring, the issue was a major one. Frank Allaun, a Labour M.P. opposed to the Community, suggested that the other members wanted to keep Britain in because 'they had their beady eyes on our oil'.[14] And even in the White Paper recommending membership, the government made its opposition to any E.E.C. interference very clear, stating that it would 'never allow [the Community] to develop in ways which could threaten our own ownership or control over our own natural resources'.[15]

And yet in the meantime the government had entered into an energy programme which potentially diminished national control over oil far more radically than anything proposed by the E.E.C. In a written answer to the House on 30 October 1974, the Secretary for Energy, Eric Varley, drew attention to an agreement which Britain had signed along with a set of other industrialized countries, including the United States and Japan, to share oil in the event of an emergency. In the event of any signatory's supply being cut in an emergency by over seven per cent, the other signatories would be obliged to apply stringent rules for sharing stocks and imports in accordance with strict formulae about who could get what. What is more the provisions would come into force automatically without requiring Parliamentary debate or consent.

There was a brief discussion on this agreement in the House on 14 April 1975 but it never created the kind of storm generated by Commission proposals on a common energy policy. Part of the explanation for this can be found in the different procedures involved rather than the different contents of the two energy programmes. Thus Varley defended the fact that there was not a debate on the emergency programme on the grounds that this was the traditional way of dealing with an agreement of this kind:

I understand that the Agreement has been laid before the House in accordance with the Ponsonby Rules. There were agreements undertaken and ratified in this way by the previous Government, and nothing is unusual about the way we are proposing to do it today. There is no comparison between the right hon. Gentleman's reference to this agreement and the European Economic Community.

In other words, the familiarity of existing procedure made it possible for Parliament to accept a proposal with far-reachig consequences without debate. By contrast, the very unfamiliarity of the Community process and the Commission within it made it impossible for the same thing to happen to E.E.C. proposals which failed then and have failed ever since to generate a common energy policy of significant proportions.

4. Open-endedness

One difference between the Community's search for an energy policy and the international agreement just referred to is that the latter was concluded for a fixed period of time. Once that period elapses, it is necessary for the contracting parties to review their acceptance of the terms and they are therefore free to rescind their agreement at that moment if they so wish. The Treaty of Rome, by contrast, states specifically (Article 240) that 'this treaty is concluded for an unlimited period' and hence establishes a policy process, whereby not only are the member states condemned to keep meeting in the search for agreements, but they are also obliged to abide by those agreements that have been made in the past, unless and until they all agree otherwise. In this case, the process is a cumulative one in which new accords are regularly being added to what is often called the 'acquis communautaire', that is to say, what the Community has already produced in the way of legislation.

The accumulation of legislation necessarily raises the question of the direction in which the Community is moving and brings us to the final challenge to the sovereignty of Parliament and the rights of the national community to determine the political direction it wishes to take. It is a necessary part of the doctrine of the sovereignty of Parliament that no Parliament can bind its successor and yet it appears that membership of the Community involves an open-ended commitment to a set of institutions and policies, whose existing shape can only be altered in the future by unanimous agreement of the member states and whose future form can only be dimly perceived at the present time. This is not to suggest that Britain or any other country is committed to stay forever in the E.E.C.[16] but it is to raise the question of the ability of any one country to control the momentum that the Community process generates.

The problem is particularly acute in that the inspiration behind the Community came from men like Monnet, Schuman and Spinelli who looked ahead to a federal process involving a clear transfer of powers from the national to the supra-national level and ending up in what was sometimes called the 'United States of Europe'. It is true that such federalist ideas have enjoyed very mixed fortunes, particularly in the recent past when there has been a more widespread feeling of immobilism within the institutional structure, but it is important not to underestimate the importance of a vision, however vague, of a different set of relations between member states and the Community lying somewhere in the future. The idea is present in the preamble of the Treaty of Rome, whose signatories expressed themselves 'determined to lay the foundations of an even closer union among the peoples of Europe' and it was made much more explicit in the final paragraph issued by the Heads of State and government after their summit conference in Paris in October 1972. They set themselves the major objective of transforming, before the end of the present decade (i.e. 1980) '. . . the whole complex of the relations of member states into a European Union (and to this end requested) the institutions of the Community to draw up a report on this subject before the end of 1975 for submission to a summit conference'. This report was produced by the Belgian Prime Minister, Leo Tindemans, and one consequence of it was that the Commission was requested to report annually on progress towards the ultimate goal of European union.[17] Whatever the difficulties that the Community is facing, a future goal involving closer integration is one that continues to animate discussion within it.

This regular theme is one that underlines again the difficulty faced in Britain of familiarization with the workings of the E.E.C.: there is something almost theological to many British observers in the concern with the concept of European union and it is a feeling of strangeness which is not restricted to those who oppose membership. Even those in favour are obliged to underline the protection afforded within the Community to those states which see any proposals as threats to their 'vital national interests'. This was noticeably the case when the Labour government called for a 'yes' vote in the 1975 referendum. In the White Paper that it produced, it referred specifically to the communiqué issued in

Paris three years before and sought to empty it of any menacing content:

> . . . the Government have established that there is no agreement in the Community on what European Union means beyond a general aspiration to closer cooperation.
> . . . the Government's view, which is shared by a number of other member states, is that closer cooperation is desirable and must be pursued in a pragmatic way, but that there is no wide support elsewhere in the Community for moves towards a centralized federal state.[18]

Such a pragmatic stance on European Union was accomplished by a determination that the Council should continue to take decisions by consensus. This means – and has meant for every British government since accession – a strict adherence to the spirit of the so-called Luxembourg compromise of January 1966.[19] At that time, France ended a boycott of the institutions by agreeing to disagree with the other member states about the use of majority voting in the Council of Ministers. She insisted that on matters of 'vital national importance', she would maintain a veto and the practice is one that since then has almost become a standard procedure in Council decision-making for any country that has perceived itself to be in a comparable situation.

Given the sensitivity of governments committed to membership to any idea that the Community might develop in ways that they could not control, it is hardly surprising that opponents of the Community have tended to stress the possibility of such developments. Left-wing critics, in particular, have argued that the integration process implies a set of one-way, irreversible measures, whose character reflects a particular model of society and whose creators are subject to a very limited form of accountability. Holland, for example, has claimed that the irreversibility involved in the Community should be distinguished from 'the fundamental and irreversible change in the balance of power in favour of working people', called for in Labour party programmes in that the latter would have to win consensus approval within the national community as a whole and could subsequently be amended by later Governments.[20] There could hardly be a clearer statement of the doctrine of the sovereignty of Parliament!

The product of a situation where the 'open-endedness' of the Community has been viewed at best with suspicion has been that it has proved very difficult to establish any kind of clear view of the direction in which British policy towards the Community should proceed. No government has produced any form of policy statement establishing priorities or seeking to define what it is that Britain should set out to derive from membership. Instead there has been a very *ad hoc* response and one within which every effort has been made to avoid too close an identification with the Community institutions, even where they might assist Britain's cause:

> In 1978 and 1979 successive British governments stepped back from exploiting the support of the European Parliament to secure changes in the Community budget, persuaded by their own fear and by the arguments of the French government that the protection of national sovereignty and the unity of the Council of Ministers must be preferred to the immediate benefits which espousal of the Parliament's intervention would bring.[21]

It may be that the reason for such coyness can be traced back to the lack of a tradition of coalition formation within British political culture but there is no doubt that the result has been to hinder the integration of Britain into the Community. The doctrine of the 'sovereignty of Parliament' clearly remains to be adapted to the circumstances of Community membership.

5. The structure of policy

The difficulties outlined in the previous section can provide only part of the explanation of the level of hostility towards the Community that exists in Britain. To offer a fuller explanation it is important to assess what the institutions of E.E.C. have brought forth in the way of policies and to consider the relationship between these policies and the interests of the United Kingdom. It is a central contention of this section that Community policies have developed in a way which has put British governments of whatever political complexion in a defensive position. Rather than engage fully in the devising of new policies, they have felt obliged to bring the debate back to the whole structure upon which the policies are based and which rests uneasily with important British interests.

The need to identify the structure lying behind Community policies is important, as it is all too easy to try and make simple links between the output of the Community and outcomes in the member states. Thus, for example, before Britain joined, it was fashionable to argue that the higher growth rates experienced in the original six as compared to Britain in the 1960s were the result of E.E.C. membership or at least that membership had had an important effect on growth.[22] The difficulty with this argument became clearer after 1973 and the dramatic rises in the price of oil. Opponents of the Community then pointed to the slowdown in the rate of growth and the increase in economic and social problems, as if the E.E.C. could itself in some way be held responsible for what was happening. On both sides of the divide, the independent impact of Community policies tended to be exaggerated or downgraded in accordance with political predilection rather than on the basis of any clear analysis of the kind of impact the Community actually has.

One comes somewhat closer to the idea of a policy structure with the claim that Britain's difficulties in relation to the Community arise precisely because she joined when she did, that the entry was far too late. The implication of such a claim is that not only could Britain have benefited from the more favourable international environment of the 1960s but that she could also have been involved in the development of policies from a much earlier stage. As it was, she only became involved at a time when the outlines of the Community's development had already been set and when any change in the outline would mean upsetting the delicate balance of advantage established between the original member states, the so-called 'acquis communautaire'.

One critical aspect of this initial structure was that it was based on what Shonfield has called 'a compact of abstention',[23] and what others describe as 'negative integration'.[24] That is to say, the governments involved agreed to abolish a whole set of restrictions on the free movement of goods, people and capital. In doing this they were following closely the articles of the Treaty of Rome which laid down clear and precise guidelines for the removal of such barriers. The Treaty had, however, much less to say about what kind of positive framework should be established once the barriers were removed and it is with this void that Community policy-makers have been grappling ever since. Thus it is one thing for the Commission to tell a national government that it should not give its fishermen fuel subsidies which unfairly discriminate against other E.E.C. fishermen; it is quite another to establish consensus on what constitutes equal treatment or unfair discrimination.

The one, most important, exception to the general picture of 'negative integration' was the setting-up of the Common Agricultural Policy (C.A.P.). The C.A.P. was established on the basis of two principles; first, that there should be *common prices* applying throughout the Community for all those products covered by the system; and second, that the Community should finance *support mechanisms*, which would guarantee that the incomes of farmers did not fall below a certain level. These principles soon became established as articles of faith, unchallengeable aspects of the 'acquis communautaire' but they have posed further headaches for the policy-making machinery. They have created the very opposite of a void; they have produced a terrifically complex structure, full of anomalies, and yet one which persists for fear of upsetting the whole structure of policy upon which the Community is based.

Both the 'compact of abstention' and the C.A.P. underline the general problem of resource distribution within the Community as compared to the member states. National governments are free to vary the way in which they generate resources and then distribute them: in accordance with their political persuasion, they can tax one or other sector within society more or less heavily, borrow more or less money and then concentrate their expenditure on defence, social services or whatever. The freedom enjoyed is certainly not absolute: past patterns of revenue collection and expenditure are an important constraint. Nevertheless, the room for manoeuvre is much more marked than in the Community, where the generation of resources and their distribution offers far less scope for political choice and where the policy structure is much more rigid. From the British point of view, the rigidity and lack of scope have proved particularly hard to accept.

To illustrate the difficulties that British negotiators have faced, it is useful to look at, in a little more detail, two particular controversies which have divided Britain very markedly from other members of the Community. The first of these is the argument over the British contribution towards the Community budget, an argument which revolves around the basis upon which the *financial* resources of the E.E.C. should be generated and distributed;[25] the second is the debate over the development of a common fisheries policy (C.F.P.), a debate which highlights the problem of establishing a system for access to and distributon of *natural* resources, which is regarded by the parties concerned as fair and equitable.[26] Both cases, in their different ways, point to important structural elements in the Community which have conflicted with British perceptions of interest; in both cases the stage was set for the clash of interests before Britain joined.

6. The budgetary problem

The budgetary problem revolves around the link between the way in which revenue is raised and revenue is spent in the Community. That link became firmly established in April 1970, when the governments of the six original member states established the system of 'own resources'. Before then the money to pay for Community policies was money that belonged to the national governments and which they contributed; after that date (though the system only took full effect on 1 January 1975) the money collected legally belonged to the Community, with the Community repaying 10 per cent of the total amount to cover the costs of collection. The sources of this revenue were clearly specified[27] in the 1970 decision and come from three sources: first, the customs duties imposed on all goods covered by the common external tariff, i.e. the tax applied to imports from outside the Community; second, the agricultural levies on foodstuffs coming from non-E.E.C. countries, calculated according to the difference between the world price and the Community price for those products; and third, a certain strictly limited proportion of the base rate of Value Added Tax collected in each member state.

There are two important features of this system of revenue collection: its automaticity in application and its restrictiveness in scope. It is automatic in the sense that the pattern of industrial and agricultural trade and the level of value added tax in each country alone determines how much each country pays without regard to any other factors: there is, for example, no effective limit to the percentage of the total contribution that any one country can provide. It is restrictive in the sense that there is no way in which the Community can generate extra resources without amending the decision taken in 1970. Effectively, therefore, only agreement amongst all the member states can create a situation whereby new policies can be financed, assuming that the pattern of expenditure on existing policies remains the same.

It is precisely these two features which have underlined the character of the budget problem for all British governments since the beginning of the 1970s. Thus Britain happens to have an economic structure which suffers under the automatic system established in 1970: the country continues to import agricultural and non-agricultural products from outside the E.E.C. on a scale larger than most other E.E.C. countries.

For a considerable time after accession, the difficulty was obscured because first, Britain obtained a five-year transitional period of adaptation to the 'own resources' system under the Treaty of Accession[28] and second, at the Dublin Summit meeting in 1975 the Prime Minister, Harold Wilson, gained agreement to a temporary corrective mechanism designed to prevent the contribution of any country exceeding its percentage value of the Gross National Product (G.N.P.) of the Community. However, in 1979, the newly elected Thatcher government drew attention to the effects of the 1970 arrangement, effects which the Prime Minister argued were extremely inequitable.

Mrs Thatcher pointed to the way in which Britain's percentage contribution to the budget had grown constantly since 1974 and by 1980 would have surpassed the percentage of her G.N.P. in the G.N.P. of the Community. Whereas in 1974, the budgetary contribution amounted to 10 per cent of the total and the national G.N.P. corresponded to 15.65 per cent of the Community G.N.P., in 1980 the value of the national G.N.P. would have increased only slightly to 16.70 per cent of the Community total, while the contribution to the budget would have doubled to 20.19 per cent. In the process the amount contributed under each of the three headings of the 'own resources' had increased markedly. By 1980 the value of customs duties would have almost doubled in the four years since 1977, reaching nearly 1,500 million units of account (or approximately £750m); the value of agricultural levies would have more than doubled in the same period to reach 405 million units of account (c. £200m); and the value of the V.A.T. contributions would have increased to over 1,200 million units of account (c. £600m). The importance of these figures emerges more forcefully when they are set against the pattern of expenditure. Here British governments have been faced with the well-known difficulty that more than 70 per cent of the Community budget has been consistently spent on agriculture. However, Britain is unable to benefit substantially from this expenditure. Only 2.7 per cent of the working population are engaged in agriculture (compared with 7.7 per cent in the Community as a whole) and the country remains a net agricultural importer. C.A.P. expenditure, by contrast, benefits countries, like France, that are net agricultural exporters and have a large proportion of their working population in agriculture.

Attempts to reduce this 70 per cent figure have been numerous but they have foundered on two points: first, the remarkably well-organized farming lobby in the Community has resisted any moves to change the character of the C.A.P. so that it ceases to be such a predominant feature of expenditure; and second, moves to expand other policy areas such as regional or social policy have come up against the limits of expenditure established in 1970. At a time when many governments, including the British one, have been trying to cut back government expenditure, the chances of increasing the overall amount of Community expenditure, which would require agreement of all states at national as well as Community level, seem very slight indeed.

The impact of this impasse can be seen when receipts and expenditure are compared to produce the net contribution of each country. In recent years, the pattern has been similar to that represented in the Commission's estimate of the situation for 1980 (see table 9).

Table 9 [29] (in £ millions)

Country	Pays	Receives	Balance	
Belgium	600	950	+	350
Denmark	240	425	+	185
West Germany	2,975	2,255	−	720
France	1,975	1,895	−	80
Ireland	90	375	+	285
Italy	1,340	1,705	+	565
Luxembourg	13	203	+	190
Holland	825	1,055	+	235
United Kingdom	2,023	1,015	−	1,008

In fact the level of Britain's budget deficit has varied over the last few years but it has consistently been an important net contributor along with West Germany. Equally consistently, all shades of political opinion have insisted that there should be a closer correspondence between payments and receipts, what has been called in French, 'juste retour'. The debate over this concept of a fair return has revealed how wide a gap there is between Britain's conception of the Community and its policies and that of Britain's partners in the E.E.C.. The partners argue against the 'fair return' on two levels: first, it is pointed out that the amount that Britain pays in could be reduced, if she concentrated her trade still further on the Community: the pattern of U.K. trade on this view is not a given towards which the Community alone is obliged to adapt itself; second, it is underlined that Britain did, after all, sign an agreement accepting the rules in force in the E.E.C. when she joined: to circumvent this agreement by appeal to a non-communautaire principle would be to undermine the whole fabric of the Community's legal order. Hence they have always insisted that any agreement to reduce the problem should be seen as an exceptional and temporary measure.

The British reply has been couched in terms of fairness. Is it fair that Britain with her weak economic position should be amongst the largest net contributors? Is there not an element of unfairness in appealing to Community principle when clear material interests in favour of the status quo underline those appeals? And is it not therefore important to find a fair and durable solution to the problem? To seek to arbitrate between these positons is a hazardous, not to say, impossible task: they derive from different starting-points and different interpretations of what the Community should look like. However, it is clear that the clash of opinions is one that has not helped to integrate Britain into the Community: it is a difference which has rankled, more or less openly, ever since Britain opened negotiations in 1970 and remains very much on the political agenda over a decade later.

7. The common fisheries policy

In a remarkably similar way, the fishing policy of the Community (C.F.P.) has provoked a continuing element of argument between Britain and her partners since 1970. As in the case of the budget, the structure of policy was decided before Britain joined and it is the character of the structure which has been at the centre of the debate ever since. As in the case of the budget, also, the debate has revolved around the criteria which should be used to determine the distribution of resources – in this case, natural rather than financial – and the extent to which 'extenuating circumstances' can dilute or direct the main thrust of a Community policy.

On 30 June 1970, the day before negotiations began with the candidate countries, the original six agreed to the basic principle which should govern the conditions under which E.E.C. fishermen could fish in the waters of other E.E.C. states. That principle was one of 'equality of access' for all Community vessels in the waters of all Community countries. The relevant regulation expressed the principle as follows:

> The system applied by each Member State in respect of fishing in the maritime waters coming under its sovereignty or within its jurisdiction must not lead to differences in treatment with regard to other Member States.
>
> In particular, Member States shall ensure equal conditions of access to and exploitation of the fishing grounds situated in the waters referred to in the previous paragraph for all fishing vessels flying the flag of a Member State and registered in the Community territory.[30]

The difficulty posed by this principle was and remains that fish are not distributed equally around the coasts of the Community and that therefore the granting of equal access threatens to upset the pattern of fishing established under a system where national governments can determine the terms of access to national waters. At the time of the accession negotiations, the problems were most obvious in the case of Norway, a country whose fishermen caught 95 per cent of their catch within Norwegian waters and where the volume of the catch totalled half as much again as the catch of that of all the original Six put together. These basic facts were undoubtedly influential in bringing about a 'No' vote in the referendum held in Norway in the autumn of 1972: 'equal access' looked likely to bring about too severe and disadvantageous a change in the distribution of this natural resource.

In Britain, the situation was less clear-cut at the time because of the division in the industry between the inshore and the deep-sea fishermen. The former made a considerable noise at the time of accession negotiations, because the bulk of their catch came from within the 12-mile zone off British coasts which would be opened up by the 'equal access' principle; the latter, by contrast, had little reason to complain as they went to fish off the coasts of the Soviet Union, Norway, Iceland, Greenland and Canada, far from the reach of E.E.C. regulations. Furthermore, the deep-sea part of the industry was thriving: in Hull, for example, the catches of the early 1970s were the largest ever recorded. When, in addition, it is remembered that the deep-sea industry, organized on the basis of shore-based companies, has generally exercised more political influence than the scattered individual owners of the inshore industry, it is possible to understand why the fishing issue, despite being the last point of dispute to be settled in December 1971, failed to prevent Britain entering the Community, as it had done in the case of Norway.

What Britain got the Community to agree to was a temporary derogation from the existing rules – the same basic principle as that applied in the budget negotiations – whereby until 31 December 1982, Britain would be able to have an exclusive six-mile limit, with the area between six and twelve miles reserved for vessels from other states that had historically fished there.[31] In other words, the principle of equal access was left intact and the awkward decision as to what to do after the derogation expired was put far into the future.

However, in the intervening period, the environment for the industry did not remain fixed: in particular, the internationally accepted rules guaranteeing effective 'open access' to all waters outside a narrow band around coastal states effectively collapsed. In the course of negotiations at the third United Nations Law of the Sea Conference (UNCLOS III), a consensus began to emerge around the notion of an Exclusive Economic Zone (E.E.Z.), extending up to 200 miles from the shores of coastal states, whose governments would have the right to determine the terms of access to resources in the sea and on the seabed. The consequences for the British industry were unfortunate in two important respects. First of all, the deep-sea industry now found itself effectively excluded from its traditional fishing grounds, as countries like Iceland claimed the right to exercise control over access to fish in waters up to 200 miles from their coasts. Second, Britain was not able to compensate for the loss by claiming undisputed sovereignty over the seas up to 200 miles from her coasts: she was obliged to accept the need to establish a shared responsibility with the Community for those waters and could not hope to persuade her partners of her right to exclude other E.E.C. vessels from waters outside the U.K. twelve-mile limit, despite the pressure of the industry for as much as a 100-mile zone.

As in the case of the budget dispute, the importance of such extenuating circumstances becomes critical in the context of concrete discussions about resource distribution. Thus if one considers the area covered by the 200-mile zone of the member states, to what percentage of the fish to be found in that zone should each member state have a right? In the course of 1980 the Commission produced figures for the average catch per country in the Community zone between 1973 and 1978 along with a proposal, presented in October, as to what each state should be entitled to catch in the zone in 1981 (see table 10).

Table 10 [32]

	Historical catch (tonnes)	October '80' proposal (tonnes)
Belgium	24,644	21,001
Denmark	316,295	294,991
Iceland	15,278	32,890
France	144,041	120,783
Netherlands	89,985	85,026
Germany	124,623	125,070
United Kingdom	273,479	309,034
Total	988,345	988,795

The October proposal offered to Britain 31.25 per cent of the total catch but was considered unsatisfactory by British negotiators for two reasons: first, it was argued that account needed to be taken of the fact that within the E.E.C. 200 mile zone, Britan contributed 56 per cent of the surface area and 60 per cent of the resources to be found in it, and second, it was claimed that Britain had lost 40 per cent of her total catch through loss of access to third country waters and that this, too, needed to be reflected in the allocation of quotas. This line of reasoning derives from a belief that Britain's possession of more fish within her waters entitles her, for that very reason, to a higher quota. However, if the original idea of the C.F.P. of 'equal access' is applied, then by itself ownership of more fish is not an argument in favour of an increased quota, particularly when the overall level of catch is not increasing and when Britain's own demands can only be met by a decrease in the catch of other countries. Once again, it is not a question of arguing that the British case is right or wrong but rather one of recognizing that British policy-makers have consistently felt that the criteria used in establishing and developing a policy have run contrary to important British interests.

8. Whither Britain and the E.E.C.?

It has been suggested that Britain's reluctance over membership of the Community can be traced to two forces: first, an inability to come to terms with the character of the Community institutions and in particular, to an adaptation of the doctrine of the 'sovereignty of Parliament' to the circumstances of membership; second, a feeling that the shape of the 'acquis communautaire' and the policies that embody it conflicts with certain important British interests and presents severe obstacles to change.

However, it remains to ask whether these two areas of difficulty are permanent features of the political landscape. Are the disputes that have marked the first decade of British membership of the Community likely to persist for the next decade, assuming that Britain remains a member? Or will those disputes come to be seen as the protracted but unavoidable consequences of a country like Britain, with its particular traditions and structures, joining as unusual an entity as the Community?

There can be no straightforward answer to these questions: rather any answer must be based on the observer's assessment of the relative strengths of the forces for continuity and change in British politics. These forces should be viewed not simply in quantitative terms, i.e. the number and distribution of ministers, members of Parliament or citizens favouring staying in the E.E.C. or withdrawing, but also qualitatively in terms of the power of competing attitudes towards the Community. In particular, it is necessary to seek to evaluate the depth of diverse feelings about the possibility and desirability of convergence between Britain and her continental neighbours.

For those who oppose membership, there are three important strands of thought in Britain which are available to support their case (or which could be said to underlie their case). The first of these is the belief that Britain is in the Community but not of the Community, that is to say, that Britain remains psychologically as well as geographically separate from the rest of the E.E.C. There is little doubt that this belief is widespread even amongst those who formally support British membership. Thus Gaston Thorn commented, on assuming office as President of the Commission in January 1981, that he was very struck by the way that British ministers in the Council of whatever political persuasion would regularly address their colleagues as 'you in the Community' and rather rarely as 'we in the Community'.[33] He was clearly alluding to the feeling of separateness, which finds an echo in calls for a looser connection between Britain and the E.E.C.

The second strand is related to the first in that it argues from separateness to superiority. Thus allegiance to the concept of the sovereignty of Parliament is based on a long historical tradition which has generated a considerable feeling of pride. Not only that, it has also generated unfavourable comparisons of continental arrangements with those in Britain. As the *New Statesman* pointed out in its leading article produced before the referendum,[34] many of those opposed to membership argued (and still do) that the other members of the E.E.C. are 'more used to abandoning their political institutions', i.e. to the loss of sovereignty, as a result of invasions that they have had to submit to: Britain's institutions are therefore seen as enjoying the qualities that time alone can impart.

The third strand combines oddly with the second in that confidence in native institutions is matched by a considerable lack of confidence in the ability of Britain to alter the shape of Community policies. Throughout the years of British membership there has been constant stress on the imbalance in the shape of the 'acquis communautaire' but the fight to alter it has been marked by a much lower level of skill or success.[35] British negotiators have had considerable difficulty in coming to terms with the rules of the Community game with the result that opponents of membership are able to underline the rigidity and therefore unsuitability for Britain of the Community structure.

All these three elements are ones that have persisted throughout the years of membership: they represent the forces for continuity in spite of British membership, and therefore conflict with that membership, whether or not those who hold such beliefs favour withdrawal or not. At the same time, there are forces for change because of British membership, which tend to form the currency of supporters of membership and which are seen as guaranteeing the long-term future of Britain in the Community. Again they revolve around three basic beliefs.

The first is the pragmatic belief that no other arrangements with the Community are either viable or sensible, that there is no longer any alternative. It evokes a plea for realism, often directed at the Labour party to persuade it to reconcile itself to membership. As one writer has put it, 'the E.E.C. is there, its decisions will affect us whether we like it or not and there is no alternative role which the U.K. can play. It is therefore necessary to make the best of a difficult position, something which, after a century of dominance, is not easy.'[36] In other words, differences like those discussed in this chapter will remain but they have got to be put up with: Britain has got to adapt.

The second belief is that, in fact, the differences between Britain and the rest of the Community are narrowing and will continue to narrow over time, reducing conflicts of interest. It is often revealed in economic analysis which points to the changing pattern of British trade. Thus whereas in 1973, 32 per cent of total U.K. trade was with the other eight members of the E.E.C., by 1980 the figure had risen to over 40 per cent. The result was to cut the proportion of goods subject to the common external tariff, coming from the world market, and hence, by this argument, to integrate Britain more firmly within the Community.[37]

The final belief is one that looks to the Community in idealistic terms as offering opportunities which are simply not available at the national level. Despite the problems that the Community faces, the belief is one that continues to exercise a degree of influence in Britain. Thus Shirley Williams writes of how the E.E.C. could develop the idea contained in the Brandt report on North-South relations of allocating a percentage of G.N.P. for the purposes of multilateral aid. Such an idea she sees as:

> a first step away from the concept of charity towards the concept of justice. . .
> No single European country, with the possible exception of Germany could hope to get any such scheme off the ground – but the Community could.[38]

All three of these beliefs constitute pressure for change, for adaptation by Britain towards the Community. By contrast, the three earlier beliefs discussed serve to hold back that adaptation, to encourage the possibility that Britain could yet withdraw. And it will be the outcome of the conflict between these beliefs that will determine the long-term future of the relationship between Britain and Europe.

To predict now that one or other set of beliefs will prevail is an impossible task but it is possible to point to the basic issue that needs to be resolved. That issue involves determining how the underlying character of the Community is to be perceived from Britain; what kind of an institution does it constitute? The two answers that can be given to this question were identified already in 1973 by Simon Z. Young in his summary of the fisheries negotiations before Britain became a member:

If the Community is seen as basically a common enterprise of states in pursuit of a recognizable common interest, which Britain shares, then this outweighs the sacrifices involved in the inevitable give-and-take of Community membership. But if this common interest is regarded as illusory or as better pursued by a looser form of inter-state collaboration than those required by Community membership, then the fisheries agreement . . . must be judged as opening the way to sacrifices of British interest which it may indeed prove possible to keep to a moderate degree but which are essentially unnecessary and not worth while in the first place.[39]

Ten years later British opinion remains very divided as to whether there is a 'recognizable common interest' or not. Until such time as the division becomes less deep on this core issue, the question of British membership of the Community will remain very much on the political agenda.

NOTES

1. Commission des Communautés Européennes (1981), *Euro-baromètre – l'opinion publique dans la Communauté Européenne*, no.15, juin, tableau no.14, 33.
2. For a recent discussion of the character and powers of the institutions, see S.Henig, *Power and Decision in Europe: The Political Institutions of the European Community* (1980).
3. A.Shonfield, *Europe: Journey to an Unknown Destination* (1972), 9.
4. J.D.B.Mitchell, 'The sovereignty of Parliament and Community law: the stumbling-Block that isn't there', in *International Affairs*, LV, 1 (1979), 37.
5. Mitchell, *ibid.*, argues that there is no *legal* conflict between the two, which has not been faced and solved in other E.E.C. countries.
6. Van Gend en Loos v. Netherlands Tax Administration IX Rec. (1963), *Common Market Law Review*, 105; for a fuller discussion of this case and Community law in general, see J.Mitchell (1974) 'European Law and National Law', in *The European Economic Community: National and International Impact*, Open University Press (1974), 40–58.
7. Quoted in Mitchell (1979), *op.cit.*, 33.
8. Quoted in Hansard Society, *The British People: Their Voice in Europe*, 1979, 27. The issue of Parliament's response to the E.E.C. is also discussed in D.Coombes, 'Parliament and the European Community', and in *The Commons Today*, ed. S.A.Walkland and M.Ryle (1981), 237–59.
9. Hansard Society *op.cit.*, 28–9.
10. D.Coombes, *op.cit.*, 245.
11. Unless, as in Denmark, there is a system whereby a powerful select

committee can instruct individual ministers as to the extent to which they can compromise in negotiations. If faced with new proposals in Brussels, they are obliged to consult the chairman of the committee before reaching agreement.

12. Treaty Establishing a Single Council and a Single Commission of the European Communities (Merger Treaty), Article 10.
13. Official Journal C73, 2.4.1981, 37 – an answer to written question no. 1848/80 by Lord O'Hagan.
14. *The Times*, 13 May 1975.
15. H.M.S.O. (1975), *Membership of the European Community: Report on renegotiation*, Cmnd. 6003, para. 108.
16. For a discussion of this issue see P.Taylor, 'The European Community and the obligations of membership: claims and counter-claims' in *International Affairs*, LVII, no.2, 236–53.
17. See, for example, Bulletin of the European Communities, Supplement 3/81, for the fifth in this series of reports.
18. H.M.S.O. (1975), *op.cit.*, para.130.
19. S.Holt, 'Policy-making in practice – the 1965 crisis' in J.Barber and B.Reed, *European Community: Vision and Reality* (1973).
20. S.Holland, *Uncommon Market* (1980), 7.
21. W.Wallace (ed.), *Britain in Europe* (1980), 7 – the book contains much material relevant to the concerns of this chapter.
22. See, for example, H.M.S.O. (1971), 'The United Kingdom and the European Communities' Cmnd 4715, paras.44–56 in Barber, and Reed, *op.cit.*, 255–60.
23. Shonfield, *op.cit.*, 11.
24. For example, D.Marquand, *Parliament for Europe* (1979), 15 ff.
25. For a further discussion of this isssue, see H.Wallace, *Budgetary Politics: The Finances of the European Communities* (1980): and the chapters by Godley and Brown in Wallace, *op.cit.*
26. For a further discussion of this policy, see the author's chapter on 'The Common Fisheries Policy' in W.Wallace, H.Wallace, and C.Webb, *Policy-Making in the European Communities* (1983).
27. See decision of 21 April 1970 on the remplacement of financial contributions from member states by the Communities' own re-sources.
28. See Articles 130 and 131 of the Treaty of Accession.
29. Quoted in the *Sunday Times* of 25 Nov. 1979.
30. Article 2(1) of Regulation 2141/70 establishing a 'common structural policy for the fishing industry', Official J., XIII, no.L 236, 27 Oct. 1970, 1.
31. See Article 110–112 of ch.3 of the Treaty of Accession.
32. Agra Europe Eurofish Report no.89, 15 Oct. 1980.
33. Quoted in *the Guardian*, 18 Dec. 1980.
34. *New Statesman*, 30 May 1975, 'The case for yes'.
35. Wallace, *op.cit.*, 5 ff.
36. D.S.Bell (ed.), *Labour into the Eighties* (1980), 5.

37. 'L'arrimage brittanique' in *30 jours d'Europe*, juillet-août 1981, 19.
38. S.Williams, *Politics is for People* (1981), 200.
39. S.Z.Young, *Terms of Entry* (1973), 102.

9 BRITISH FOREIGN POLICY: TRADITION AND CHANGE

J.E.Spence

'Why, sometimes I've believed as many as six impossible things before breakfast.'
Through the Looking-Glass

1. The pragmatic tradition: virtues and vices

MOST commentators on the wavering course of British foreign policy since the war agree on one proposition: too much has been attempted with too few resources, largely because successive governments have failed to recognize the true nature of Britain's decline from the status of a power of the first rank and have correspondingly neglected to make the fundamental adaptations in interest and commitment that such a recognition entails. The academic literature on the subject has spawned titles which are in themselves an eloquent testimony to this theme: *Descent from Power, Imperial Sunset, The Collapse of British Power, The Long Recessional*, etc.,[1] and it is rare to find such unanimity on a topic of scholarly concern. As one recent writer has put it, 'there are only two super powers in the world, and Britain is not one of them. To Americans, this will seem a statement of the obvious. To many British people, it sums up their decline in national status.'[2] These words, written in 1981 a year before that extraordinary – some would say aberrant – manifestation of British power in the Falklands crisis, imply that the British have, in fact, come to terms with decline. Why, then, has this recognition taken so long? What incentives and constraints have governed the formulation and conduct of British foreign policy during the post-war period?

The contemporary analyst has of course the twin advantages of hindsight and detachment from the press of day-to-day politics. Inevitably, retrospective judgments about a country's foreign policy or any other aspect of its political life derive from a natural and quite proper desire for some explanation, some pattern that can be imposed on what at the time may have seemed to be a welter of unrelated events, 'one emergency following upon another'.[3] And yet H. A. L. Fisher's phrase might well earn the wry consent of the decision-maker as he grabbles with the flood of telegrams, the pressures of time and energy, the 'play of the contingent and the unforeseen'.[4] It serves, too, as a timely warning to the analyst who might otherwise be tempted to offer an explanation which credits politicians with skills and a degree of control they cannot – given the intractable nature of the international environment – possess. Further, we must avoid criticizing politicians for not behaving in a manner consistent with some abstract, rational calculation of what should constitute the national interest over the long term. As Hedley Bull has remarked with respect to the great issues of peace and war (and his words apply, less dramatically, to the humdrum world of everyday diplomacy):

> The decisions of governments on matters of peace and war . . . do not always reflect a careful weighing of long-range considerations, or a mastery of the course of events: the questions which strike the historian of these decisions a generation afterwards as important appear crudely answered or, more often, not even asked: the governments appear to him to stumble about, groping and half-blind, too preoccupied with surviving from day to day even to perceive the direction in which they are heading, let alone steer away from it.[5]

It is too easy to forget that politicians have to cope with an international environment where power and influence is unequally distributed between independent units, the individual (and at times collective) reactions of which are more difficult to predict, far less control than the aspirations and demands emanating from the relative calm and consensus of a domestic political order. 'The enterprise is to keep afloat on an even keel . . . [for] . . . there is neither harbour for shelter nor floor for anchorage, neither starting place nor appointed destination.'[6] This assumption, it could be argued, has governed the thinking of generations of British foreign policy-makers although it may, given its status as an inarticulate major premise, appear to downgrade too severely the role and importance of more self-conscious ideologies such as 'imperial status', 'world role', 'European partnership' or 'Atlantic Community'. Oakeshott's metaphor (admittedly wrenched out of context) does, however, alert us to the deeply ingrained empiricism so characteristic of the British approach to the external world.

Yet for many analysts empiricism is not enough. Kenneth Waltz's definition of the concept and his trenchant criticism of its application in practice effectively summarizes a dominant theme of much of the post-war critique of British foreign policy:

> The empiric leans on precedent, carefully digests past experience, and cautiously takes one step at a time. This may or may not be a good way of proceeding; it is surely a conservative way. How serviceable it is will depend on the problem at hand and the conditions that prevail . . . The effect of proceeding empirically is to suppress assumptions without eliminating them and to focus upon means without relating them adequately to military and political conditions, economic capability, and changes in technology.[7]

Implicit in this argument is the further assumption that a concentration upon 'means' has led to a neglect of the 'ends' of policy as defined over the long term. Yet as Waltz himself points out (with a touch of exasperation), 'As Britain has declined in the world, Englishmen have devoted more and more attention to defining her role. The more definitions one reads, the harder it becomes to understand just what the role is supposed to be.'[8] Certainly the academic literature,[9] the pages of Hansard and the speeches of foreign statesmen[10] are littered with references to Britain's inability to find such a role as well as suggestions of what it might be. John Strachey's remarks in 1953 provide a good example:

> We must concentrate. We must stop stationing all our available forces – land forces, at any rate – all over the world . . . what this means is a radical revision of the tradition of our world defence

policy. It means ceasing to try to behave as if we are still the leading world empire. From the date . . . of India's assumption of independence a reorientation of our whole attitude was absolutely necessary.[11]

But given the strength of the empirical tradition in the making of British foreign policy, it is hardly surprising that the argument about role was largely rhetorical. Whether in power or in opposition, both the major political parties have had little alternative but to adapt as best their leaders could to events largely outside their immediate and direct control. No sooner was a role defined than domestic economic circumstances or external pressures appeared to undermine it. This in part both explains and justifies the high degree of bipartisanship characteristic of British foreign policy during the post-war period. As the cold war gathered pace in the late 1940s, the Labour government, under the direction of Attlee and Bevin, quickly abandoned any hope that Left could more fittingly speak unto Left and instead followed policies with respect to the United States and the Soviet Union that its Conservative successors could accept and build upon without hesitation. Similarly, the Labour party in the 1950s shared with the Conservative government of the day an enthusiasm for the Commonwealth as a 'third force' capable of acting as a bridge between East and West until division appeared between and within the two parties over the merits of entry into Europe and its effects on the Commonwealth in the early 1960s.[12]

Thus a combination of internal and external pressures forced a common perception of British interest on the leadership of both political parties: for the Labour party, except for a minority on the extreme Left, this meant an abandonment of any attempt to define a role for Britain in terms of a specifically 'socialist' foreign policy as the inter-war ideals of collective security, faith in international organization and disarmament gave way to a recognition of the balance of power and the role that alliances and weapon systems must inevitably play as the price of security, however precarious, in a hostile world. Similarly, despite some kicking and screaming from the Right wing of the party and blind alleys such as Cyprus, Suez and Aden, the Conservative acceptance and acceleration of the decolonization process (especially during the partnership of Harold Macmillan and Ian Macleod in the 1958–60 period), following the precedent of Indian independence set in 1947 by their Labour pre-decessors, is a striking example of bipartisanship in external affairs.

What is forgotten by academic critics who lament Britain's failure to define a clear and precise role in foreign affairs, is that states are not 'actors' on some notional stage, speaking well-rehearsed lines, making their moves, exits and entrances with impeccable timing and flair. The term may have some limited value as a description of a state's performance in, say, the 'theatre' presented by a dramatic debate in the United Nations,[13] or more sensibly, as a metaphor describing the behaviour of protagonists in a crisis which, like the plot of a well-constructed play, often appears in retrospect to have a prelude, a *dénouement* and some ultimate resolution, often tragic. Yet the term remains seriously misleading in the realm of foreign policy analysis: it assumes that a role once defined can be self-sustaining, impervious to erosion by time and circumstance, that a state can 'plough a lone furrow in pursuit of its particular interests'.[14]

This criticism applies equally to those politicians who pleaded for a re-definition of Britain's role and those who persisted in believing that a world role was still possible, albeit on slightly reduced terms. For John Strachey, as we have already noted, a new role meant 'ceasing to try to behave as if we are still the leading world empire'.[15] But this advice was as much rhetorical as Harold Wilson's assertion in November 1964 that 'we are a world power and a world influence, or we are nothing'.[16] Strachey's arguments and those who echoed its sentiments in the 1950s and 1960s seemed at first sight sensible enough: recognize that Empire was an illusion and find a less demanding role for Britain. But this assumed that the Imperial slate could be wiped clean and a new start made rather like – to continue the theatrical metaphor – a stage manager who clears the set before embarking on a new production. What critics ignored was that decolonization was not a process that could be concluded within a short time span. In fact it took over 25 years before the task of withdrawal from Empire finally was done. As we shall argue later, the process – precisely because it was relatively slow as compared with the French experience – brought certain advantages. Costs there were, too, not least the fact that the transformation of Empire into Commonwealth, in itself a major and fundamental adaptation to reduced economic and political circumstances, hindered adaptation in other spheres of interest precisely because the process was not smooth and straightforward, but slow and subject to violent fits and starts, in the Middle East and South East Asia in particular.

It is the haphazard nature of the process that critics fix on when they stress the failure of Britain to find a new, more viable role. No doubt it would have been easier to do so had politicians of both parties been willing and able to admit publicly that the work of decolonization was essentially a negative exercise, a 'clearing of the decks', a necessary prelude to the definition of a new and different role. But the formulation of foreign policy is rarely that easy and straightforward; a candid admission that the Empire was finished, that the emergent Commonwealth had no political or economic substance, no significant contribution to make to sustaining Britain's role in the world, was impossible while the process of decolonization continued its long-drawn-out course. Instead, the illusion of a new 'role' was needed to soften the blow to national pride that loss of Empire inevitably represented and speech after speech by successive British Prime Ministers and Foreign Secretaries extolled the value of the Commonwealth as an effective substitute for what had gone before. In 1955, for example, we find Anthony Eden claiming that 'the British Commonwealth and Empire is the greatest force for peace and progress in the world today'.[17] Seven years later Denis Healey, then in Opposition, argued that 'we have to restore the faith of our friends in Asia, Africa, Australia and New Zealand in our ability in this country to make the Commonwealth the nervous system, the spinal column, of a new world order'.[18] Then again, Sir Alec Douglas-Home speaking in the House of Commons in 1964 asserted that 'if people are searching for a new role for Britain, this is it'.[19] And as late as 1975 James Callaghan reiterated this theme, asserting that 'we have country by country connections throughout the world. We have the experience . . . *we have the policy* which can enable Britain to make a contribution out of all proportion to our individual size and power to the problems facing the world . . . we may have found [our] role. . . We are the bridge builders.'[20]

Why has there been this traditional obsession with 'role playing'? Was the emphasis on the Commonwealth, for example, simply rationalization of declining status, 'a natural inclination of the weak to define influence in terms of moral force, for they have little of any other kind'?[21] This is a plausible argument and one not inconsistent with Christopher Hill's view that the 'quest for a unique role, like the pursuit of the Holy Grail, is a fatal distraction to politicians with responsibilities . . . [that] . . . roles are package-deals of ideas which not only suppress contradictions and simplifications in the interests of a central, predominant concept, but also exclude phenomena not caught in their particular net.'[22] This is a perceptive comment on the attempt in the 1950s and 1960s to breathe life into the multi-racial

Commonwealth as a major vehicle for a new and vigorous role for Britain in world affairs. Some, however, go further and argue that it was not so much the practical difficulty involved in trying to elaborate a single well-defined role for Britain (in substance rather than at the level of rhetoric) that inevitably complicated policy-making, but rather the confusion of roles that resulted from trying to maintain the Commonwealth connection, the 'special relationship' with the United States and a variety of links with Europe. In other words it was the attempt to operate a foreign policy within the so-called 'three circles' of interest which inhibited Britain from rationalizing its interests and commitments in some order of priority. This is a persuasive claim but not persuasive enough. It leaves out of account – as we shall later argue – the exigencies of the time, the presssure of circumstance and, in particular, Britain's unique position during the first post-war decade. Britain's foreign policy was set in a mould compounded of past practice and traditional ideas which proved extremely difficult to break in later years.

But it may be that some fundamental modification of a state's interests and their incorporation into a new, less demanding role is only possible after some traumatic experience profoundly altering the nation's outlook and expectations. French policy after 1958 is often cited as an example. General de Gaulle's attempt to make France the leader of *Europe des Patries* and the latter a putative great power, following the domestic agonies of colonial war in South East Asia and Algeria, reveals – it is claimed – a statesman single-mindedly wrenching his countrymen from an out-moded colonial role into a new appreciation of their state's destiny. Yet the notion that France divested itself of its colonial incubus in favour of a new and purposeful European role is a half-truth at best. Roles of this kind are elusive creatures even for the most far-sighted states-man. France has, in fact, retained a major neo-colonial presence in most of its former colonies, while de Gaulle's attempt to project his country as an independent agency of national liberation from the Atlantic to the Urals (even unto Quebec!) was quickly abandoned by successors who expressed their nationalistic impulses much closer to home. Britain in the same period underwent no similar traumatic experience, unless we so regard the Suez crisis of 1956 and Harold Macmillan's decision to apply for entry into Europe in the later years of the decade. But even here, as we shall argue presently, old roles co-existed with attempts to find new ones – a point not lost on a French government quick to capitalize on what seemed to be a confusion of objectives and long-term commitment.

These general observations on the scope and substance of British foreign policy in the post-war period are offered by way of preliminary to more detailed analysis of the way in which Britain has coped with particular issues. The emphasis so far has been placed on the empirical strain in the British conduct of foreign affairs, the tendency towards bipartisanship and finally by what in retrospect appears to have been a mistaken faith in the benefits of role definition. This may seem a harsh judgment and it deserves qualification insofar as the widespread belief in the new Commonwealth as a substitute for Empire, while creating problems of a very different kind, nevertheless served to cushion the shock of imperial decline. The burden of the argument that follows is that the political, economic and psychological constraints on policy-makers nearly always outweighed whatever incentive there was to break free from the past, and it is this factor above all which induces caution in any judgment made with the 'irresponsible' advantage of hindsight.

2. The three circles

Winston Churchill's famous definition of the aspirations of British foreign policy makes a useful starting-point for analysis of the major themes that have dominated conduct of external affairs in the post-war period. Speaking at the 1948 Conservative party conference he said:

> As I look upon the future of our country in the changing scene of human destiny I feel the existence of three great circles among the free nations and democracies . . . the first circle for us is naturally the British Commonwealth and Empire . . . Then there is also the English-speaking world in which we, Canada, and the other British Dominions play so important a part. And finally there is United Europe. These three majestic circles are co-existent and if they are linked together there is no force or combination which could overthrow them or ever challenge them. Now if you think of the three interlinked circles you will see that we are the only country which has a great part in every one of them. We stand, in fact, at the very point of junction, and here in this Island at the centre of the seaways and perhaps of the airways also we have the opportunity of joining them all together.[23]

Yet even as he spoke, economic circumstances, the policy of the

Labour government, and the pace of events abroad were busy undermining the validity of his vision. The decision to grant independence to India, Pakistan, Ceylon and Burma in 1947 had removed at a stroke the strategic asset of the Indian army and set a precedent which at the time few acknowledged, but was ultimately to prove irresistible for the pace and scope of decolonization elsewhere and especially on the African continent. The new multi-racial Commonwealth of the 1950s and 1960s was to prove a frail vessel for the expression of British power and even those Dominions which had shared a common economic and strategic interest with Britain in the inter-war period had long since gravitated to the United States for the provision of their security.[24]

With regard to the second 'great circle', that relating to the United States, the Labour government could claim that its policy between 1945 and 1951 had succeeded in 'joining them altogether' at least insofar as Europe and the United States were concerned. Yet success here was paradoxically a result of relative weakness rather than the exercise of independent action by a great power. It is true that Ernest Bevin, the Labour Foreign Secretary, had played a crucial role in persuading the Truman administration to abandon its short-lived desire to retreat from the burdens of super-power status. But the two circles of Europe and North America intersected in a way which demonstrated Britain's inability to play the role of the great power of former years. By promoting and participating in the Brussels Treaty of 1948,[25] Bevin was in effect acknowledging that Britain could no longer play its traditional role of 'balancer', standing aloof from Europe until it was time to redress an unfavourable balance by throwing its weight on to the side of the weaker coalition. Hence Britain was committed in advance to a particular group of allies and the edifice was complete with the incorporation of the United States and Canada into the wider alliance of the North Atlantic Treaty Organisation in 1949.

British diplomacy in these early post-war years could not easily be faulted. Its government was the first to recognize that the war-time co-operation of the 'Big Three'[26] could not long survive the peace. Its achievement in persuading the Western democracies of the need to react vigorously to the brutal manifestation of Soviet power in Eastern Europe demonstrated conclusively that the lessons of appeasement in the 1930s had been well learnt. The fact that Britain had felt obliged in 1947 to ask the United States to take over its traditional responsibilities in Greece and Turkey and underwrite the economic recovery of Europe through the provision of Marshall Aid was an admission that Britain could no longer act independently without the support of its more powerful American ally. Thus Churchill and others might claim the advantage of a 'special relationship' with the United States, but it was hardly a relationship of equals and in the crucial area of atomic weapon development did not exist at all following the passing of the McMahon Act by Congress in 1946. Its true significance arose from the circumstances of the immediate post-war period: Britain alone among the major European allies had emerged from the war as an unoccupied power but without the economic resources to rebuild the shattered economies of Western Europe. But it did have a sufficient reserve of diplomatic and political skill to enable its government to take the lead in the task of winning a massive American commitment to the maintenance of Western European security.

But this innovative role implied a demanding corollary: as the one stable European ally to emerge relatively unscathed from the trauma of war, and one with considerable interests and commitments scattered across the globe, there was a clear obligation to help the United States maintain order whenever and wherever Western interests were threatened outside the strictly European parameters of NATO. And rearmament began in earnest in 1950 on the outbreak of the Korean war on the assumption that NATO had to be still further strengthened if Russian-sponsored aggression in the Far East was not to spread to Western Europe. Thus, the 'special relationship', a product of intimate war-time collaboration, seemed to British politicians a natural and essential link that need not be discarded in favour of an exclusively European role.

The Attlee government has often been accused of throwing away the chance of establishing Britain as a European power first and foremost. Instead – so the argument runs – it attempted to maintain a fading imperial role and a privileged position *vis-à-vis* the United States. Europe – according to this view – was the only 'circle' that mattered in the long run and the opportunity was squandered because of the illusion of a world role. Thus Peter Calvocoressi has argued that 'the intellectual and emotional resources which had gone into thinking about world affairs – whether about running the Empire or getting rid of it – could have been switched to thinking about Europe's affairs and to deciding a role for Britain in Europe'.[27] What this criticism ignores, however, is that foreign policy-making is not an exact science, capable of devising neat, 'rational' solutions based on some obvious set of costs/benefit criteria and immediately applicable in the short term. 'Getting rid' of an Empire was bound to take time, given a 'habit of mind' which not unreasonably believed well into the 1950s that a colonial territory had to demonstrate a degree of economic and political viability before independence could be granted.[28] And colonial ideology was supported in the 1950s by economic interdependence: between 1950 and 1954, 49 per cent of British imports came from the Empire/Commonwealth while the latter took 54 per cent of British exports.[29]

Yet another 'habit of mind' with its roots deep in the empirical tradition was the wide-spread hostility, shared by both Labour and Conservative politicians, to theories of European integration involving a commitment to supra-national institutions. These had been developed in Europe as an alternative to the traditional pattern of state behaviour which – it was claimed – had led to the carnage and bloodshed of two world wars. As such these theories derived from a different historical experience, a key element of which had been Franco-German enmity over many decades, and their application in the structure of the European Coal and Steel community (established in 1950) was designed to remove the 'sinews of war' from exclusively national control. Thus statements such as 'if European integration is to make fresh advances it must become a reality both in practice and in the will of the individual'[30] had an unwelcome and un-British Hegelian ring about them deeply at odds with the British commitment to the notion of state sovereignty and national independence.

Thus, as Waltz remarks, 'to lead Europe, from her reduced position of power, Britain would have had to abandon British ideas and alter British commitments in order to become herself more European'.[31] This strategy was in practice not a valid option, however appealing in theory both at the time and in retrospect.

Thus stripped of its rhetorical overtones, Churchill's definition of the three circles of British interest was in effect an assertion of the British claim to exercise influence on a global scale, despite or rather because of the poverty of its power and resource base. Influence was, therefore, regarded as a substitute for power, but the distinction was rarely clear to the electorate, and successive governments latched on to the term as one providing substance for a new 'role' in world affairs. What *was* clear was the extent of Britain's economic weakness and the major constraint this imposed on foreign policy, whether defined in the traditional terms of independence, power and self-assertiveness, or those implying a capacity to deal with the three circles of interest as areas in which an influence at least could be cultivated. Consider the position in 1945: some 11½ million tons of merchant shipping had been sunk by enemy action, the stock of housing and industrial plant had been battered by Nazi air attacks and little had been done to replace obsolete manufacturing plant. As Kennedy points out 'about 10 per cent of Britain's pre-war national wealth had been destroyed at home . . . overseas debts had increased nearly fivefold, to £3,355 million, and capital assets worth £1,299 million had been liquidated . . . In all, Britain had lost about one quarter (£7,300 million) of its pre-war wealth.' His conclusion, if sombre, is telling: '[Economic] difficulties have overshadowed, ominously, continually, restrictively almost every consideration of the country's external role and have thus been the greatest influence of all in its decline as a major power.'[32]

The erosive effect of economic weakness was truly exposed in the 1950s and 1960s, a period of repeated sterling crisis and continual pressure on the balance of payments. It was in this period that the three circles of influence, far from displaying a harmony of purpose (however compelling as parameters because of past practice and inescapable current commitments), began to rub discordantly together to produce inconsistency in policy and a string of dilemmas never satisfactorily resolved.

Waltz has argued that 'the one clear peacetime case in this century of policy not muddled into and made simply in reaction to events was the firm decision to withdraw from India and to hasten the conversion of Empire to Commonwealth'.[33] This judgment neglects the empirical strain in British foreign policy-making after 1945 to which Waltz – as we noted earlier – rightly draws attention. It ignores the fact that in practice the process of decolonization was 'responsive rather than anticipatory'.[34]

British policy-makers were subject to contradictory pressures: on the one hand those emanating from a variety of nationalist groups scattered across the Empire and challenging the morality and, more important, the will of the British to maintain colonial rule; on the other the necessity, for example, of maintaining a military presence east of Suez as a means of shoring up a precarious regional order which, if left unprotected, might fall prey to Soviet subversion. Thus the commitment to decolonization (in the terms that Waltz defines it) had to be balanced against the contribution British policy-makers felt obliged to make to the general defence of Western interests in distant areas. And who else but Britain could make that contribution given the preoccupation of her European allies with economic recovery from the ravages of war? Only France, presumably, in the period up to 1960, but its governments (and there were many) were themselves deeply involved in successive bouts of colonial war in Indo-China and Algeria and could do little to help.[35]

Thus a 'global' rather than a purely European role was in a sense forced upon Britain and this in turn led to further contradictions. The bases to which Britain attached importance in pursuing this role (Singapore, the Canal Zone, Cyprus, Aden) became an obvious target of nationalist agitation and propaganda in the colonial struggle, reducing their value as defensive bastions against external threats. Similarly, Britain's adherence to SEATO and CENTO in 1954 was based on the assumption that South East Asia and the Middle East could be defended by an alliance mechanism based on that which provided security for Western Europe. What this assumption neglected, however, was that a military alliance made in a political vacuum and without a core of economic viability (unlike the area covered by NATO) lacked credibility.

The second difficulty was that this 'peace-keeping' role was continually subject to economic constraint. Between 1956 and 1962 British conventional forces were cut from 800,000 to 375,000,[36] but this cut in capability was not the product of a reasoned cut in commitment. Given the pressures of nationalist hostility, given persistent balance of payment difficulties and the failure of the British economy to generate sufficient resources, it is hardly surprising that Britain was ultimately forced to give up its peace-keeping function.

In retrospect the many campaigns that Britain fought in Asia, Africa, the Caribbean and the Middle and Far East were delaying actions designed to prepare the ground for an ultimate transfer of power to an indigenous majority.[37] Politicians at the time might declaim 'thus far and no further' as they tried to stem the loss of one base after another;[38] they might similarly rationalize such retreats when they did, in fact, occur by arguing that changes in military technology, for example, no longer required a physical military presence. As John Garnett has perceptively concluded, 'throughout the post-war period no British government succeeded in synchronizing Britain's defence policy outside Europe . . . with the process of decolonization or the relative decline of British power'.[39] But the task was probably impossible from the start: the Empire could not be liquidated overnight. British policy-makers remembering the precipitate withdrawal from Palestine in 1948 and the resulting conflict between Jew and Arab (not to mention the bloody struggle between Hindu and Muslim in the wake of the British retreat from India) were clearly under some obligation to transfer power in a context of relative stability. Hence 'the armed forces were often left to "hold the ring" against indigenous rioting and terrorist activity as politicians worked out their time-tables of withdrawal'.[40]

3. Nuclear weapons and foreign policy

It could be argued that the development of an independent nuclear deterrent was in one sense an attempt to escape the confusion of roles and the contradictions that resulted from the pressure to decolonize on the one hand and the commitment to make a contribution to the defence of Western interests across the globe on the other. The decision to build an atomic bomb by the Attlee government in 1947 was sensible enough: the United States was not yet committed to the defence of Europe, there had been a unilateral cut-off by the United States in the atomic war-time collaboration between the two powers and Britain 'stood vulnerable and alone'.[41] The Labour govern- ment reasoned – correctly as it turned out – that the demonstration of an independent British atomic capability would help restore the war-time 'special relationship' to which Britain attached immense importance as no other significant alliance partner was available. The continuation of the atomic programme and its subsequent transformation into a nuclear one in the early 1960s complicated the Churchillian aspiration (shared by his successors) to reconcile the competing claims of the 'three circles' of foreign policy.

Earlier we remarked on the post-war tendency to substitute 'influence' for 'power' in the conduct of British foreign policy. The history of the independent nuclear deterrent is one example of a self-conscious attempt to have both – and on the cheap. Pierre, for example, argues that 'a prime incentive for the nuclear force was the belief that nuclear weapons were "cheaper", that they could provide more security for less money and man-power'.[42] Further, that Britain's emphasis throughout the 1950s on a 'declaratory strategy of nuclear deterrence' arose from 'her inability to meet the rearmament goals originally set after the outbreak of the Korean war without a serious dislocation of the economy'.[43] Thus during the decade following the publication of the Global Strategy Paper in 1952, the contribution British nuclear weapons could make to the West's deterrent strategy was continually stressed. This posture appeared to gain in substance after 1958 when American cities were seen as vulnerable to the newly-developed I.C.B.M.s of the Soviet Union and the American nuclear guarantee of British interests seemed less certain. In the 1960s nuclear weapons were seen as adding substantially to British power, providing a capability for the defence of both British and Commonwealth interests wherever these might be threatened. This concentration on a nuclear rather than a conventional military role for Britain was spelt out in Duncan Sandys' Defence White Paper of 1957: the result was the abolition of conscription, a decision which made it difficult to meet the increasing number of calls on Britain's conventional forces to cope with 'brush fire' conflicts, for example in Kuwait, Brunei, Aden, and at the same time maintain a respectable contribution to NATO.[44]

This policy was continued by the Labour government elected in 1964. As Waltz explains, quoting Denis Healey in 1965, 'Commonwealth ties as well as nuclear weapons would enable Britain "to make a contribution towards peace-keeping in vast areas of the world"'[45] – a revealing comment on how Britain contrived to combine the 'circle' of Commonwealth 'influence' with nuclear capability. (Precisely how nuclear weapons were to deter 'brush fire' conflicts was never satisfactorily spelt out.)[46] A year later in 1966, Healey, with less justification than his Labour predecessors in the 1945–51 period, claimed 'There is at least agreement between the two sides of the House that Britain's world-wide role is an essential role which Britain must perform and which, indeed, no other country is capable of performing if Britain does not.'[47] But this 'world wide' role was short-lived: in 1967–8 the constraint of economic crisis once again forced a radical revision of British overseas defence commitments and Harold Wilson's government had no alternative but to announce a withdrawal from East of Suez.

No such revision took place with respect to nuclear capability. The rationale remained the same throughout the lifetime of both the Conservative and Labour governments before and after 1964: the deterrence of Soviet aggression on the Central European front and the influence that a deterrent gave its possessor on the formulation in theory and the conduct in practice of American nuclear doctrine in a crisis. To military advantage was added diplomatic and political utility. Nuclear weapons, it was claimed (especially by Conservative politicians), enabled Britain to have influence in Washington,[48] to have a 'seat at the top table' at summit conferences and in disarmament negotiations and perhaps serve as a basis for the establishment of a European deterrent force, combining French and British components and giving Britain the capacity to influence both political and strategic developments in Europe.

The clearest exposition of the diplomatic 'advantage' of nuclear weapons was to be found in Coral Bell's *The Debatable Alliance*[49] where it is claimed that 'the case for British nuclear weapons has always been, essentially, that lack of them meant total diplomatic dependence on the U.S.'.[50] Certainly much was made of this argument by Sir Alec Douglas-Home in the run-up to the general election of 1964 in contrast to Harold Wilson who initially promised to re-negotiate the Nassau Agreement of 1962 and who, when in power, promoted the idea of an Atlantic Nuclear Force (A.N.F.) to which the British Polaris system would be assigned. This never materialized, principally because of President Johnson's antipathy and growing American involvement in South Vietnam.

The difficulty arising from the efforts of British politicians to define a role requiring the continued possession of a nuclear capability is well illustrated by Harold Macmillan's failure to gain British membership of the E.E.C. in the early 1960s. He is often credited with being the first post-war British Prime Minister to have the courage and foresight to recognize that Britain could no longer maintain its traditional policy of operating within the 'three great circles' of interest and commitment. The Suez disaster – it is often alleged – was a turning-point for him in this respect: that military adventure had demonstrated once and for all that Britain was no longer a great power, capable of acting independently. The Commonwealth had revealed itself as a hollow sham hopelessly divided over the merits of British military intervention, and in the case of India and Canada a source of bitter criticism. The United States, by threatening to withdraw support for sterling, had forced withdrawal from the venture while the British nuclear deterrent had singularly failed to influence the attitude of either friend or enemy during the crisis. The contradictions in the 'three circles' posture were clearly exposed as Macmillan struggled to reconcile joining the E.E.C. with the re-assertion of the special relationship with the United States and the continued protection of Commonwealth agricultural interests and those of the European Free Trade Association (EFTA),[51] established in the late 1950s as a counterweight to the E.E.C.

Yet Macmillan's first objective following his assumption of office in 1957 was to restore good relations with the United States. Second, his government pressed on with the development of the Blue Streak nuclear delivery system as the core of the independent deterrent. Following its cancellation in 1960, agreement was reached with the United States to purchase the Skybolt system. Thus when in July 1961 Macmillan announced that his government proposed to open negotiations for admission to the E.E.C., it seemed to many (and especially to the French President, General de Gaulle) that British policy was still dominated by the 'three circles' concept and all that implied in terms of the maintenance of some form of great power status.

This view received ample confirmation with the Nassau agreement of 1963 which, following the cancellations of Skybolt, provided for British purchase of the Polaris missile system from the United States on the understanding that the 'submarines would be assigned as part of a NATO force . . . except where Her Majesty's Government may decide that supreme national interests are at stake'.[52] Macmillan claimed that this arrangement combined 'interdependence' and 'independence', but the distinction was lost on de Gaulle who justified his subsequent veto of British entry into the E.E.C. by citing British dependence on the United States for the supply of the Polaris missile as clear evidence that Britain remained an Atlantic rather than a European power. As Pierre perceptively remarks, 'Britain looked to Europe for her future *economic* partners – and simultaneously looked to the United States for her future *strategic* partner. These two major strands of foreign policy, if pursued, were likely to conflict.'[53]

The Labour government of 1964–70 continued the nuclear policy of its Conservative predecessors but was no more successful in sorting out the muddle arising from persistent attempts to maintain a role supported by nuclear capability.

Shortly after he assumed the premiership in 1964, Harold Wilson, deprecating the view that nuclear weapons provide influence, asserted that:

> when we argue about our right to a central place, whether in the
> Alliance, whether in the United Nations, whether in world affairs
> generally, about our influence, about our presence at the top table,
> and all the rest of it, let us recognize that our rights depend on this
> world-wide role, that it is a distinctive role and that no one else can
> do it.[54]

This hardly squares with his efforts to promote the Atlantic Nuclear Force, a primary incentive for which was his belief that by doing so he was offering the United States and the NATO alliance as a whole a better alternative to the American sponsored proposal to establish a Multilateral Nuclear Force (M.L.F.). Nor was it consistent with the view expressed by his Secretary of State for Defence, Denis Healey, who – as noted earlier – extolled the advantages of nuclear weapons in backing up British diplomacy and military operations in Commonwealth trouble spots.[55] Wilson's statement is a classic example of the Labour government's desire to have things both ways: wanting a world-wide role but at the same time concerned not to make too much of the contribution nuclear weapons could make to giving substance to that role – presumably because to stress their significance would create difficulties with the left wing of the party which was still committed to unilateral nuclear disarmament.

Reviewing this period of British foreign and defence policy, it is hard to escape the conclusion that the cultivation of a nuclear role did not give Britain that independence in foreign policy which it was so often justified as doing. It is true that Britain was an influential partner of the United States in the negotiations that led to the Test Ban Treaty of 1963 and the Non-Proliferation Treaty of 1968. It may be – though it is hard to prove conclusively either way – that Britain's nuclear armoury contributed to the general deterrence strategy of the West insofar as it represented – depending on the nature of an American response to the threat of Soviet aggression – both an additional and an alternative threat to Russian cities, adding an extra increment of uncertainty to Soviet calculations and risk-taking. To this extent, then, nuclear weapons might be regarded as providing a basis for an independent 'defence' policy in times of acute crisis. But it is surely significant that it was never invoked either as deterrent or defence in protecting Commonwealth interests for which conventional forces were much more important in coping with 'brush fire' wars.

Moreover, in the day-to-day conduct of diplomacy in normal times, the record suggests that Britain – unlike France (whose deterrent was genuinely independent both with respect to origin and potential use), gained relatively little political leverage in the United States or in Europe through possession of a nuclear capability. Indeed, the reverse was the case, as de Gaulle demonstrated in vetoing both the 1961 and the 1967 applications to join the E.E.C. Nor did the 'top table' argument fare any better in practice: Britain has been conspicuously absent from such summits between the super powers as well as the U.S.–Soviet negotiations in both rounds of the Strategic Arms Limitation Talks (SALT I and II). One obvious difficulty has been the fact that Britain has lacked the 'bargaining counters', measured in terms of missiles and warheads, the currency of such negotiations. As this analysis has tried to show, Waltz may be exaggerating when he claims that Britain in the 1960s became a 'nuclear satellite of the United States',[56] but his judgment is closer to the mark than Coral Bell's view that lack of nuclear weapons meant 'total diplomatic dependence on the U.S.'.[57]

Interestingly, the Campaign for Nuclear Disarmament (C.N.D.) in the 1960s shared their Conservative and Labour opponents' view about the ends of British policy even if the movement disagreed radically about the means. For the C.N.D. the price of a British influence over the attitude and opinions of other governments, especially those in the Third World, was the unilateral abandonment of a nuclear posture. Indeed, a 'neutralist' stance in foreign policy, it was alleged, would provide an effective leadership role among the non-nuclear, non-aligned powers – apart from setting a good moral example to those states already in possession of the bomb or about to acquire it. This bipartisanship on the necessity for a role for Britain (with or without the military means to give it substance) stretched across even the most ideologically hostile frontier, that between the extreme Left and extreme Right of the British political spectrum. There was, however, a small minority on the Left who disagreed in principle with this view, arguing with impeccable logic if not much understanding or appreciation of the global range of British interests, that giving up the bomb was a necessary preliminary to a profound contraction of those interests, a retreat into 'Swedish' or 'Irish' style of foreign policy behaviour and a complete abdication of any kind of influence anywhere.

The course of British foreign policy up to 1973 and Britain's entry into the E.E.C. suggests that policy-makers were compelled by economic circumstances and unexpected developments in the external world to modify substantially the assumptions that had prompted Churchill's vision of a 'three circles' role for their country. Perhaps it is not surprising that British politicians hankered after new roles, some means of exercising influence in areas where their predecessors had once exercised real authority and power. Forced to recognize that a major conventional *and* nuclear capability was beyond British resources, politicians clung to the latter as providing a stable and less expensive means for the exercise of that elusive 'influence' so long sought after in the post-war years. It would, however, be facile to condemn without reservation successive governments for indulging in the search: Britain's problems throughout this period were essentially those of a middle range power, possessing substantial economic and political interests in distant parts of the globe and concerned to provide a stable environment for their assertion and protection. Those interests could not be abandoned overnight, indeed their maintenance was vital for domestic well-being. And despite accession to the Treaty of Rome in 1971, Britain was still left with interests and resulting commitments that were to preoccupy its leaders into the next decade.

4. The 1970s and beyond
New constraints

The international environment in which Britain had to operate in the 1970s was very different from that of earlier decades. The former lacked the paradoxically comforting certainties of the intense cold war atmosphere of the 1950s. Then, at least, the enemy was clearly defined; the U.S. seemed confident of its capacity to play Britain's nineteenth-century role as the guarantor of world order; China and Japan had not yet emerged as major actors in international society; the Third World was busy seeking the political kingdom and hopes were high that stable government and economic development would follow colonial emancipation. There was above all – in the Western world at any rate – a sense of confidence in the capacity of the developed states to maintain and increase levels of material prosperity. Indeed, this was regarded as an entirely legitimate preoccupation of governments, summed up in Harold Macmillan's phrase, 'you never had it so good'. And this optimism was paralleled by Harold Wilson's emphasis in the 1960s that Britain's economic growth would be stimulated by the exploitation of 'the white hot heat of technology'.

By the mid-1970s, however, the international system was plagued by doubts of a kind that had received scant attention in earlier decades. In some quarters, ecological fears about the industrial world's capacity to survive replaced the traditional concern with the threat of nuclear destruction; the Vietnam experience and the disillusion induced by Watergate called into question the global reach and commitment of American foreign policy and even the legitimacy of its institutional framework. The gulf between Congress and the executive (over what response to make to the establishment of a Cuban presence in Angola in 1975, for example) suggested that it might become increasingly difficult for the United States to act decisively and with speed – not only in the obvious area of crisis management, but also in coping with longer-term problems such as the Soviet naval presence in the Indian Ocean. The vulnerability of many Western states to the new-found bargaining power of the oil-producing states; the growth of world-wide inflation on a scale dwarfing the economic difficulties facing Britain in the 1950s and 1960s; the parallel growth of internal disaffection (Ulster, for example) and terrorism in the interstices of the international system – all these developments (and it would be a brave man who tried to establish the connection between them) represented, in varying degree, obstacles to the maintenance of that precarious world order to the support and consolidation of which Britain had been committed since 1945.

Britain and the Commonwealth

What were the implications of these changes for the 'three circles' of traditional British commitment? With respect to the Commonwealth, the process of decolonization was well nigh complete with the major exception of Rhodesia; all that remained were scattered dependencies such as Gibraltar, Hong Kong and the Falkland Islands, none of which wanted independence because of the propinquity of a large and powerful neighbour nursing long-standing ambitions of ultimate incorporation of these tiny imperial outposts. The 'old' Commonwealth, especially Australia and New Zealand, although still dependent on the United States for the maintenance of their security (witness the former's support for American policy in Vietnam) diversified their foreign policies to establish new regional commitments.

For the newer Third World members of the association, the Commonwealth retained its importance in two important areas:

(1) as a forum (through meetings of prime ministers and finance ministers) for exchanges of views on North/South economic issues in particular, and one free of the ideological posturing characteristic of more structured organizations such as the United Nations. There are, too, a host of formal and informal associations linking Britain

with the rest of the Commonwealth: the Association of Commonwealth Universities, the Commonwealth Legal Conference, and the Commonwealth Parliamentary Association – all obvious examples of low key but useful co-operation. These, *inter alia*, are supported by the Commonwealth Secretariat established in the 1960s to promote such linkages involving large numbers of individuals whose interests are professional rather than overtly political.[58]

(2) as a mechanism for maintaining anti-colonial pressure on Britain to promote political change in Southern Africa. Third World members had used the Commonwealth nexus to promote decolonization in the 1950s and 1960s and in the next decade both Conservative and Labour governments were exposed to continual pressure from the front-line states (Zambia, Tanzania and Botswana) to move Ian Smith, the Rhodesian premier, into conceding majority rule. Similarly Britain was (and still is) an active member of the Contact Group of Western governments established by the United Nations to promote the independence of Namibia from South African rule. Here, too, the African Commonwealth states played a key role in monitoring progress and acting as surrogate spokesmen for the variety of national movements in the struggle with their white counterparts in Salisbury and Pretoria.

Indeed, British involvement in Southern Africa at a variety of levels – political, economic and diplomatic – is a telling example of the difficulties governments face in adapting to reduced circumstances. Those who over the decades have appealed for an abandonment of global pretension have often in the same breath called for Britain to exercise its moral and political 'responsibility' for promoting change in areas like Southern Africa. British governments have had little alternative but to do what they can in this respect; to ignore developments in the region, to leave the protagonists to their own, often violent, devices would put substantial economic and other interests at risk. Thus British policy since 1970 has been based on the assumption that negotiated settlements rather than a continuation of violence in Rhodesia and Namibia, for example, was the better alternative.

In the 1950s and 1960s American presidents had been content to follow a British lead on African issues, but following the establishment of a Cuban military presence in Angola in 1975, the United States – principally through the shuttle diplomacy of Henry Kissinger – belatedly involved itself in Southern African affairs. A joint diplomatic initiative with Britain followed, designed to settle the lingering Rhodesian conflict between the Smith régime and the African Nationalist Movement, providing a good example of the 'special relationship' in action. Yet it was left to Britain as the responsible colonial power, in association with her Commonwealth partners among the front-line states, to end the Rhodesian civil war and devise a constitutional formula for independence on the basis of the Lancaster House Agreement of 1980. And it is significant that the diplomatic groundwork for the achievement of Zimbabwean independence in March 1980 was laid at the Lusaka Commonwealth Conference of 1979. This last major act of decolonization was thus the product of a combination of Anglo-American and Commonwealth diplomacy, a vindication of the belief that Britain was more than just a European power, but rather one with important extra-European interests that could only be asserted and defended in association with traditional allies. By the time of the Lancaster House Agreement, Britain had been a member of the E.E.C. for nearly a decade; but it was also a power with extensive interests in Southern Africa and these could not be lightly cast aside.

Britain and South Africa

This particular case study clearly illustrates the difficulties facing a state like Britain under pressure from a variety of sources to promote peaceful change in a distant society, but no longer able and willing to endure a replay of the Anglo-Boer war.

Yet British policy-makers from 1974 onwards, following the collapse of Portuguese rule in Angola and Mozambique and the outbreak of widespread disturbances in urban South Africa in 1976, came to believe that a policy of inaction would greatly damage British interests in the long run. Hence Britain's participation with its Western allies and the United States in particular in the search for an appropriate strategy to ease the transition from white supremacy to black majority rule. British (and by definition Western) policy towards South Africa has had to be devised within parameters set by the combination of rapid external change in South Africa's immediate environment and the pressure generated by internal dissent.

The dilemma facing governments is that the time-scale for the implementation of a degree of acceptable change is inevitably longer than that of the black majority. If dramatic measures such as sanctions or, alternatively, support for the liberation movements are to be excluded, Britain has no alternative but to rely on a combina-

tion of diplomatic and economic pressures coupled with induce-
ments to the white minority to accept the need for meaningful and
credible changes in the structure of their society. Here attention has
been rightly focused on the role that Western firms operating in
South Africa could play in improving wages and employment
practices, although it was recognized that the political consequences
of such action would be felt only over the long term. Thus it is worth
noting the initiative taken by David Owen, the British Foreign
Secretary in 1976, to promote an E.E.C.-backed code of conduct for
European companies operating in South Africa, designed to harmo-
nize policies on the wage levels and conditions of work of their
employees. Indeed, Dr Owen's comment might well be taken as a
concise summary of current official thinking in the West on what can
usefully be done with the resources currently available to their
governments:

> We have an unrivalled opportunity to take up our economic
> inheritance in South Africa and use it as a catalyst for change.
> [The E.E.C. has real leverage and should apply it in a sensible
> way by] extending the political arm of its economic power.

It is fashionable in Marxist circles to interpret Western policies as
motivated entirely by economic self-interest and indifference to
moral dimensions. No one would dispute the importance of such
interests, but it is surely worth stressing that one important reason
for past inhibition and present uncertainty is the question of what
can be done both to protect these interests and at the same time to
help the deprived majorities to attain their political and economic inheritance. And there are few clear historical parallels to offer guidelines to policy-makers. After all, what Britain is being asked to do is to
manipulate the pace of internal change in a society, the political
tradition of which is the product of a peculiar historical experience
and one very different from that which led to the creation of the
liberal-democratic state in Europe and North America.

Certainly societies can have change and transformation imposed
upon them: the traditional techniques for doing so involve either
occupation (as in the case of Eastern Europe after the Second World
War), or war and defeat which, in the case of Japan, Italy and
Germany, led to the creation of new political institutions on the
ruins of the old and an ultimate shift in prevailing political and social
values. Neither of these apocalyptic options are at present open to
Britain and the West *vis-à-vis* Southern Africa. Hence the search for

more refined instruments of pressure in the hope that the use of the blunter weapons of violence and revolution can be successfully forestalled.[59]

Britain and the E.E.C.

Britain's performance as an E.E.C. member during the last ten years has been extensively discussed elsewhere in this volume, but some general observations are relevant to the theme of this particular chapter. Paul Kennedy's comment is especially perceptive:

> Britain *still* occupies a role in the world out of all proportion to its area and population. Consequently, the country's 'Janus-face', scrutinizing and attempting to influence European developments but simultaneously peering with concern at events in Africa or North America, will preserve the ambivalences which have long existed in British attitudes towards external policy.[60]

One important 'ambivalence' arises from the fact that entry into Europe has greatly accelerated the blurring of the traditional distinction between foreign and domestic policies. Foreign policy in a European context now begins at home, and a wide variety of economic and social issues are the subject of bureaucratic concern and regulation in Brussels. Ministers and civil servants from virtually every department of state commute regularly to Brussels to engage in discussions with their opposite numbers on topics such as fishing rights, agriculture, commercial and legal practice, etc. – all in the name of the harmonization of economic and social behaviour. (The European Court of Human Rights, for example, has heard cases emanating from Britain on the legal status of birching in the Isle of Man and the principle of the closed shop in trade unions.) Foreign policy in the European context has thus become increasingly technical and its impact on individuals leads in many instances to irritation and indifference. Hope has faded that in time the E.E.C. would assume the status of a new super power capable of mediating East/West conflict and promoting in the process a genuine sense of European identity. Yet, paradoxically, continued membership of the E.E.C. has become a major issue in the electoral debate between the political parties, making nonsense of the conventional wisdom that foreign policy issues count for little in party contests.[61] The goodwill towards the European experiment symbolized by the two-to-one majority in favour of European membership in the 1975 referendum dissipated rapidly as both Labour and Conservative governments took a strongly nationalist line in negotiation with their European counterparts over such contentious issues as the Common Agricultural Policy. Mrs Thatcher, in particular, from 1979 bluntly asserted the British interest in reforming this policy, and it is clear that European entry 'has not so far provided Britain with the new power base, the fresh sense of international purpose'[62] which its supporters had always claimed as the chief justification for concentrating on a European as distinct from a wider role in international politics.

This conclusion should hardly surprise us. Those who in the past passionately advocated Britain's entry into Europe overestimated the extent to which economic integration would act as a catalyst for political union and the creation of a common foreign policy capable of managing external crisis on the basis of a common interest. (The disarray into which the E.E.C. states were thrown following the OPEC oil price rise in 1973 and the failure to agree on a long-term strategy to deal with problems posed by the 'violent equilibrium' of Southern Africa are cases in point.)

Nor did supporters of the European ideal recognize that Britain, despite its late conversion to membership of the Community, could not simply shrug off the traditional responsibilities in areas of conflict elsewhere. And the failure of Europe to unite politically and present a united front in its dealings with the external world made adaptation correspondingly more difficult. After all, a key argument in favour of British accession to the Treaty of Rome was that these wider responsibilities could more appropriately and less expensively be exercised within a European framework in which the E.E.C. states would agree on a common approach to issues affecting their interests in the Third World, the Middle East and Southern Africa, for example. Failure has meant that Britain has had to follow a relatively independent policy, often in association with the United States – and no amount of European summitry can disguise the extent to which discussion on these occasions has been concerned with reconciling individual state interests on matters affecting the internal (monetary reform, agricultural policy, etc.) rather than the external relations of the Community as a whole.

Nuclear policy in the 1980s

Britain's nuclear role has also been affected by the lack of progress towards European political unity. Both the Labour government

(1974–9) and its Conservative successor under Mrs Thatcher continued to maintain the independent nuclear posture: the former authorized a modernization of the Polaris programme in the mid-1970s and the Conservatives opted for an expenditure of £7500 millions to purchase the new Trident system from the United States.[63] The latter will be operational from the early 1990s and is designed to give Britain nuclear capacity well into the twenty-first century. Thus the 'special relationship' with the United States has been maintained in the realm of defence while the presence of conservative administrations in both London and Washington has meant the growth of a common outlook on relations with the Soviet Union, especially with respect to arms control negotiations in the 1980s.

Two observations are relevant here: one reason for persisting with the nuclear role (though by no means the only or most important one) has been the expectation that it might in time form the basis for joint Anglo-French collaboration, providing a foundation for a European deterrent to give substance and credibility to a European defence and foreign policy. But this assumes progress at a 'constitutional' level and the fact that this has not occurred has, in any case, negatively reinforced the British decision to persist with a nuclear capability as both symbolic and practical demonstration of Britain's role as a major power with interests and commitments beyond Europe.

Second, nuclear weapons have become a major issue in the inter-party debate on defence and foreign policy generally. The Conservative decision to embark on a new and more expensive nuclear programme in 1981 excited public controversy on a scale unknown since the C.N.D. first focused attention on the issue in the late 1950s. Indeed, the fact that E.E.C. membership and the relevance of nuclear weapons for British foreign and defence policy have both become matters of contention between government and opposition parties is clear evidence of the break-down of the traditional bipartisan approach to crucial issues of foreign policy and represents a strikingly new feature of the British political scene.[64] Similarly, the debate over the wisdom of stationing American cruise and Pershing missiles on British soil was a reflection of party division on the viability of the 'special relationship' with the United States and especially its nuclear component.

Yet if past experience is any guide, it was probable that any new Labour government would find itself under great pressure from both the United States and its own military advisers not to abandon the nuclear deterrent without gaining some significant *quid pro quo* from the Soviet bloc following negotiations of mutually agreed arms reductions. It would be one thing to cancel Trident well before delivery took place; quite another to scrap unilaterally the existing Polaris system and compel simultaneous withdrawal of American weapons and personnel from British bases without doing consider- able damage to the credibility of the NATO alliance as a whole and Anglo-American relations in particular.

The Falklands crisis (1982)

No discussion of British foreign policy in the post-war period would be complete without some reference to the Falklands crisis of March/June 1982. For nearly 20 years the Foreign and Common- wealth Office had advised ministers that a transfer of the islands to Argentine sovereignty was the only policy consistent with the need to protect British interests in Latin America in general, given 'long term financial weakness and the consequent shortening of the reach of Britain's armed forces'.[65] That commitments had to be reduced to match the available resources was an assumption – as we have seen – that increasingly governed British foreign and defence policy from the mid-1960s, but it was one which Parliament resolutely refused to accept with respect to the future of the Falklands. Ministers who raised the issue in the Commons invariably faced a hostile reception from backbenchers on both sides of the House.[66] What this con- certed opposition failed to acknowledge, however, was that Britain's claims to the Falklands could only be effectively maintained if there was equal willingness to commit resources either to reduce the growing economic dependence of the islands on the Argentine or, alternatively, to deter and defend against any attempt at forcible occupation by the latter's forces.

This is yet another example of that confusion of purpose which has been characteristic of British foreign policy during the last 30 years. At the same time it demonstrates that the process of cutting back commitments to match resources, while a rational and sensible enough strategy, is often at the mercy of intangible factors such as a lingering but nonetheless passionate attachment to a seemingly dated imperial peacekeeping role, compounded of sentiment, a sense of responsibility for kith and kin and a belief in a specifically British obligation to resist aggression. With respect to the Falklands, practice fell short of aspiration in the years preceding the crisis. Thus the decision taken to withdraw the survey ship *Endurance* from the South Atlantic, the recommendation to give up the survey base on South Georgia, the removal of full British citizenship from some of the islanders, all contributed greatly to the Argentinian perception that Britain lacked the will and the means to resist a take-over.[67]

That a British task force could be assembled at short notice in April 1982 paradoxically owed something to the fact that the policy of reducing defence capability to conform with Britain's NATO role as a regional power committed exclusively to the defence of Europe had not been fully implemented. The reduction in naval capability which Mrs Thatcher's government embarked upon in 1981[68] (and in particular the proposed sale of the anti-submarine warfare carrier *Invincible* to Australia and the closure of the Chatham dockyards) evoked considerable protest among backbench Conservatives and the government's defence advisers whose arguments in favour of a wider defence capability to sustain an extra-European role was strengthened by the successful re-occupation of the Falklands.

To quote Lawrence Freedman, 'defence policy prior to April 1982 can be seen as following NATO orthodoxy by concentrating on land and air forces capable of blocking a conventional invasion of West Germany, backed up by a nuclear deterrent. Therefore, the most significant feature of the Falklands War was that it was fought well out of the NATO area and with the Royal Navy the lead service. It was precisely the war for which Britain was planning least.'[69]

In effect the crisis revived debate about Britain's external role, demonstrating yet again how difficult (some would say undesirable) it has been to devise a long-term strategy, a 'role' that would allow for the 'contingent and unforeseen' in the conduct of external affairs. And regardless of whether such a strategy is possible or desirable, the popular support Mrs Thatcher's Falklands policy generated complicated matters insofar as it suggested a deep-seated impatience with the 'rationalists' in the Foreign and Commonwealth Office and elsewhere: in particular their insistence that Britain must adapt to its new and reduced status as an island off the coast of Europe with little prospect of influencing the pace of world events unless in association with its European partners. That Europe has signally failed to produce a sense of external identity has only served to strengthen that perception. On the other hand, President Reagan's support, however belated, for the British position on the Falklands issue together with the wide-spread approval of the Commonwealth, could be regarded as justification for the persistent refusal of British governments to jettison those links entirely in favour of an exclusively European role.

5. Conclusion

That Margaret Thatcher's government, elected in 1979, was hostile to a narrowly European role is clear. Speaking at Chatham House in September 1982, the Foreign Minister, Francis Pym, remarked:

> But I do not regard Britain as simply a regional power which should concentrate on a few areas of clear economic and political concern to us and avoid involvement in other issues where our interests do not appear to be so directly engaged. This would be to turn our back on our history and our traditions, to take an unnecessarily shortsighted and narrow view of national interest, and to waste the assets built up by our long years of action on the world stage. We are obviously not a superpower, but we are a world power; and it is not in any sense an anachronism or an anomaly that we are one of the five permanent members of the Security Council.[70]

The reference to Britain's status as a world power is one which could have been made at any time over the last 30 years. It reveals very clearly the long-standing assumption that having a contribution to make to the maintenance of international order is *the* major interest of British foreign policy. And this is one which must be sustained regardless of whether the state's economic interests (and these are, in any case, considerable and widely scattered) are directly at stake. In effect, Mr Pym was asserting the traditional view of the substance of British foreign policy and one sharply at odds with the verdict of both the Duncan Report of 1969 and that of the Central Policy Review Staff of 1977.[71] Both these inquiries called for a diminution of British diplomatic activity, and the C.P.R.S. report in particular stressed the need for Britain to concentrate its diplomatic resources on the promotion of economic interest in those areas of the world where trade and investment were of the greatest importance to domestic economic growth.

By contrast the argument of this chapter has been that radical shifts in British policy have proved very difficult to make. This is partly because the liquidation of empire takes time and cannot be carried through in neat, well-ordered stages to conform with some pre-ordained definition of a post-colonial role. Second, the legacy of decolonization in areas such as the Middle East, Africa (especially the southern third of the continent), and the Indian Ocean raised problems of legitimate concern to British interests – both political and economic – and this was especially true of those conflicts which have acquired cold war overtones.

Thus Britain, throughout the post-war period, has felt obliged to exercise a degree of global responsibility despite the decline in economic power and military capability. Even when a self-conscious effort has been made (as in the retreat from East of Suez in 1967), new international problems have arisen elsewhere requiring a significant British involvement for their resolution. The Rhodesian issue, for example, preoccupied policy-makers throughout the 1970s; Rhodesia's transformation into an independent state has not ended the need to cultivate a British interest in Zimbabwe, and developments in Namibia and South Africa will, no doubt, require a continuing British involvement for some time to come. An uneasy balance has had to be struck between exerting an influence on events affecting the global order and resources available for exercising that influence. The difficulty is that the terms of the balance are constantly shifting under the pressure of sudden, unexpected developments in the external world. Hence pragmatic reaction has been the dominant theme of policy. And indeed, could it have been otherwise, given the anarchic nature of international society – a condition of politics which inevitably reduces any attempt at role definition designed to cope with the long term to a rhetorical exercise at best?

Furthermore, it could be argued that Britain does, in fact, have resources of diplomatic skill and experience which retain their value in promoting not only British interests but those of the West in general in areas beyond a purely European context. And although we should be wary of exaggerating the significance of intangible factors (such as 'the English language, the BBC World Service, parliamentary government, legal processes, sport, university structures, intellectual and literary exchanges', to quote Paul Kennedy's impressive list,[72] all of these do contribute in ways impossible to quantify to the image of Britain in the eyes of foreign governments and peoples. It is, after all, plausible that American popular support for Britain in the Falklands crisis and its impact on President Reagan's 'even-handed' approach to the protagonists owed something to factors of this kind, to that hidden, unquantifiable goodwill, appropriately surfacing in a moment of crisis after 30 years of skilful diplomatic cultivation of the 'special relationship' between the two countries.

Finally, it is worth stressing that despite an overwhelming impression of having 'muddled through' the difficulties and dangers of the post-war period; despite an exaggerated confidence in the political and diplomatic advantages of an independent nuclear deterrent and the technological and economic errors made in maintaining one; despite, too, an excessive pre-occupation with the search for a new 'role' – the British political system has remained stable and its style of life humane and civilized. Moreover, the British people have escaped the traumas endured by France and the United States as their governments struggled to escape 'imperial' commitments in Algeria and South-East Asia. As Kenneth Waltz perceptively remarks 'most of these are not inspiring ways of adjusting to decline in a country's international status, but they are benign'.[73]

NOTES

1. F.S.Northedge, *Descent from Power: British Foreign Policy, 1945–73* (1974); M.Beloff, *Imperial Sunset* (1969); C.Barnett, *The Eclipse of British Power* (1972); L.W.Martin, *British Defence Policy: The Long Recessional*, Adelphi Paper (1969); A.Verrier, *Through the Looking Glass – British Foreign Policy in the Age of Illusions* (1983).

2. G.Smith and H.W.Polsby, *British Government and it Discontents* (1981), 54.

3. H.A.L.Fisher, *A History of Europe* (1936), v.

4. Fisher, *op.cit.*, v.

5. H.Bull, *The Control of the Arms Race* (1961), 49.

6. M.Oakeshott, 'Political Education' in *Rationalism in Politics* (1962), 127.

7. K.N.Waltz, *Foreign Policy and Democratic Politics: The American and British Experience* (1967), 157–9.

8. Waltz, *op.cit.*, 241.

9. See e.g. C.Hill, 'Britain's elusive role in world politics', *British J. of International Studies* (1979), 249–59; also J.Barber, 'Britain's place in the world', *British J. of International Studies*, VI (1980), 93–110.

10. N.B.Dean Acheson's famous comment in 1962 that 'Britain has lost an Empire but not yet found a role.' (Speech at West Point, 5 Dec. 1962).

11. Quoted by J.C.Garnett, 'British Strategic Thought' in J. Baylis (ed.), *British Defence Policy in a Changing World* (1977), 168. Presumably the Royal Navy still had a global role to play!

12. Hugh Gaitskell's claim in 1962 that Britain could not turn her back on 'one thousand years of British history' could have been made with equal feeling by Edward Heath's Conservative critics of the latter's enthusiasm for British entry into Europe.

13. See C.C.O'Brien and F.Topolski, *The United Nations: sacred drama* (1968).

14. Barber, *op.cit.*, 93.

15. Garnett, *op.cit.*, 168.

16. P.Kennedy, *The Realities behind Diplomacy: Background Influences on British External Policy, 1865–1980* (1981), 375–6.

17. Waltz, *op.cit.*, 240.

18. Waltz, *op.cit.*, 241.

19. Waltz, *op.cit.*, 241.

20. Hill, *op.cit.*, 253.

21. Waltz, *op.cit.*, 241.

22. Hill, *op.cit.*, 250, 257.

23. Waltz, *op.cit.*, 226–7.

24. N.B. the signing in 1949 of the Anzus Pact in terms of which the United States effectively replaced Britain as the guarantor of Australasian security.

25. This consisted of Britain, France and the Benelux countries and was the precursor to NATO.

26. In March 1946, in a speech at Fulton, Missouri, Churchill warned that an 'iron curtain' was about to divide Europe in two.

27. J.Frankel, *British Foreign Policy 1945–1973* (1975), 228. For a similar view see J.P.Mackintosh, 'Britain in Europe: historical perspective and contemporary reality', *International Affairs*, XLV (1969), 250.

28. David Goldsworthy has effectively demonstrated that it was only in the late 1950s that gradualism was replaced as the criterion for the grant of independence to a colonial territory by the view that 'all that mattered was that an indigenous elite, with some degree of local support, should exist and be willing to take over'. See his *Colonial Issues in British Politics 1945–1961 – from 'Colonial Development' to 'Wind of Change'* (1971), 361.

29. Kennedy, *op.cit.*, 335. By 1966–8, however, exports to the Commonwealth had fallen to 29 per cent while those to Europe had risen to 20 per cent. See Mackintosh, *op.cit.*, 251.

30. Waltz, *op.cit.*, 252, quoting the E.E.C.'s first General Report.

31. Waltz, *op.cit.*, 229–30.

32. Kennedy, *op.cit.*, 317–18, 320.

33. Waltz, *op.cit.*, 303.

34. Garnett, *op.cit.*, 169.

35. This view prevailed well into the 1960s. See e.g. the 1966 *Defence Rev.* which claimed that 'maintenance of peace around the world . . . "above all justifies our military presence outside Europe".' Waltz, *op.cit.*, 156.

36. J.Baylis, 'British Defence Policy' in *Contemporary Strategy: Theories*

and Policies, eds. J.Baylis, K.Booth, J.Garnett, P.Williams (1975), 274.

37. As Baylis points out, 'between 1947 and 1967 the military were involved in maintaining order at one time or another in British Guiana, British Honduras, Kenya, Aden, the Gold Coast, in Hong Kong, Jamaica, the Cameroons, Zanzibar, Borneo, Tanganyika, Uganda and Mauritius. In the Far East also British troops successfully fought a protracted counter-insurgency campaign in Malaya against Communist guerrillas between 1948 and 1960 which enabled the colony to progress smoothly to independence with a relatively stable democratic régime.' *op.cit.*, 271.

38. N.B. the statement about Cyprus by a Conservative junior minister in 1954 that 'there are certain territories in the Commonwealth which, owing to their particular circumstances, can never expect to be fully independent', Kennedy, *op.cit.*, 334.

39. Garnett, *op.cit.*, 169. One writer has described this process as 'the "search . . . for handholds" by a country sliding downhill', Kennedy, *op.cit.*, 372, quoting B.Porter, *The Lion's Share: A Short History of British Imperialism* (1975).

40. Baylis, *op.cit.*, 271.

41. A.J.Pierre, *Nuclear Politics. The British Experience with an Independent Strategic Force 1939–70* (1970), 305.

42. Pierre, *op.cit.*, 308.

43. *Ibid.*

44. See A.J.R.Groom, 'The British Deterrent' in Baylis, *op.cit.*, esp. 129–39.

45. Waltz, *op.cit.*, 155.

46. See, however, P.Johnson, 'The Tories and the Bomb', *New Statesman*, 9 Oct. 1964, 546–7, where a potential deterrent role for Britain's nuclear force under a new Labour government is described.

47. Waltz, *op.cit.*, 155–6.

48. N.B. Sir Alec Douglas-Home's defence of this proposition with respect to the negotiation of the Test Ban Treaty: 'I was in the negotiations all through on the nuclear Test Ban Treaty. I have no doubt whatever that we would never have got that treaty unless the United Kingdom had been in a position to intervene from knowledge and had a status which could not be denied. We would not have got it if it had not been that we were a nuclear Power.' *H.C.Deb.*, 704 (17 Dec. 1964), col.588. Quoted in Waltz, *op.cit.*, 151.

49. C.Bell, *The Debatable Alliance: An Essay in Anglo-American Relations* (1964).

50. Bell, *op.cit.*, 125.

51. See Waltz, 225–6, for a detailed analysis of this issue.

52. L.Freedman, *Britain and Nuclear Weapons* (1980), 18.

53. Pierre, *op.cit.*, 317.

54. Waltz, *op.cit.*, 155.

55. *Ibid., passim.*

56. Waltz, *op.cit.*, 152.
57. Bell, *op.cit.*, 125.
58. See J.E.Spence, 'The future of the Commonwealth', *The Ditchley J.*, III (1976), 68–79. The author is grateful to the Ditchley Foundation for permission to quote extracts from this article.
59. See J.E.Spence, 'The West and South Africa', *The Ditchley Journal*, IV (1977), 15–30. The author is grateful to the Ditchley Foundation for permission to quote extracts from this article.
60. Kennedy, *op.cit.*, 382.
61. For a perceptive analysis of the influence of public opinion on defence policy-making see D.Capitanchik, 'Public Opinion and Popular Attitudes towards Defence', in Baylis, *op.cit.*, 255–79.
62. Smith and Polsby, *op.cit.*, 77.
63. See J.Baylis, 'Britain and the Bomb', in *Nuclear War and Nuclear Peace*, eds. G.Segal, E.Moreton, L.Freedman, J.Baylis (1983), 116–52.
64. See Capitanchik, *op.cit.*
65. 'Britain's Foreign Office', *The Economist*, 27 Nov. 1982, 26.
66. 'From Lord Chalfont in the 1960s to Mr Nicholas Ridley and Mr Richard Luce in 1981–82, ministers recall their Falklands parliamentary question times as the worst moments of their foreign office careers.' 'Britain's Foreign Office', *op.cit.*, 27.
67. 'Britain's Foreign Office', *op.cit.*, 28.
68. In June 1981 it was decided to reduce frigate and destroyer strength from 60 to 42. The Navy, in effect, 'took 57 per cent of the cuts in planned expenditure'. See L.Freedman, 'British Defence Policy after the Falklands', *The World Today*, CCCVIII (1982), 332. See also Defence Estimates 1981, Cmnd.8212-I (April 1982).
69. L.Freedman, *op.cit.*, 333.
70. 'British Foreign Policy: Constraints and Opportunities', *International Affairs*, LIX (1982–3), 2.
71. Report of the Review Committee on Overseas Representation, Cmnd.4107, 1968–9 (1969); Review of Overseas Representation. Report by the Central Policy Review Staff (1977). N.B. M.Donelan's comment: '. . . a country beyond its commercial, financial, social and military policies, has also a foreign policy which is the sum of all of them, but on a higher level of politics'. *International Affairs*, XLV (1969), 607.
72. Kennedy, *op.cit.*, 382.
73. Waltz, *op.cit.*, 306.

CONCLUSION

J.E.Spence and R.L.Borthwick

IT IS DIFFICULT to know what future historians will make of the period of British government that followed the general election of 1979. That election produced a government determined to alter the direction in which British government had moved over the previous 40 years: a social democratic consensus based on Keynesianism was to be replaced by a more vigorous style deriving from a different political tradition.

Already it is clear that much less has changed than is often believed. Mrs Thatcher's government, despite firm statements to the contrary, made many concessions to the aforementioned consensus (as in its treatment of the National Coal Board and British Steel). As with the Nixon administration it is perhaps a case of: 'Watch what we do, not what we say.' In some areas there has been change; the growth of the civil service has been checked and many of its comfortable assumptions queried. Indeed, from the point of view of the bureaucracy the Thatcher government may well be one of the most radical it has had to deal with. There is a school of thought which believes that Labour governments are thwarted in their efforts by a conservatively inclined bureaucracy. The evidence to support this view has always been patchy, but it must now be apparent that governments of the Left have no monopoly of the capacity to irritate the Whitehall machine. The Thatcher administration has taken cost-cutting in the civil service more seriously than its predecessors and the 'MINIS' development referred to by Peter Jackson in his chapter has been given more encouragement. Moreover, there is clearly more interest in giving muscle to the Prime Minister's office than has been shown for some time, thereby presumably making the Prime Minister less beholden to advice from the departments of state. The appointment in 1982 (following the Falklands crisis) of Sir Anthony Parsons as Mrs Thatcher's Personal Adviser on Foreign Policy is a case in point.

None of this is necessarily to suggest that the growth of the state is about to be reversed dramatically. It is unlikely that more than marginal adjustments can be made to the present balance between the public and private sectors in the United Kingdom. What may well have happened, however, is that, outside a section of the political Left, the confident faith in the continued growth of the public sector has been shattered.

As Rodney Barker points out in his interesting and controversial chapter of this book, the social democratic state is facing new challenges. However, we would be more optimistic than he is about its capacity to cope with those challenges. Certainly there is nothing in the world at large to encourage the belief that other systems cope better with these challenges than does liberal democracy. There are obviously connections here with the notion that populations are becoming harder to govern, particularly in western democracies. Certainly in Britain, as in the United States, it is not difficult to point to evidence that citizens are less tolerant of government shortcomings, less willing to be led and more likely to reject incumbent governments. In part this has to do with the issues raised by Wyn Grant in his chapter: that, for example, the business of governing has become more complicated, and more groups see themselves as having a legitimate voice in determining the decisions of government. However, it does not follow that the social (or liberal) democratic state has failed or that capitalism has likewise revealed its inability to cope with the world of the late twentieth century.

It may be true that there are new issues such as race or sex arising in politics, but it could equally be argued that they are old issues and it may be doubted whether they present greater challenges now than they did at, for example, the start of the twentieth century. In part this lack of faith in the ability of the modern state to cope with problems derives from the mistake of seeing it as an instrument of class exploitation. Of course to those who hold this view it is of little use to offer evidence to the contrary. Those who do not see the state in class terms are deluded or suffering from false consciousness; they lack the insight into their own condition that has revealed to the elite who possess not merely insight into the truth but also an understanding of the requirements of history, against which it is presumably futile to struggle. Such a vision is powerful but narrow and does less than justice to the complexity of the real world. Perversely the British people, who have never neatly fitted into the Marxian view of the system, show a diminishing interest in class-based politics.

Equally, they show less interest in shifting from the middle ground of British politics than some would wish and others affect to believe.

Not all would agree with the view expressed in the first chapter that the state has become a more coercive instrument in British society. It is probably true that the topocratic state has grown: the power of groups employed by the state, such as civil servants, social workers or hospital ancillary workers, is more obviously and directly exercised than would formerly have been thought acceptable. In that respect the power of the state has at times been exercised on behalf of its employees rather than on behalf of its subjects. But the pattern is mixed and we would not want to erect any conspiracy theory of the growth of private interest in public clothing.

Coercion viewed in the narrow sense of police power also deserves a different interpretation. Some commentators in their criticism of the police have confused cause and effect. The police can hardly be said to have initiated a change in their methods of dealing with political demonstrations. What has changed is the willingness of participants in such demonstrations to resort to violence. In such circumstances the police are compelled to consider different tactics and a different scale of protection. What we have seen in recent years has been the determination of groups on the Right to hold provocative marches and an equal determination on the part of groups on the Left to prevent them doing so, and even to prevent them from holding political meetings at all. In the course of trying to maintain the peace the police have found themselves assaulted with a variety of weapons, such as petrol bombs, which would until recently have been thought quite alien to the British political tradition. Larger police presences have therefore been required, but this hardly equals greater coercion. For example, anyone over the age of 35 is likely to be aware that a much greater police presence is now required at professional football matches in this country than would have been thought necesssary until about 15 years ago. However, it would hardly follow from that evidence that the police are now a more coercive force than they used to be.

Of course the state or its agents may occasionally do foolish things; it is the strength of the social democratic state that in such cases complaint will very likely be made and enough fuss created for some redress to take place. In that regard the liberal/social democratic state represents a system of tolerance and openness which has the breadth and stability to survive onslaughts on it by those who would use it to further their own particular ends.

Modern British government, as H.M. Drucker argues in his chapter, has been based on a particular type of party system. That system of two dominant parties has clearly been under greater challenge in the past few years than at any time since Labour replaced the Liberal party as one of the two major parties in the first quarter of the century. The enthusiasm which followed the establishment of the Social Democratic party and the success which the party enjoyed in such by-elections as Crosby and Glasgow, Hillhead (in alliance with the Liberals) have been too great to be sustained. Given the general volatility of British politics in recent years, some fluctuations are inevitable. It seems unlikely, however, that British politics will return to a simple model of two dominant parties. In part this is because the decline in support for the Labour and Conservative parties is sufficiently long-term not to be attributable to merely temporary events. As H.M.Drucker points out, the decline is especially worrying for Labour: not only has it failed in a period of mass unemployment to recover from its 1979 position which in itself was its poorest electoral performance since the 1930s, but its capacity for internecine warfare shows little sign of abating. Moreover, in recent years its leader has shown little capacity to gain public approval, achieving lower scores in the opinion polls than any other leader of the opposition since measurement of this began. No doubt some of Labour's difficulties can be laid at the door of the Falklands issue. Whatever the consequences of this for British foreign policy, a matter discussed by J.E.Spence in his chapter, and whatever the final verdict of British opinion on the issue, there is little doubt that its short-run effect has been to boost the fortunes of the government of the day and to give back to the British people some of their sense of national pride and self-respect.

The appeal of the Labour party has almost certainly been further weakened by defections, particularly of some of its more popular figures, to the S.D.P. In addition, the full impact of its constitutional changes has yet to be felt. So far the party has withstood only a contest for the deputy leadership under the new rules involving the trade unions and the constituency parties as additional elements in the selection process. What the effect on the party will be of a contest for the leadership itself remains to be seen, but, if the 1981 deputy leadership election is any guide, it will very likely exacerbate the divisions within the party. Moreover, the new procedure carries with it the distinct possibility that a future election of this sort will produce a winning candidate who is unacceptable to the majority of the parliamentary party. Such an outcome raises a serious constitutional issue: does the Labour party's new selection procedure conflict with the demands of a parliamentary system? At the very least such an outcome would place the monarch in a difficult position if Labour were to be in a position to form a government. (There are, in addition, growing demands in the Labour party for the composition of a future Cabinet to be decided much more by the party, rather in the way that the composition of the Shadow Cabinet is influenced substantially by elections within the Parliamentary party.)

The monarch may in any case become more involved in political controversy in the next few years if we do indeed move into an era where single-party government becomes less common. It is not yet possible to say whether we are moving into a period of multi-party government or whether we are witnessing the replacement of one major party by another. However, with both the S.D.P. and Liberal parts of the Alliance committed to electoral reform, the prospects of some change in the electoral system might be thought brighter than for many years. If it were to be conceded by one of the major parties as the price of Alliance support for a coalition – which seems the most likely possibility – then we might well move into an era where post-election bargaining became a more normal and acceptable part of government building.

As Geoffrey Alderman points out in chapter 2, such a change in our arrangements would affect profoundly most aspects of the political system. Not only might it help to provide a period of more centrist government, which arguably is what a majority of the electorate want, but it would also have a profound effect on the operation of Parliament and government generally.

Already Parliament is a much less docile body than it was in the first 25 years after the end of the Second World War. The spirited behaviour of the 1970s which, as we have seen, involved a government being defeated on major issues and finally being obliged to call a general election after losing a vote of confidence, has, understandably, not been followed to the same degree in the 1980s, but even there, with an apparently safe majority, the government has suffered occasional defeat and been obliged to make other concessions to avoid that possibility. As important in the long run is likely to be the growth in interest in committee activity: the 1979 system of committees has breathed life into the Commons' powers of scrutiny as well as renewing interest in securing more effective control of public expenditure. Not only, as Peter Jackson points out, is this a matter of making parliamentary control more real but also of bringing more of public expenditure within the ambit of parliamentary scrutiny. It is symptomatic of certain attitudes in British government that someone who is, allegedly, Parliament's watchdog – the Comptroller and Auditor General – should be chosen not by Parliament but by the government. It is surprising that this system of selection has survived until the 1980s and the efforts of the chairman of the Public Accounts Committee to secure an effective Parliamentary voice in such matters is a crucial test of the House of Commons' willingness to give substance to the forms of its institutional prerogatives.

The 1970s were a period of severe strain for some of the conventions of Cabinet government. In his chapter James Barber discusses the changing relevance of the arguments about the power of the cabinet *vis-à-vis* the Prime Minister, offering a valuable critique of current interpretations. What has also become clear is that the convention of collective ministerial responsibility is under considerable strain. The referendum debate of 1975 produced the clearest failure of the doctrine since 1932. The devolution referendum of 1979 also revealed breaches of the doctrine. In both cases the damage was caused and limited by the resort to the device of the referendum. In the short run it enabled both sides within the Government of the day to take refuge in accepting the wisdom of consulting the people. (Although no further referendums have been held since 1979, those we have had are unlikely to be the last.)

In less dramatic ways too collective responsibility is less impressive than it used to be. In both Labour and Conservative governments of recent years the public has had ample opportunity to become aware not only of the existence of deep divisions within the Cabinet on major issues of policy but also to learn in some detail about the precise composition of the different sides in the argument. A less deferential media (reflecting perhaps a less deferential society) has shown that, thanks to investigation aided by leak, it is no longer possible to maintain the doctrine of collective responsibility in its pristine form. Nor have governments shown themselves any more loyal and cohesive in retrospect. The public have been treated to the spectacle of certain members of the 1974–9 Cabinet trying to disavow their responsibility for decisions to which they were party and over which they did not feel obliged to resign.

Individual ministerial responsibility likewise survives as a doctrine with less than full authority behind it. In this case it could be argued that the change has taken place over a much longer period. Few would now claim more for the doctrine than that it is a means of ensuring answerability by ministers in parliament. (Even here there are limits: some subjects are not answered on and the choice is the executive's – M.P.s have no power to compel ministers to answer.) In that respect it still exists as a device to shield civil servants but without much implication that ministers should resign when things go wrong – the Foreign Office resignations at the outset of the Falklands crisis notwithstanding. The doctrine has undoubtedly been affected by various changes in British government in recent years. The investigations of the Parliamentary Commissioner for Administration have inevitably brought more scrutiny of civil service decisions and the extension of the select committee system in the Commons has brought more public testimony from civil servants and, perhaps more important, more public attention to that testimony.

Indeed, life in general has become more difficult for civil servants – and for others. Not only are M.P.s showing less willingness to defer to civil service leadership, but, as Michael Shackleton has shown, British membership of the European Communities has posed difficulties for both government and Parliament in their efforts to look after British interests and to secure public scrutiny of decisions made, or about to be made, in the institutions of the Community. Parliament has faced the additional challenge of a directly elected European Parliament. On the whole only the House of Lords has responded positively to this. Not only have they made a more effective attempt than the Commons to scrutinize European matters, but they have also tried to build links with British members of the European Parliament.

It could also be argued that life has been made more difficult for the civil service by the failure of the national economy to grow at previous rates or even at times to grow at all. Not only are their numbers, remuneration and pension schemes more challenged than in better times, but they are more likely to be blamed for the quality of decision-making. The fact that they are able to prevent the public being aware of the advice they give to ministers likewise is less well-received when the whole system appears to be under strain. Critics have also drawn attention to the composition and structure of the service; and to the ability of the service apparently to deflect demands for change. Many would argue that more needs to be done to achieve a more open and a more diverse bureaucracy.

As noted earlier, the power of government departments is likely to be affected by the development of a more substantial Prime Minister's department. The arguments for this are of long standing. Equally the ability of the system to absorb outside influences is also well established: witness the fate of the Civil Service College (which has, in effect, become a mechanism for in-house training) and the Central Policy Review Staff (Think Tank), the voice of which was arguably much weakened by civil service colonization.

Finally, with respect to the conduct of foreign policy, one significant development has been the growth of intense party debate over the merits of the E.E.C., the morality and utility of nuclear weapons and, following the Falklands crisis, the role of the Royal Navy as the backbone of British defence policy. These divisions of opinion, reflected in extensive media coverage and the growth of radical 'peace' movements such as the C.N.D., do not correspond to any profound disagreement about the ends of British foreign policy. Rather it is about the best means of asserting that influence in world affairs to which politicians of all persuasions have aspired since 1945, despite a decline in the resources – economic and military – traditionally deemed necessary for such a role.

Yet, while the debate on the E.E.C. and the relevance of nuclear weapons is likely to intensify during the remainder of the decade, it seems unlikely that a retreat into Little England will occur. That 'habit of mind' which for so long has sustained a British commitment to help preserve a precarious world order will persist. As J.E.Spence argues in his contribution to this volume, a self-conscious abdication of that commitment was never really possible in the past. What, however, has been finally acknowledged is that Britain cannot act alone without the support of traditional allies; this may be the most significant lesson of the Falklands crisis of 1982 and those which may yet arise in, for example, the Middle East and Southern Africa. Responsibility without power is an unenviable role for a medium power; its worst effects may be substantially mitigated, however, if the burden can be shared by the like-minded states of the Western alliance. Whether there will be a common approach to external problems and, moreover, a willingness to act decisively within the E.E.C. framework remains a speculative but crucial question.

These essays have tried to highlight what we see as some of the more important aspects of contemporary British government. They were conceived in the spirit of trying to understand the impact of the growth of the state on British politics and the responses to the effects of that growth as these were revealed in the early 1980s. They are published at a time when that growth, and its inevitability, has been challenged. The ideological argument between those who would extend the power of state very much further and those who would roll it back will no doubt continue. Whether the future lies with these groups or with others who seek merely to make existing arrangements work more effectively and more responsively (and ultimately more sensibly) is for others to decide.

SELECT BIBLIOGRAPHY

1 The rise and eclipse of the social democratic state.

K.Dyson, *The State Tradition in Western Europe* (1980).
I.Gough, *The Political Economy of the Welfare State* (1979).
R.Miliband, *The State in Capitalist Society* (1969).
F.G.Poggi, *The Development of the Modern State: a Sociological Introduction* (1978).

2 The electoral system

G.Alderman, *British Elections: Myth & Reality* (1978).
V.Bogdanor, *The People and the Party System* (1981).
F.W.S.Craig, *British Electoral Facts 1885–1975* (1975).
S.E.Finer (ed.), *Adversary Politics and Electoral Reform* (1975).
I.McLean, *Elections* (2nd edn., 1980).
The Report of the Hansard Society Commission on Electoral Reform (1976).

3 Parliament

J.Morgan, *The House of Lords and the Labour Government, 1964–1970* (1975).
P.Norton, *The Commons in Perspective* (1981).
P.G.Richards, *The Backbenchers* (1974).
M.Rush, *Parliament and the Public* (1978).
S.A.Walkland, *The Legislative Process in Great Britain* (1968).
S.A.Walkland and M.Ryle (eds.), *The Commons Today* (1981).

4 The power of the Prime Minister

W.Bagehot, *The English Constitution*, with an introduction by R.H.S. Crossman (1963).

R.Blake, *The Office of Prime Minister* (1975).
R.Crossman, *Inside View* (1972).
A.King (ed.), *The British Prime Minister* (1969).
J.Mackintosh, *The British Cabinet* (1968).
H.van Thal (ed.), *The Prime Ministers* (2 vols, 1974 and 1975).

5 The evolution of the political parties

D.Ashford, *Policy and Politics in Britain* (1981).
S.H.Beer, *Britain Against Itself* (1982).
V.Bogdanor, *The People and the Party System* (1981).
S.E.Finer, *Adversary Politics and Electoral Reform* (1975).
A.Gamble, *Britain in Decline* (1981).
B.Hindess, *Parliamentary Democracy and Socialist Politics* (1983).

6 The role and power of pressure groups

A.Cawson, *Corporatism and Welfare* (1982).
F.Field, *Poverty and Politics* (1982).
W.Grant and D.Marsh, *The C.B.I.* (1977).
R.King and N.Nugent (eds.), *Respectable Rebels* (1979).
K.Middlemas, *Politics in Industrial Society* (1979).
J.J.Richardson and A.G.Jordan, *Governing under Pressure* (1979).

7 Fiscal crisis and parliamentary democracy

J.Buchanan and G.Tullock, *The Calculus of Consent* (1965).
D.Coombes and S.A.Walkland, *Parliaments and Economic Affairs* (1980).
P.M.Jackson, *The Political Economy of Bureaucracy* (1982).
J.P.Mackintosh, *The House of Commons and Taxation* (1972).
A.Robinson, *Parliament and Public Spending* (1978).
A.Wildavsky, *Budgeting: A Comparative Theory of Budgetary Processes* (1975).

8 Britain and the E.E.C.

D.Coombes, 'Parliament and the European Community', in *The Commons Today*, ed. S.A.Walkland and M.Ryle (1981).
F.E.C.Gregory, *Dilemmas of Government: Britain and the European Community* (1983).

Hansard Society, *The British People: Their Voice in Europe* (1977).
R.J.Lieber, *British Politics annd European Unity: Parties, Elites and Pressure Groups* (1970).
A.Shonfield, *Europe: Journey to an Unknown Destination* (1972).
W.Wallace, *Britain in Europe* (1980).
W.Wallace, H.Wallace and C.Webb (eds.), *Policy-Making in the European Communities* (1982).

9 British foreign policy: tradition and change

J.Baylis, *British Defence Policy in a Changing World* (1977).
'British Foreign Policy to 1985' (series of 8 articles), *International Affairs*, LII (Oct. 1977), LIV (Jan., Apr., July, Oct. 1978), LV (Jan., Apr. 1979).
J.Frankel, *British Foreign Policy 1945–1973* (1975).
P.Kennedy, *The Realities behind Diplomacy: Background Influences on British External Policy 1865–1980* (1981).
F.S.Northedge, *Descent from Power 1945–1973* (1974).
A.J.Pierre, *Nuclear Politics: the British Experience with an Independent Strategic Force, 1939–1970* (1972).
K.N.Waltz, *Foreign Policy and Diplomatic Politics: The American and British Experience* (1967).

INDEX

and Boundary Commission, 29
civil rights in, 14–15
nationalism, 17
and plurality system, 23, 107,
 111
and PR, 24, 27, 41
representation at Westminster,
 41
under-represented, 30
and voting, 34
nuclear policy, 220–2, 238
nuclear weapons, secrecy surrounding, 17

Ombudsman (Parliamentary Commissioner for Administration),
 59, 237

Parliament
as talking shop, 52
and boundary revisions, 31–2, 44
and broadcasting, 57, 58, 67
and control of expenditure, 147–
 8, 152, 155–8, 236
decline in power, 74, 150, 160
decline in status, 64–5
and economic policy, 150, 152–4
and EEC, 167–8, 169–72, 174–6
history in relation to socio-
 economic affairs, 148–9
and influence in Britain, 147–8
few extremists in, 105
and legislation, 52–3, 59–61, 150
Lords' reform, 68–70
political parties' view, 49–50
and public sector employment
 and pay, 158
and pressure groups, 140
relations with executive, 50–2,
 53–4, 65, 74, 147, 155, 161,
 235
role of, 49–50, 51–2, 148, 152
Plaid Cymru, 22, 24, 30, 43–4, 107,
 111
plurality system of voting, 23–5, 39,
 41–3

police power, 15–16, 233
political demonstrations, 15–16
political parties
change of balance between, 110–
 11
changed by changing Britain,
 115–16
differences between, 106–7, 117
differences in organization, 106
ideology, 117
local activists, 117–18
polarization, 113
and pressure groups, 140–1
rebellion, 111–13
state financing, 38
perceptions of, 106
political scientists, traditions in
 U.K., 4
pressure groups
acceptance of government authority, 105
and Civil Service, 139
CND, *see* Campaign for Nuclear
 Disarmament
and corporatism, 127–8
and collective opinions, 126
definitions, 123–5, 138
and government, 51, 114, 126,
 138
and elections, 36–7, 124
environmental groups, 125, 141
and EEC, 141–2
insider groups, 132–3, 134–6
and media, 135, 136, 141
and opinion-making, 141–2
outsider groups, 133–4, 136–8
relationship with state, 125–6,
 159
strategies, 132–8
Prime Minister, 73–101
and Cabinet, 73–75, 81–2, 83,
 85–6, 98
and Civil Service, 94, 131
constraints, 94–5
control of own supporters, 75
differences between Labour and